Software Reliability

ACHIEVEMENT AND ASSESSMENT

Members of CSR

B.G. ANDERSON
British Aerospace Dynamics Group

T. ANDERSON
University of Newcastle upon Tyne

R.E. BLOOMFIELD
Central Electricity Generating Board

C.J. DALE
National Centre of Systems Reliability

B. DE NEUMANN
GEC Research Laboratories

J.E. DOBSON
University of Newcastle upon Tyne

G.D. FREWIN
Standard Telecommunication Laboratories

C.H. GRIBBLE
Ferranti Computer Systems Ltd

L.N. HARRIS
British Aerospace Dynamics Group

M.A. HENNELL
University of Liverpool

B.A. KITCHENHAM
The City University, London

B. LITTLEWOOD
The City University, London

J.A. McDERMID
York University

G. PALMER
The City University, London

A.A. WINGROVE
Royal Aircraft Establishment

Software Reliability

ACHIEVEMENT AND ASSESSMENT

EDITED BY
B. LITTLEWOOD
MSc, PhD
The City University
London

Blackwell Scientific Publications
OXFORD LONDON EDINBURGH
BOSTON PALO ALTO MELBOURNE

Editorial offices:
Osney Mead, Oxford, OX2 0EL
(*Orders*: Tel. 0865 240201)
8 John Street, London, WC1N 2ES
23 Ainslie Place, Edinburgh, EH3 6AJ
52 Beacon Street, Boston
Massachusetts 02108, USA
667 Lytton Avenue, Palo Alto
California 94301, USA
107 Barry Street, Carlton
Victoria 3053, Australia

First published 1987

Set by Setrite Typesetters Ltd
Hong Kong
Printed and bound
in Great Britain

DISTRIBUTORS

USA and Canada
Blackwell Scientific Publications Inc.
P.O.Box 50009, Palo Alto
California 94303
(*Orders*: Tel. (415) 965-4081)

Australia
Blackwell Scientific Publications
(Australia) Pty Ltd
107 Barry Street
Carlton, Victoria 3053
(*Orders*: Tel. (03) 347 0300)

British Library
Cataloguing in Publication Data
Software reliability : achievement and assessment.
1. Computer programs —
Reliability
I. Littlewood, B.
005'.3 QA76.6
ISBN 0-632-01573-X

Library of Congress
Cataloging-in-Publication Data
Software reliability.
1. Computer software —
Reliability. I. Littlewood, B.
(Beverley)
QA76.76.R44S65 1987 005
87-971
ISBN 0-632-01573-X

Contents

Preface

The reliability of software is already of public concern. It is likely that this concern will increase greatly over the next few years. These observations stem partly from the dramatic roles, often of a life-critical nature, that software is increasingly being called upon to play. More important in this public perception, however, is the *ubiquity* of software. We are all now exposed to computer systems in our daily lives, and this exposure grows apace. Malfunctions in these systems are now visible directly to the public: gone is the time when we were insulated from the machines by a protective screen of experts.

It seems inevitable that there will be increasing demands for the software engineering community, in the wide sense, to be more accountable to the public. More specifically, the days are numbered when we can get away with the kinds of disclaimers which today too often accompany software. In this context, it is vital that we have ways of achieving adequately reliable delivery of software functionality, and that we can assure ourselves that such adequate reliability has been achieved in particular cases. Someone, sooner or later, is going to grasp the nettle of offering an explicit undertaking about the behaviour of the software they supply. It would be nice to believe that this initiative will come from the UK, since much of the best research in the reliability area has been carried out here. At the very least, the UK software industry must be in a position to act when these demands are made.

Our intention in organizing this workshop was to make available accounts of the best current practice as well as pointers to what is likely to be available shortly. The workshop was held at the University of Keele in April 1985 and was supported by the Alvey Directorate and the US Army European Research Office. We are grateful to both organizations for their help in making possible the workshop and this volume.

As the title of the workshop implies, the contributions roughly divide into those concerned primarily with the *achievement* of product reliability, and those whose main concern is its *measurement*.

On the achievement side, the first chapter by Nancy Leveson is concerned with the special problems of making systems safe. This is an issue which is likely to become increasingly important as computer systems are introduced into more life-critical contexts. In Chapter 2, Mike Hennell examines the ways in which testing is related to requirements and specification. He treats two problems: that of establishing that the stated requirements are indeed an accurate reflection of the actual (abstract) requirements, and that the specification is a correct interpretation of the stated requirements. In Chapter 3, Gillian Frewin discusses some of the ways in which quality plans can be used to co-ordinate activities both within a project and between projects within a company. In Chapter 4, Tom Anderson begins by commenting on the traditional practice of providing reliability in computing systems by fault *avoidance* and fault *removal*. He suggests that, although these techniques will continue to be necessary, there will be an increasing need to supplement them by techniques of fault tolerance. In Chapter 5, Alan Wingrove examines the ways in which the final reliability of a software product depend on the management of its development. In Chapter 6, Alec Stewart presents a formal description and proof mechanism for the development of concurrent systems. In Chapter 7, Peter Humphreys discusses some of the difficulties facing current users of software which is required to have high reliability. He points to the difficulty of measuring high reliability and suggests ways forward via qualitative analysis of the development process. In Chapter 8, Barbara Kitchenham continues in a similar vein but is concerned with general commercial software rather than the specialized needs of very high reliability applications. She describes types of metrics useful to project managers and gives examples of their use with ICL.

There follow several chapters dealing with the measurement of reliability. In Chapter 9, Wolfgang Ehrenberger relates his experiences with software verification and validation in the nuclear industry, contrasting systematic approaches with those with large statistical tests involving many thousands of test cases. In the next chapter, Chris Dale addresses the problem of data requirements for software reliability prediction. He treats two situations: the first in which it is required to make predictions in the very early stages of the life-cycle, based on *process* measurement; the second when the *product* itself exists and direct measurement of its behaviour is possible. In Chapter 11, Bev Littlewood considers some modelling approaches to this second problem of evaluating product reliability. He shows that the reliability measures emanating from different models can vary greatly in their accuracy, and describes some new tools which allow a user to examine the accuracy of the measurements of a particular program. The next two chapters, by Bernard de Neumann and Bernard Anderson, describe some novel mathematical approaches to the reliability measurement problem via information theoretic concepts such as entropy. An important objective of this work is to move away from the highly parameterized approach of the earlier models. In Chapter 14, Norman Harris discusses some philosophical issues associated with the use of models in reliability.

Finally, in two short chapters, Gunnar Hagelin and Jon Davies give examples of the development of reliable computer systems. The first of these concerns a safety system for railways, the second reliable funds transfer between major banks.

My job in editing this volume has been helped by many others, and I would like to take this opportunity to thank them all. Firstly, of course, my thanks and appreciation must go to the contributors for the work represented here; to the members of CSR whose efforts ensured the success of the workshop and who assisted in reviewing the draft material; to Shirley Craig for carrying out the Herculean task of checking the references; and to Dominic Vaughan and Fiona Needham at Blackwell, for their patience and understanding. Most importantly, I wish to thank Grace Palmer for the contribution she made to the workshop and my rôle as editor.

B. Littlewood
London, 1987

Chapter 1

Building Safe Software

N.G. Leveson
Information and Computer Science Dept, University of California, Irvine, California 92717, USA

1.1 INTRODUCTION

For the most part (excluding military applications), computers have been used in situations where failures and incorrect outputs could cause annoyance and loss of money, but usually not of human life. Most safety-critical activities of complex systems have been controlled by mechanical devices and/or humans. Extensive techniques and procedures have been devised to ensure safety in these systems including (for mechanical devices) design techniques such as interlocks and (for humans) elaborate training, checklists, and human factors research. Hazard analysis and risk assessment procedures were developed to attempt to ensure that risk of serious accidents was reduced to an acceptable level. As the systems grew in complexity, system safety engineering also developed as a unique area. Government certification and licensing authorities established criteria for design and evaluation of safety-critical systems.

Two factors have arisen which have greatly complicated this problem. First, microprocessors became small and cheap enough to make it economically profitable to replace the mechanical and human safety systems with programmable electronic devices. Second, the complexity of some of the systems we are attempting to build is so great that humans and mechanical devices are not capable of providing the control necessary to operate them effectively and safely. Computers are increasingly being used to monitor and control critical functions in such systems (e.g. advanced aircraft, air traffic control).

The result is that a new concern has arisen in both the areas of system safety and computer-science — how can we build these computer-controlled systems so that risk is minimized? Risk assessment and hazard analysis techniques need to be enhanced to include software. Government certification and licensing authorities need to devise new standards and procedures. And new concerns and issues arise for those building the software and computer hardware. This paper will discuss some of the new issues for the software engineer and describe a methodology under development which attempts to provide help in building safety critical software systems.

1.2 SOFTWARE ISSUES

A system or subsystem may be described as *safety-critical* if an execution time failure can result in death, injury, loss of equipment or property, or environmental harm. The bad news is that current software engineering technology cannot guarantee that the required ultra-high reliabilities of these systems can be achieved for software (or, for that matter, even measured). In fact, available evidence indicates that current software reliability figures are, at best, orders of magnitude less than required (Dunham & Knight 1981).

Since computers have been used in critical systems for several years, if there was a problem then it should have surfaced by now. Software has been used extensively for safety-critical functions in space and large military systems. And indeed, software faults are believed to account for many operational failures in these systems (Bonnett 1984). Just a few examples are:

- In a fly-by-wire flight control system, a mechanical malfunction set up an accelerated environment for which the flight control computer was not programmed. The aircraft went violently out of control and crashed (Frola & Miller 1984).
- In a fly-off test between two different types of air launched cruise missiles, eight out of 20 flights were reported as unsuccessful due to flight control computer software errors (Anon 1980).
- A computer-controlled automatic throttle system malfunctioned, forcing an aircraft off the deck of an aircraft carrier (Frola & Miller 1984).
- A wing-mounted missile failed to separate from the launcher after ignition because the external stores sequencing program signalled the rack-retaining mechanism to close before the rocket thrust built up sufficiently to clear the missile from the wing. The aircraft went violently out of control (Frola & Miller 1984).
- A short circuit distorted some of the temperature readings in a nuclear power plant, causing the computer to think that the coolant was growing too cold. The computer speeded up the reaction in the core, the reactor overheated, the pressure in the core went up to the danger level, and then the reactor automatically shut down. The computer, apparently now 'puzzled,' correctly ordered the pressure relief

valve to open, but incorrectly ordered it to remain open until things settled down. This error caused pressure to drop so quickly that it automatically caused high pressure injection to come on, flooding the primary coolant loop — including the core, steam tubes and pressurizer. A valve stuck and 43 000 gallons of radioactive water were dumped on the floor of the reactor building. Fortunately it was not worse; after several minutes an operator noticed the computer's error in keeping the relief valve open, and closed the valves manually. Had the frequent injunction been followed that the computer knows best and that the (dumb) operators should keep their hands off the system until its routines are carried out, the sump would have overflowed and there would have been a wet reactor (Perrow 1984).

What can be done? One option is not to build these systems or not to use computers to control them. This is an option that should not be dismissed lightly. Realistic estimates should be made of the reliability achievement possible with computers, and these should be compared to more conventional control alternatives. It is possible that the risk of using a computer in a system may be unacceptable when weighed against the higher reliability (but perhaps greater cost) of not using one.

But computers will be used in many systems because there may be very good reasons to use them, and few acceptable alternatives. So new approaches may be necessary. One approach is to consider reliability in a less absolute sense. Most software reliability models treat all faults and failures identically. But the consequences of various faults may vary enormously from minor annoyance to catastrophe. It seems reasonable that if we are unable to assure that all possible failures are eliminated, at least we can concentrate on the high-cost failures. That is, even if all failures cannot be prevented, it may be possible to ensure that the failures that do occur are of minor consequence or that even if a potentially serious failure does occur, the system will 'fail-safe' (in a manner which will not have catastrophic or serious results).

The approach is useful under the following circumstances:

1 not all failures are of equal consequences; and

2 there are a relatively small number of failures that can lead to catastrophic or serious results.

Under these circumstances, it is possible to augment traditional reliability techniques which attempt to eliminate all failures, with techniques which concentrate on the high-cost failures. Note that there is no implication here that traditional reliability techniques should be replaced. Every effort still needs to be used to attempt to ensure that the computer system is as reliable as possible. This is especially true since the new techniques which will be discussed in this paper are no more perfect than the other more traditional techniques. The new techniques also assume that good software engineering methodology has been applied to the design and development of the computer system. But in systems where catastrophic failure is possible, it is often necessary to invest extra effort to ensure that the system is safe.

The new approach often involves a 'backward' analysis which starts with determining what are the unacceptable or high-cost failures and then ensuring that these particular failures do not occur, or at least minimizing the probability of their occurrence. Another way of looking at this is that a 'forward' approach would ensure that all possible reachable states of the system are correct whereas a backward approach would ensure that incorrect states are not reachable. This is only practical under the above assumptions, i.e. that there are a relatively small number of failures which are unacceptable, and that these can be identified. In practice this is usually the case, even in complex systems. For example, this approach has been applied to nuclear power plants, commercial aircraft, and missile defense systems.

Another necessity for any viable approach to these problems is that it should take a 'systems' view. The problems described above are systems problems, not necessarily just computer problems. A computer is merely one component of a system. Attempts to concentrate solely on one component without regard for its interaction with other components will lead to problems when the computer is integrated into the system. A too narrow focus on technical problems within the computer alone can lead to software which is often less effective than possible, sometimes useless, and occasionally dangerous. For example, most verification and validation efforts concentrate on proving the correspondence between the source code and the software specification and much progress has been made in eliminating software implementation faults. Unfortunately, studies show that a majority of the failures in production software systems stem from requirements and specification problems (Boehm *et al.* 1975, Endres 1975, Lipow 1979). In addition, Iyer & Velardi (1983) examined software errors in a production operating system and found that 11% of all software errors and 40% of all software failures were hardware related.

These results are not surprising from a systems engineering viewpoint. Many, if not most, serious accidents are caused by complex, unplanned and unfortunate interactions between components of the system, and by multiple failures. That is, most accidents originate in subsystem interfaces (Ericson 1981, Frola & Miller 1984). Software failures and software-induced system failures may be caused by undetected hardware errors such as transient faults causing mutilation of data, security violations, human mistakes during operation and maintenance, errors in underlying or supporting software systems, or interfacing problems with other components of the system; these include timing faults. Therefore, techniques used to build software for embedded systems, especially with respect to analysis and verification, are going to have to consider the system as a whole (especially the interactions between the components of the system or subsystem), and not just the software in isolation.

The members of the Irvine Safety Project have been considering these problems and looking at techniques which might be useful in this new approach to reliability. The ultimate goal is to provide a methodology, called Murphy, which will include an integrated set of tools for building safety-critical real-time software. There are currently three main areas of research:

1 *Software hazard analysis and requirements specification*: What kinds of system models and analysis tools are most useful? How can software requirements be derived from these system models? How can the model and requirements be analysed to ensure important reliability and safety properties?

2 *Verification, validation and assessment*: How can safety properties be identified, specified, and formally verified? What techniques appear the most promising? How can they be implemented so that they can be used in industrial environments and not just in university research labs? How can the reliability and safety of software be accurately measured and assessed? Is this possible? Is it feasible?

3 *Software design and run-time environments*: What techniques and environments are most appropriate? How can the software detect unsafe states during execution and prevent accidents? What types of self monitoring, external monitoring, fail-safe, and software design techniques can be used and are most effective? How can the results of the software hazard analysis be used to aid in the design of the software, especially with regard to handling execution-time fault detection and recovery?

In order to provide an idea of some of the work which has been done, two techniques will be briefly described: software fault tree analysis and Petri net safety analysis techniques.

1.3 SOFTWARE FAULT TREE ANALYSIS

Fault tree analysis is an analytical technique used in the safety analysis of electromechanical systems, whereby an undesired system state is specified and the system is then analysed in the context of its environment and operation to find all credible sequences of events which can lead to the undesired state (Vesely *et al.* 1981). The fault tree is a graphic model of the various parallel and sequential combinations of faults (or system states) that will result in the occurrence of the predefined undesired event. The faults can be events that are associated with component hardware failures, human errors, or any other pertinent events. A fault tree thus depicts the logical interrelationships of basic events that can lead to the undesired event.

The basic procedures for extending fault tree analysis to software were developed in 1981 (Taylor 1982, Leveson & Harvey 1983). The goal of the technique is to verify that the software will not cause accidents or, alternatively, to find software failure modes or run-time conditions which could lead to accidents. Results of the analysis can be used to determine software safety requirements from system safety requirements, to detect software logic errors, to identify multiple failure sequences involving different parts of the system which could lead to an accident, to guide in placement and content of critical run-time checks, to determine the conditions under which fail-safe procedures should be called, and to facilitate thorough testing by pinpointing critical functions and test cases. If used in conjunction with a system simulator, the interfaces of the software parts of the fault tree can be examined to determine appropriate simulation states and events. Since fault tree analysis was originally used to analyse safety in electromechanical systems, the technique being developed has the advantage of being able to link together the software system and the controlled system at the interfaces of the two, allowing the system to be analysed as a whole. It can be used at various levels and stages of software development. The procedure was originally applied successfully to the guidance and control software of a scientific satellite (Leveson & Harvey 1983).

The analysis process starts with a categorized list of system hazards identified by the system safety engineer in a process called *preliminary hazard analysis*. The software hazards are derived from the preliminary system hazard analysis to determine the software safety requirements. The basic procedure involves assuming that the hazard has occurred, and then working backward to determine the set of possible causes for the condition to occur. The root of the fault tree is the hazardous event. Necessary preconditions are described at the next level of the tree with either an *And* or an *Or* relationship. Each subnode is expanded in a similar fashion. Figs. 1.1, 1.2 and 1.3 show part of a fault tree for a patient monitoring system.

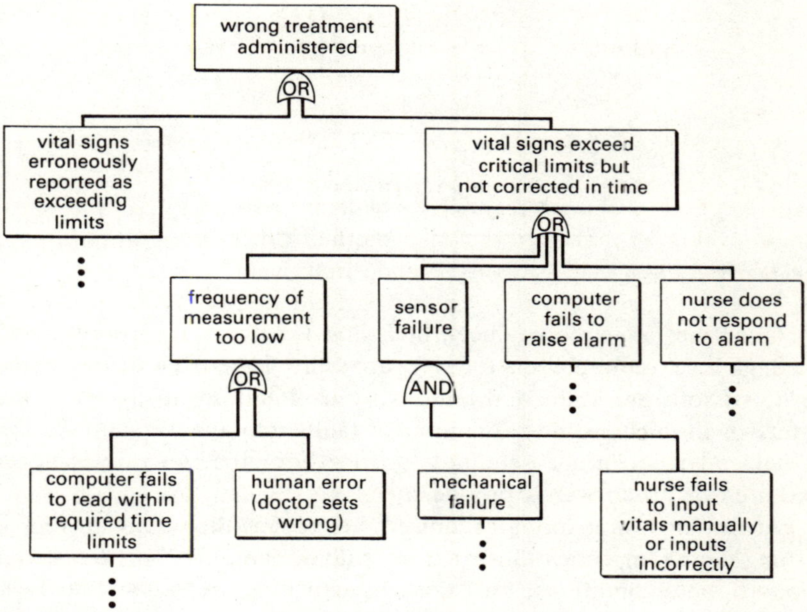

Fig. 1.1. Top levels of patient monitoring system fault tree.

```
(1) A: = F(Y);
(2) B: = X−5.0;
(3) If A > B then
       Sub 1;
    end if;
```

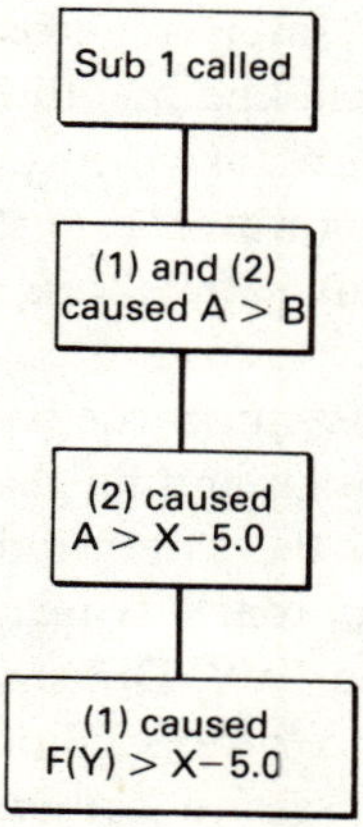

Fig. 1.2. Fault tree for several assignment statements.

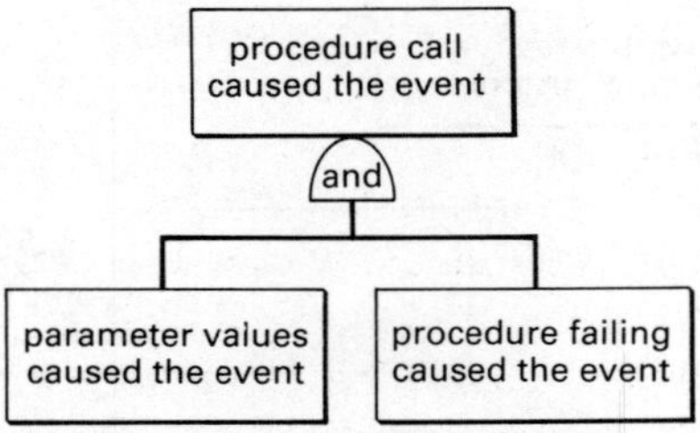

Fig. 1.3. Fault tree for a procedure call.

Once the fault tree has been built down to the software interface, the high level requirements for software safety have been delineated in terms of software faults and failures which could adversely affect the safety of the system. Software control faults may involve:

- failure to perform a required function, i.e. the function is never executed or no answer is produced;
- performing a function not required, i.e. getting the wrong answer or issuing the wrong control instruction or doing the right thing but under inappropriate conditions, for example, activating an actuator inadvertently, too early, too late, or failing to cease an operation at a prescribed time;
- timing or sequencing problems, e.g. it may be necessary to ensure that two things happen at the same, at different times, or in a particular order;
- failure to recognize a hazardous condition requiring corrective action;
- producing the wrong response to a hazardous condition.

Note that while the functional or *mission* requirements often focus on what the system *will* do, safety requirements usually include what the system will *not* do — including means for eliminating and controlling hazards and for limiting damage in case of an accident. An important part of the safety requirements is the specification of the ways in which a system may fail safely, and to what extent failure is tolerable.

As the software development proceeds, software fault tree analysis can be performed on the design and finally the code to verify that the software does indeed satisfy the safety requirements. The basic technique used is the same approach which has been used in formal axiomatic verification (Hoare 1969, Dijkstra 1976), but applied slightly differently than is common in 'proofs of correctness.' The set of states or results from a software system can be divided into correct and incorrect. Formal proofs of correctness strive to verify that given a precondition which is true for the state before the program begins to execute, the program will halt — and a postcondition will always be true of the state once the program halts. For continuous, purposely non-halting programs, intermediate states may be considered. The basic goal of safety verification is more limited. Given that the incorrect states are divided into two sets — those which are considered safe and those which are considered unsafe — proofs of safety attempt to verify that the program will never allow an unsafe state to be reached (although they say nothing about incorrect but safe states).

Since the goal in safety verification is to prove that something will not happen, it is useful to use proof by contradiction. That is, it is assumed that the software has produced an unsafe control action, and it is shown that this could not happen since it leads to a logical contradiction. Although a proof of correctness should theoretically be able to prove that the software is safe, it is often impractical to do this because of the sheer magnitude of the proof effort involved and because of the difficulty of completely specifying correct behaviour. In the few safety proofs which we have performed, the proof appears to involve much less work than proof of correctness (especially since the proof procedure can stop as soon as a contradiction is reached on a software path). It is often also easier to specify safety, especially since the requirements may be actually mandated by law or government authority, as with nuclear weapon safety requirements in the USA.

Constructs for some structured programming statements are shown in Figs. 1.4, 1.5 and 1.6. In each, it is assumed that the statement caused the critical event. Then the tree is constructed considering how this might have occurred. An example of the procedure (taken from Leveson & Stolzy, 1983) is shown in Fig. 1.7. An Ada program segment is shown which iteratively solves a fixed point equation. One possible top-level (loss event) for the segment is that no answer is produced in the required time period — and the answer is critical at this point. This loss event corresponds to the *while* loop executing too long (shown in Fig. 1.8 as 'Max' iterations).

In general, the software fault tree has one or both of the following patterns:

1 A contradiction is found as shown in the left branch of Fig. 1.8. The building of the software fault tree, for this path at least, can stop here since the logic of the software cannot cause the event. This example does not deal with the problem of failures in the underlying implementation of the software, but these are possible. There is of course a

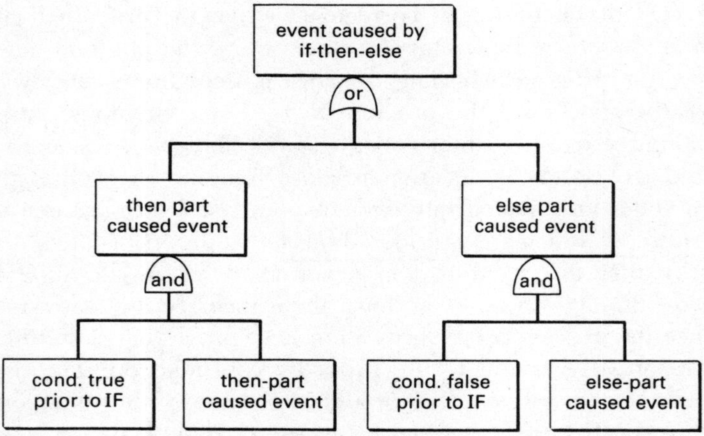

Fig. 1.4. Fault tree for an if-then-else statement.

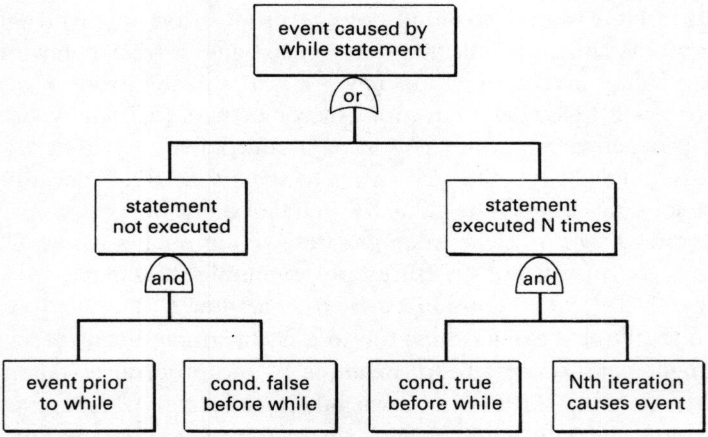

Fig. 1.5. Fault tree for a while statement.

practical limit to how much analysis can and need be done, depending on individual factors associated with each project. It is always possible to insert assertions in the code to catch critical implementation errors at run-time, which is especially desirable if run-time software-initiated or software-controlled fail-safe procedures are possible. Note that the software fault tree provides the information necessary to determine which assertions and run-time checks are the most critical, and where they should be placed. Since checks at run-time are expensive in terms of time and other resources, this information is extremely useful.

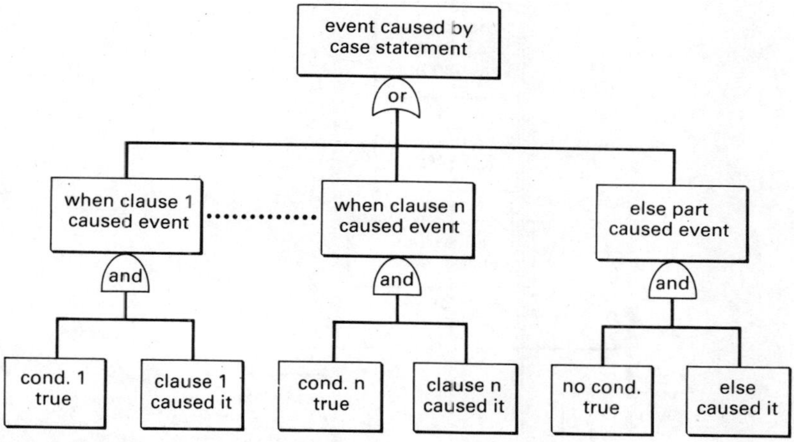

Fig. 1.6. Fault tree for a case statement.

```
get (X, Eps);
Err := Eps;
I:= 0;
while Err ≥ Eps loop
   New X := F(X);
   Err := abs(X − New X);
   I:= I + 1;
   X := New X;
end loop;
```

Fig. 1.7. Example of Ada code.

2 The fault tree runs through the code and out to the controlled system or its environment. In the example of Fig. 1.8, the fault tree shows one possible path to the loss event, and changes are necessary to eliminate the hazard. One appropriate action in this case may be to use run-time assertions to detect such conditions and to simply reject incorrect input or to initiate recovery techniques. Another possibility is to add redundant hardware, e.g. sensors, to eliminate incorrect input before it occurs.

We have defined software fault tree analysis constructs for nearly all of Ada, although timing aspects are not yet handled (Leveson & Stolzy 1983). A new project has been started to investigate the verification of the computer software/hardware interface using fault trees. This would allow, for example, verification that certain types of credible hardware failures will not cause the software to do anything dangerous. We are also implementing a tool to aid in the analysis process.

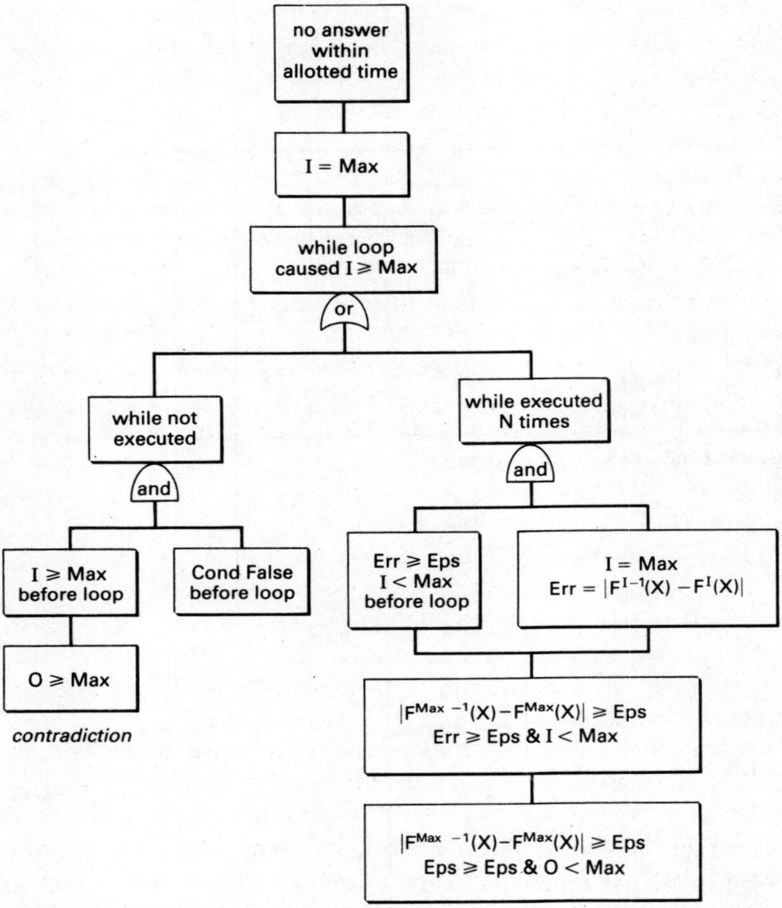

Fig. 1.8. Fault tree for example in Fig. 1.7.

1.4 TIME PETRI NET SAFETY ANALYSIS PROCEDURES

Because of some limitations of fault tree analysis (especially with regard to timing analysis), we have been developing Time Petri Net analysis procedures to determine software safety requirements (including timing requirements) directly from the system design, to analyse a design for safety, recoverability and fault tolerance, and to guide in the use of failure detection and recovery techniques (Leveson & Stolzy 1985a, Leveson & Stolzy 1985b). Procedures are currently being developed to measure risk.

In a Petri net (Peterson 1981), the system is modelled in terms of conditions and events. If certain conditions hold, then an event or 'state transition' will take place. After the transition, other (or the same) conditions will hold. A condition (called a 'place' in Petri net terminology) is represented by a circle, 'O', and an event or transition by a bar, '—'. An arrow from a condition (or place) to a transition indicates that the condition is an input, or precondition, to the transition. Similarly, a postcondition is indicated by an arrow from the transition to the condition. Figure 1.9 shows a simple example. It says that if conditions A and B hold, then the transition can 'fire.' After it fires, then conditions B and C will hold.

The Petri net model can be 'executed' to see how the design will actually work. 'Tokens' represented by a dot, '•', are used to indicate that a condition is currently true. Thus if a condition holds, it will contain a token. In the example in Fig. 1.10, transition t_1 cannot fire because P_1 does not have a token. But all the preconditions for t_2 are currently true (i.e. P_2 and P_3), so t_2 can fire. Figure 1.11 shows the next state of the Petri net. When t_2 fires, the tokens are removed from the preconditions and a token is deposited in each of the postconditions. In the example, the only postcondition is P_5. Note that it is possible for the same condition to be both a precondition and a postcondition for a transition. If a transition has no preconditions, then it can fire at will.

During the execution of the Petri net, the 'state' of the system at any time consists of the set of conditions which contain tokens. Starting from some initial state, the Petri net model can be executed showing all the legal states (sets of conditions) that the system can 'reach.' This information can be depicted graphically in a 'reachability graph', i.e. a graph that shows the possible state sequences from a given initial state. If the design is non-deterministic (i.e. the order of

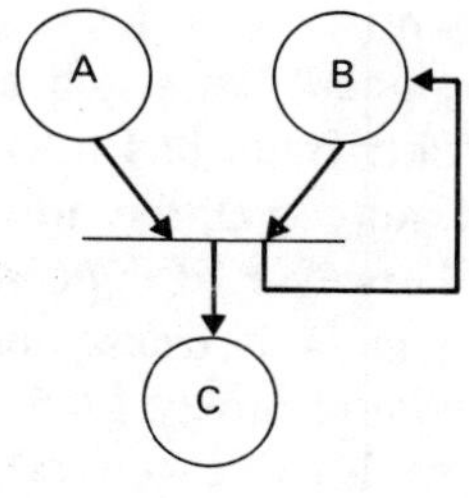

Fig. 1.9. Time Petri net analysis.

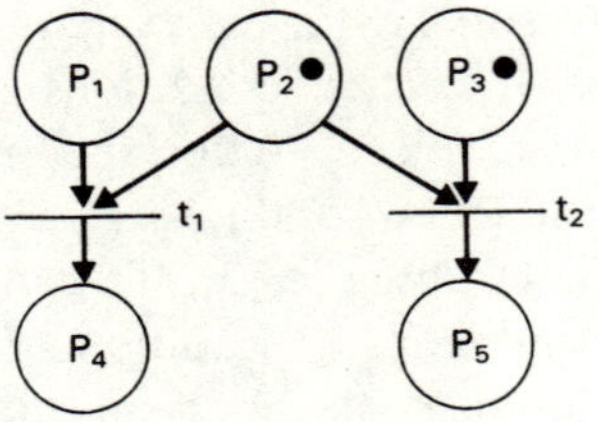

Fig. 1.10. Example of a Petri net.

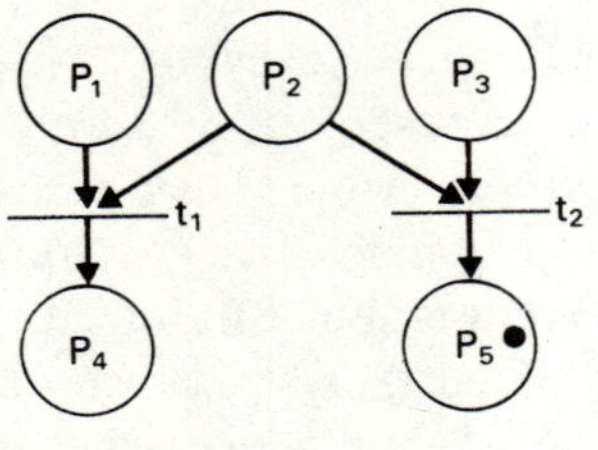

Fig. 1.11. The next state.

the transitions or events is not constrained by the design), then the graph will have branches for the different possible orderings of events. Figures 1.12 and 1.13 show a Petri net and the corresponding reachability graph for a simple model of a railway crossing, where the left part of the model represents the train, and the middle part represents the actions of the computer which is controlling the crossing guard gate (on the right). The reachability graph shows that the design is flawed from a safety standpoint, since it is possible for the train to be at the crossing and the crossing guard gate to be up at the same time. That is, there are two reachable states where both P_3 and P_{11} hold. Note that it also shows the sequence of events which can lead to this hazard so that appropriate measures can be taken to avoid it.

Although creating the entire Petri net reachability graph will show whether the system as designed can reach any hazardous states, the reachability problem for Petri nets has been shown to be time- and space-hard. Therefore, it may well be impractical to generate the entire reachability graph. However, it is possible to use the same type of backward analysis used in fault trees, and we have developed an algorithm to do this (Leveson & Stolzy 1985a). The algorithm requires only a small part of the graph to be generated in most cases.

Briefly, the algorithm starts with the set of unsafe conditions. For each member of this set, the immediately prior state or states are

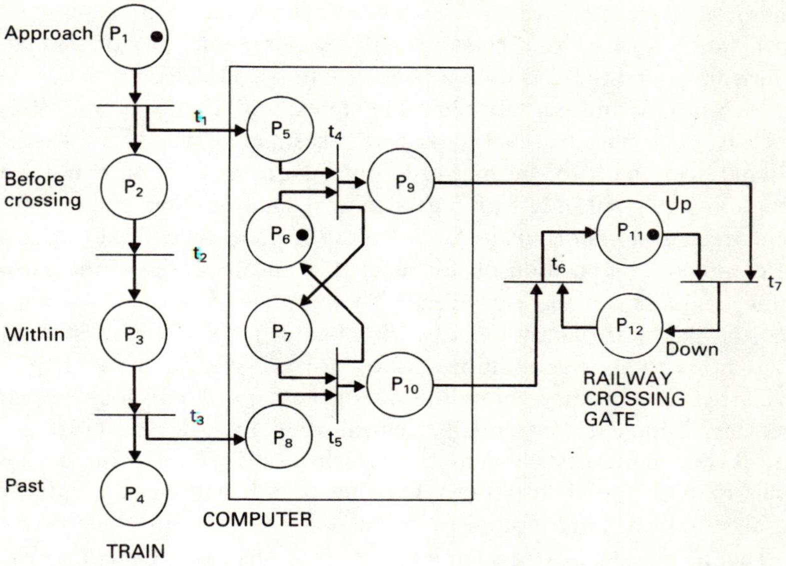

Fig. 1.12. A Petri net graph.

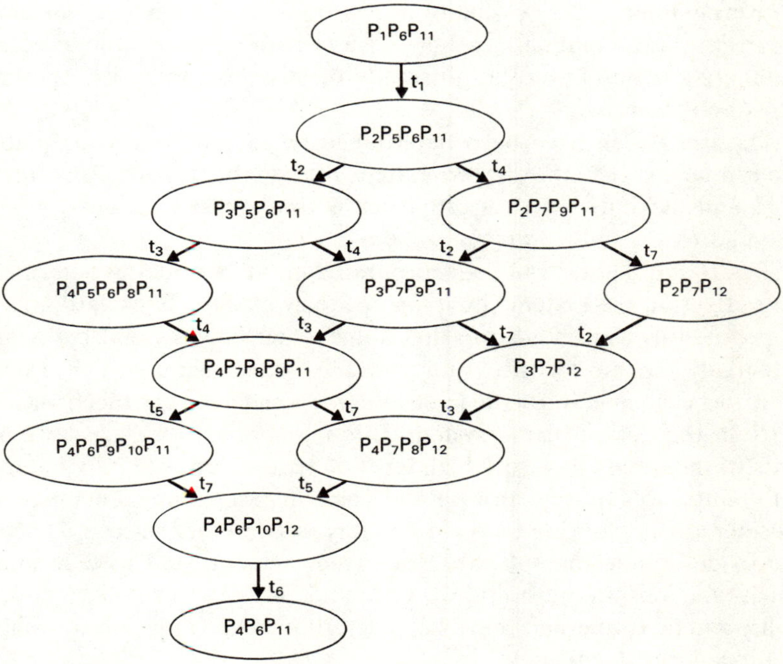

Fig. 1.13. Reachability graph for Fig. 1.12.

generated from the inverse Petri net. Each of these 'one-step-backward' states is then examined to see if it is potentially a *critical state*: a state from which there is both a path or paths from which it is possible to reach unsafe and perhaps also safe states, and a path or paths from which it is possible to reach only low-risk states. This can be used to eliminate one path to the high-risk state. Note that we start not with complete states but only with partial states. That is, some conditions in the state are unimportant as far as safety is concerned, and therefore the complete composition of the reachable unsafe states is not known at the beginning of the algorithm (the complete states from which to start the backward analysis). The 'don't-care' places in each state are 'filled in' with those conditions which are possible in the process of executing the algorithm. Note that it is necessary only to look forward one step from each potentially critical state in order to label it as critical (i.e. there exists a next-state which is safe). This is true because if this path also leads to an unsafe state, then it will be eliminated by the algorithm in a later step.

The technique is conservative; i.e. in order to reduce the large amount of computing to produce the complete graph, a larger number of critical states maybe identified than actually exist. But it does no harm to eliminate the possibility of an accident which would not have occurred. Also, eliminating a non-existent path may have the effect of eliminating or lessening the possibility of mishaps caused by run-time faults and failures.

Hazards which have been determined by the analysis to be plausible can be eliminated by appropriately altering the design (using interlocks and lockouts) to ensure that paths (sequences of events) which will lead to the hazard are not taken.

Faults and failures can be incorporated into the model to determine their effect on the system (Leveson & Stolzy 1985b). Backward analysis procedures can be used to determine which failures and faults are potentially the most costly, and therefore which parts of the system need to be augmented with fault-tolerance and fail-safe mechanisms. Early in the design of the system, it is possible to treat the software parts of the design at a very high level of abstraction, i.e. only failures at the interfaces of the software and non-software components may be considered. By working backward to this software interface, it is possible to determine the software safety requirements and to determine which functions are most critical. Formal definitions of safety, recoverability and fault-tolerance have been determined and appropriate analysis procedures delineated.

Timing can be added to Petri net models by putting minimum and maximum time limits on transitions or by putting times on conditions. Either way, it is possible to determine worst case timing requirements so that, for example, watchdog timers can be incorporated into the design if necessary. Finally, when probabilities are included in the model, minimal cut sets and other probabilistic information is obtainable.

1.5 CONCLUSIONS

Using current software engineering technology, the ultra-high reliability required for safety-critical software systems is not assurable. However, new approaches are possible which, although not assuring high-reliability, can help to assure adequate safety. This paper has described a research project underway at the University of California, Irvine, to provide a methodology to help build safety-critical software systems. Only a small part of the methodology (two hazard analysis techniques) was described. Other parts include tools to aid in formal verification and validation of safety, measurement and assessment of reliability and safety, and software design and execution-time environments, e.g. software fault tolerance (Leveson 1983, Knight *et al.* 1985, Knight & Leveson 1986), execution-time assertions to detect unsafe states (Leveson & Shimeall 1983), monitors and safety kernels (Leveson *et al.* 1983).

References

Anon (1980) *Aviation Week* **Oct. 6**, p. 7.

Boehm B.W., McClean R.L. & Urfrig D.B. (1975) Some experience with automated aids to the design of large-scale reliable software. *IEEE Trans. on Software Engineering* **SE-1** (1), pp. 125–133.

Bonnett B.J. (1984) Software assurance for safety and security critical systems. *Proc. COMPCON Fall* **84**, p. 352.

Dijkstra E.W. (1976) *A Discipline of Programming*. Prentice-Hall.

Dunham J.R. & Knight J.C. (eds.) (1981) Production of reliable flight-crucial software. *Proc. Validation Methods Research for Fault-Tolerant Avionics and Control Systems Sub-Working-Group Meeting*. Conf. Publication 222. NASA.

Endres A. (1975) An analysis of errors and their causes in system programs. *IEEE Trans. on Software Engineering* **SE-1** (2), pp. 140–149.

Ericson C.A. (1981) Software and system safety. *Proc. 5th Int. System Safety Conf.* **1**(1), pp. III-B-1–III-B-11.

Frola F.R. & Miller C.O. (1984) *System Safety in Aircraft Management*. Logistics Management Institute.

Hoare C.A.R. (1969) An axiomatic basis for computer programming. *CACM* **12** (10), pp. 576–580, 583.

Iyer R.K. & Velardi P. (1983) *A Statistical Study of Hardware Related Software Errors in MVS*. Stanford University, Center for Reliable Computing (TR 83-12).

Knight J.C. & Leveson N.G. (1986) An experimental evaluation of the assumption of independence in multiversion programming. *IEEE Trans. on Software Engineering* **SE-12** (1), pp. 96–109.

Knight J.C., Leveson N.G. & St. Jean L.D. (1985) A large scale experiment in N-version programming. *15th Int. Symp. on Fault-Tolerant Computing*, pp. 135–139.

Leveson N.G. (1983) Software fault tolerance: the case for forward recovery. *Proc. AIAA Conf. on Computers in Aerospace.*

Leveson N.G. & Harvey P.R. (1983) Analysing software safety. *IEEE Trans. on Software Engineering* **SE-9** (5), pp. 569–579.

Leveson N.G. & Shimeall T.J. (1983) Safety assertions for process-control systems. *13th Annual Int. Symp. on Fault-Tolerant Computing*, pp. 236–240.

Leveson N.G. & Stolzy J.L. (1983) Safety analysis of Ada programs using fault trees. *IEEE Trans. on Reliability* **R-32** (5), pp. 479–484.

Leveson N.G. & Stolzy J.L. (1985a) Analysing safety and fault tolerance using time Petri nets. In Ehrig H. *et al.* (eds.) *Proc. Int. Joint Conf. on Theory and Practice of Software Development* (*TAPSOFT*) 2. Lecture Notes in Computer Science **186**, pp. 339–355. Springer.

Leveson N.G. & Stolzy J.L. (1985b) Safety analysis using Petri nets. *15th Int. Symp. on Fault-Tolerant Computing*, pp. 358–363.

Leveson N.G. *et al.* (1983) Design for safe software. *AIAA Space Sciences Meeting.*

Lipow M. (1979) Prediction of software failures. *Journal of Systems and Software* **1** (1), pp. 71–75.

Perrow C. (1984) *Normal Accidents: Living with High-Risk Technologies*. Basic Books.

Peterson J.L. (1981) *Petri Net Theory and the Modelling of Systems*. Prentice-Hall.

Taylor J.R. (1982) *Fault Tree and Cause Consequence Analysis for Control Software Validation*. Riso National Laboratory, Denmark (RISO-M-2326).

Vesely W.E. *et al.* (1981) *Fault Tree Handbook*. US Nuclear Regulatory Commission (NUREG-0492).

Chapter 2

Requirements, Specification and Testing

M.A. Hennell

Dept of Statistics and Computational Mathematics, University of Liverpool, Liverpool L69 3BX, and *Liverpool Data Research Associates Ltd, 131 Mount Pleasant, Liverpool L3 5TF*

2.1 INTRODUCTION

In the literature there appears to be a belief that it is possible and even desirable to be able to state software requirements precisely and succinctly at the initial stage of the software development process. That there are projects where this is true is probably beyond dispute. Nevertheless, it is the author's belief that there is also a considerable body of software where this is either impossible or undesirable. The implications of these latter aspects may make the use of particular testing techniques inappropriate for those projects. In this paper it will be assumed that some proportion of the requirements can be stated.

The next problem is to understand what is meant by the term 'testing'. There is a collective wisdom to the effect that testing an entity is a process of showing that the entity satisfies certain constraints. There is also the acceptance that from time to time the entity being tested may actually break, but this is highly undesirable because another must then be made. In the case of software a repair is usually initiated. In a software environment the origin of these constraints will be the requirements. The requirements themselves originate from diffuse sources:

- users;
- managers;
- finance;
- laws;
- society and professional standards.

The views of users are that the delivered software should be useful in their working environment, that it should not cause unpleasant changes in work style, and that it should be effective. Traditionally, testing has been directed to this last problem. The views of managers are equally diffuse; the managers of the users require specific qualities such as usability, reliability, efficiency, etc. The managers of the producers require maintainability, readability, enhanceability, etc. Some requirements arise from financial constraints. For instance, using existing computers, with existing personnel, within a particular budget and time-scale.

There is also the need to ensure that legal constraints are not violated. The consequences of legal issues are not well understood and thus the form of the corresponding requirements is also unknown. However, an example of these would be the basis for a defence suit if a software system inadvertently wiped a large and valuable data-base clean! As more cases come to court, more knowledge will be obtained about these requirements.

The requirements imposed by society are aspects such as preventing user blindness arising from flicker on displays, or preventing sterility arising from high X-radiation from screens. Again, these requirements are not well understood. Testing is the only mechanism which in any way can handle the diversity of these requirements. In this context testing will be carried out using many different tools, techniques and methods. Some of these may involve sophisticated mathematical techniques, while others may be of the suck-it-and-see variety. The choice of the methods used will be based purely on commercial considerations of costs versus 'market edge'. Testing will principly involve validation as defined by the IEEE, but very little verification as defined by the same source (see Appendix). The reason for this is that there are almost no known techniques for taking the output from one particular phase and asking whether it is consistent with the output from the previous phase. Such a technique requires inverse transformations, and few of these exist. For example, knowledge is needed of:

- which line of high level code generates the machine code instruction which has caused a system error flag to be raised;
- which part of the design notation is associated with a particular line-of-code;
- which part of the specification is the target of a particular component of the design;
- which user requirement leads to a particular component of the specification.

What can or cannot be reasonably achieved will be discussed in the following sections. The basic entities on which testing is founded are rules, structure and weaknesses. Thus if there are a set of rules which apply to a particular phase, the most obvious action is to check that these rules are obeyed. This operation of checking may be highly complex and even beyond human capability, e.g. checking consistency in a large system.

The structure may be that of the data or the program representation (i.e. design, code, etc.). The way in which structure is exploited is as follows. First, the structure is checked to ensure that it satisfies specific rules. Second, it is assumed that the structure present is actually wanted, and the testing is directed to demonstrating that this particular structure does actually perform some task as required. The exploitation of structure requires a method by means of which the structure can be detected systematically. Then there must be a means whereby tests can be assessed in terms of, and directed towards, a specific structure.

From experience it will be found that particular aspects of the developmental process will be prone to errors. These are areas of weakness and if they can be classified or categorized, steps can be taken to ensure that careful checking can take place in these areas. Individual weaknesses of personnel can also be emphasized.

In the presence of methods for software development without a formal base, only knowledge of weak areas can be exploited. This can only be practised systematically, however, if a careful record and analysis is made of the occurrence of errors. In general, weaknesses in the methods used will be identified by the number of errors which arise in these areas. The more formal the methods become, the more rules apply and the greater the extent of the structure imposed. Note, however, that increasing formality does not necessarily mean that a greater degree of mathematics is required. For example, the Jackson method is not particularly mathematical to the user, but it does have an underlying mathematical basis.

The most important aspect of testing is that, whatever its achievements, it is quantified. In this way all interested persons will know what has been done, and on the basis of their knowledge and experience can infer the impact of this testing on the requirements.

2.2 REQUIREMENTS AND SYSTEM SPECIFICATION

Most software projects arise from requirements expressed in natural language, either orally or textually. If these requirements are expressed textually in a requirements specification, then there are a number of validatory processes which can take place. First, the documents can be checked for correct spelling and grammar (exploitation of rules). It is the author's belief that many errors detected at present by formal methods can also be detected purely by improving the text, either manually or automatically. Many variants of ambiguity can be detected automatically (Mander & Presland 1980). In general, no other method can be certain to detect such occurrences. The reason for this is that taking a particular interpretation may not lead to any inconsistencies or consequential errors. There also appears to be no way to identify those aspects which have been forgotten or are not understood.

Exploitation of structure can be achieved by checking each unit of text (sentence, paragraph, etc.) to ensure that it has some relevance to the topic. Further structure can be imposed by indenting, sectioning and so on.

There are, in general, two types of specification relevant to software development. The first is the statement of the user's view, as noted above, in documents referred to as a requirements specification. These documents must clearly be validated by users since only they know what they want. A further check by some less biased source is also necessary in order to try to ensure that the stated wants closely pertain to the user's needs. The second specification is drawn up from the software producer's view, and as such it is a technical document which restates the requirements in a form meaningful to software developers. It is not clear that this step is always achievable.

Formalizing the requirements (in total or in part) presents a new viewpoint (Jones 1980). Attention is concentrated on specific issues and the consequences of particular aspects can be studied. Formalization itself cannot guarantee to detect errors, nor can it prove that the requirements specification is correct: it merely demonstrates consistency. The value of consistent requirements will clearly depend on the nature of the project. Conversely, the difficulties caused by inconsistent requirements will depend on the extent of the inconsistency. Formal methods are thus one weapon in the armoury of the software tester. The trade-offs between the costs and effectiveness of formal methods have yet to be established. There are areas of software development, such as mathematical software, where even the possession of an accurate formal specification does not seem to greatly simplify development.

Testing a specification will not find all the possible errors. For instance, combinatoric effects are unlikely to be encountered. Also, the ultimate interrelationship of the various aspects of the specification may not be known until the implementation is complete. These interrelationships may be determined by the specific details of the design. Errors of this type can with justification be said to be design errors, in the sense that the design failed to keep separate issues which should be separate. However, where is the fault if it is not possible to produce such a design given the other requirements (such as cost)?

As a cautionary note it is unwise to depend heavily on any method or notation which requires a knowledge of functionality. There is no known way in which details of functionality can be extracted from natural language text with any degree of certainty. Contrary to the views expressed in many books (De Marco 1979, Jackson 1983), functions cannot be deduced necessarily or exclusively from the use of verbs.

2.3 DESIGN

Proceeding beyond a software specification leads to the design phase. There are numerous techniques on the market (Jackson & Simpson 1975, SofTech 1976, Gane & Sarson 1979, Yourdon 1980, Jackson 1983). The tester needs to know for any particular design method what rules should be satisfied, what structure should result and what weaknesses are known. A careful analysis of the above methods for example shows that only the Jackson and MASCOT methods have any significant rules at all. The others are mainly hand-waving and rules of thumb. Even these latter aspects are open to criticism since there is no experimental analysis to support their use. All the design methods give rise to identifiable structures, and these can be utilized by the tester. For example, in the Jackson method the design results in a program structure which is essentially tree-like. Departures from this structure can be detected automatically in resultant code.

It is worth noting that analyses of software have indicated that as much as 50% of the code is introduced purely for housekeeping purposes and as such is not traceable directly to any aspect of the specification (Howden 1980, Boehm 1981, Hennell *et al.* 1984a).

In general, however, there is relatively little which can be accomplished in the way of systematic validation for most of the current design methods. Design is the Achilles heel of software development. The implication of this, together with the possibility of much of the design not being directly related to the specification, is that testing the code is of paramount importance.

2.4 IMPLEMENTATION

Testing at this stage is therefore critical since it is the last point where remedial action can be taken without the eventual purchaser being aware. It is late in the life-cycle but not too late.

When a design is finally transformed into code all the errors of the previous phases are documented. Fortunately, testing code is an area where expertise has now reached a satisfactory state. Structural testing as embodied in static analysis, code auditing and dynamic analysis is widely practised (Hennell *et al.* 1984b). Nevertheless, there is an on-going need to continue experiments to isolate the most cost-effective practices.

It is at the implementation stage that the majority of software requirements can be most easily checked. This, however, implies that requirements should have been stated in the requirements and project specifications. In the former case they will be stated from the view-point of the user, while in the latter the viewpoint will be that of the software implementer. An example might be reliability, which a user might see as being available 98% of switched-on time, or alternatively two days between failures.

The technology for translating the users' or managers' views of these requirements into terms meaningful in a software implementation is still inadequate. In the above example, it is still not known precisely what standards the software must achieve in order to be certain that the external reliability criteria are satisfied. Such an external view will probably imply that many criteria must be satisfied. An example in this case would be the managerial requirement of readability, which would probably imply control of style and layout, simple control flow, data flow and minimum complexity.

In general, the bridge between the external and internal views can be bridged in two ways. The first is by experience, in which the use of particular techniques is correlated with the perceived properties. This process takes many years and requires careful control and experimentation. The second way is to link the two views by a mathematical model. Unfortunately very little progress has been made up until now, although many ideas are being explored.

From experience it is known that most managerial requirements can be met by a combination of techniques. The success of these may well depend on the nature of the software and the application area. For example, it is known that very high quality structural testing does indeed tend to produce highly reliable software in an environment where either:

1 the structure of the inputs is accurately known; or

2 the requirements were well understood and there is very little missing code.

In achieving these requirements through the use of testing techniques, the question of economics arises. The effect of the previously mentioned gap between the external and internal view is that the satisfaction of the specific requirements may only be achieved by a measure of overkill. For example, 98% up-time may actually be achievable by quite a low level of systematic structural testing, whereas in practice the tendency is to proceed to the higher levels just in case these should actually prove to be inadequate. This possible overkill costs money and it is highly desirable to be able to reduce this burden.

The greatest deficiency now is in the area of acceptance testing; it is desirable to be able to demonstrate that the software performs the tasks that its users require. This process might be summarized by demonstrating that the software performs the desired functions. Throughout the literature much emphasis is placed on the word function and its adjectival form, functional. Unfortunately, there is no method which will derive software functions. Functional testing cannot be quantified and hence cannot be claimed as a systematic testing strategy (Hennell *et al.* 1984b).

2.5 MAINTENANCE

Maintenance is the final stage of the software life-cycle and is usually the largest. In a number of large projects it has been shown to be far the most expensive phase. Whether this is true for smaller projects is not so clear. For very small projects it is certainly not true. The cross-over point is not known. Clearly, reliability is a function of the use of the software and the expectations of its users. Testing in this phase can be separated into two concerns. The first is to ensure that the maintained software is at least as reliable as before changes were made. This is the attempt to preserve what was already achieved. Regression testing is the usual term for this process. The second concern is to demonstrate that the changed components perform according to the new view. Modern structural testing techniques are ideally suited to these two tasks.

Areas where current testing techniques are hopelessly inadequate involve such issues as user interface, high complexity from combinatorial explosions, and timing problems.

2.6 GENERAL ISSUES

When testing issues are being considered by a particular software developer for a particular project, information on the relative costs of different strategies is desirable. It is not obvious, for instance, that seeking errors in the specification is necessarily cost-effective. For example, in an environment where the specifications are constantly changing, is it cheaper to largely ignore the possibility of errors and only check the finalized system? If the code has already been written (and rewritten), then finding errors at this stage may be highly efficient. Equally obviously, if the specification is to be frozen, a careful validation will ensure that subsequent activities will not proceed along erroneous lines.

As a general principle it appears that software developers should concentrate on isolating the really important requirements, and use these to build a strong framework from which software to implement the remaining requirements can be hung. Those requirements which are subject to disagreement, inadequate knowledge, moving application areas etc., and which will consequently be subject to change, can then be hung loosely on to this framework. The consequent cost of changes and errors can then be minimized. In the author's experience this is what happens when software developers construct subsequent systems of a type already known to them. Unfortunately there is no method which adequately catches the flavour of this approach.

2.7 SUMMARY

The quality required for a resultant product is a function of the application area and the required business image of the developer. There are situations where minimal testing is entirely satisfactory. There are others, such as nuclear reactor safety control systems, where one would hope that no possible testing activity has been neglected.

Testing has been performed at early points in any definition of the life-cycle, but its value depends very heavily on the methods of software production. If these methods are rich in rules and structure then testing will be highly effective and, more importantly, can be quantified. If there are insufficient rules and structure then testing becomes a matter of luck and skill.

Finally, testing is the ultimate protection of a software developer. It can be used just prior to delivery to ensure that, notwithstanding the great care taken in the production process, the finished product can perform at least some of its functions without generating errors. This gives both the developer and the customer confidence that the software is of the required standard.

2.8 APPENDIX

IEEE definitions from standard glossary of software engineering terminology:

Validation: 'The process of evaluating software at the end of the software development process to ensure compliance with software requirements.'

Verification: 'The process of determining whether or not the products of a given phase of the software development cycle fulfil the requirements established during the previous phase.' There are some additional (specific) components which are not consistent with this definition.

References

Boehm B.W. (1981) An experiment in small-scale application software engineering. *IEEE Trans. on Software Engineering* **SE-7** (5), pp. 482–493.

DeMarco T. (1979) *Structured Analysis and System Specification*. Prentice-Hall.

Gane C. & Sarson T. (1979) *Structured Systems Analysis: Tools and Techniques*. Prentice-Hall.

Hennell M.A., Hedley D. & Riddell I.J. (1984a) Assessing a class of software tools. *Proc. 7th Int. Conf. on Software Engineering*, pp. 266–277.

Hennell M.A. *et al.* (1984b) *Report to the U.S. Army under contract DAJA 37-81-C-0736*.

Howden W.E. (1980) Functional testing and design abstractions. *Journal of Systems and Software* **1** (4), pp. 307–314.

Jackson K. & Simpson H.R. (1975) *MASCOT: A Modular Approach to Software Construction Operation and Test*. RRE (Technical Note 778).

Jackson M.A. (1983) *System Development*. Prentice-Hall.

Jones C.B. (1980) *Software Development: A Rigorous Approach*. Prentice-Hall.

McCain R. (1985) A software development methodology for re-usable components. *Proc. 18th Annual Hawaii Int. Conf. on System Sciences*.

Mander K.C. & Presland S.G. (1980) *An Introduction to Specification Analysis — SPAN*. SCM Dept, University of Liverpool Report.

SofTech (1976) *An Introduction to SADT*. SofTech (Document 9022–78).

Wolverton R.W. (1974) The cost of developing large-scale software. *IEEE Trans. on Computers* **C-23** (6), pp. 615–636.

Yourdon E. (1980) *Structured Design Workshop. Ed.2.1.*

Chapter 3

Quality Plans as a Means of Coordination, and Engineering Improvement

G. FREWIN
STC (Standard Telecommunication Laboratories Ltd), London Road, Harlow, Essex CM17 9NA

3.1 INTRODUCTION

The subject of the CSR workshop was the achievement and assessment of software reliability. However, 'Reliability' is only one of a group of desirable qualities which are required in products and this paper is directed towards the general management of all those qualities. The approach suggested is intended for the quality manager, or quality engineer, whose responsibilities and areas of influence lie within the technical management of one or more project teams: it is less appropriate for the kind of external and administrative control exerted by traditional quality control functions. In particular, established 'Quality Control' tends to aim for consistency and stability, while the style of quality management discussed below is highly reactive and open to the introduction of alternative tools and methods, even, if found necessary, in the course of a project.

The areas urgently needing management and control systems include:

- the perception and specification of a customer's real needs;
- translation of that specification into a conforming design;
- maintaining that conformity throughout the development processes;
- product and sub-product demonstrations (tests) which provide convincing indications of the product and project having met their requirements;
- ensuring that the tests and demonstrations are designed and controlled, so as to be both achievable and manageable.

The problems of gaining control in all these areas are compounded and complicated by the richness of software's possible functionality, the multiplicity of different approaches and uses that can be associated with any one product, and the many possible methods and means for making the transformation from a concept into a working product.

It is suggested below that the most promising mechanisms for gaining and improving predictability and controllability of software qualities are quality plans (with their subsidiary documents: testing plans and data plans), and their use as a means of coordination within projects, across projects and between organizations. The contents of the plans are not discussed in detail in this paper, since several standards presently either exist or are in preparation. It is assumed that readers will either be using quality plans already, or will be able to locate enough background material to be able to follow the discussion and, perhaps, go on to use quality planning in future.

Given that many organizations are already using quality plans, it might be asked why it has been felt necessary to produce this paper? There are three main reasons: first, that many software procurers and developers do not appear to recognize the value of such plans; second, that a high proportion of plans which are produced at the beginning of projects are either not followed through or are not fully recorded; and third, that much data of general value and interest is not used to its fullest extent in its parent projects and/or is never made known outside those projects. Thus this paper has taken on the form of lists of uses for quality plans, test plans and data plans, presented in the hope that they will reach some of those who need them, as well as others who already use quality plans and will be encouraged to make their own experiences and results more public.

3.2 ORGANIZING FOR COORDINATION

Effective coordination can only be introduced and practised if the environment and supporting structures exist. Of these, probably the most important is the presence of a general understanding of the potential for benefit, and the will to seek and achieve it. To make the coordination work, all those involved must be prepared to question and evaluate every aspect of what they are doing, and must be ready to both give and to accept suggestions and information outside their normal field of interest and authority. (It should be noted that these objectives are very similar to those found in quality circles.) Creating and maintaining this openness and critical examination is a worthwhile challenge for quality management.

3.2.1 Roles and responsibilities

The *Customer* (or user, or person representing customer/user interests) has a particular role, which is discussed below — otherwise, apart from the two special roles of test coordinator and data coordinator, the effect is mainly of extending the roles usually played by project management into the additional responsibilities and opportunities of quality planning.

The *Test Coordinator* is expected to ensure that every specific statement of intent in the product requirement, specification and design, is matched by a well designed (cost-effective, convincing, self-reporting, etc.) test, measurement or demonstration. Further, that the supporting structure of reporting procedures, test controls, and necessary tools and equipment, are in place to enable those tests to be run — and to ensure that they (plus others made necessary by changes or observations during development) *are* all run and reported at appropriate points in the development.

Collected data will be chiefly used in project planning, process planning, process control, tool and method evaluations, and product release/acceptance. The *Data Coordinator* ensures that the physical and administrative structures for data collection exist and are documented in the quality plan, receives and validates the data during development, and through analysis and communication ensures that the meaning of the information is known to all with a use for it, in time for its effective application. The data coordinator may use information from more than one project and more than one source — for example, projects running in parallel, historical records, and information from external sources — in order to ensure that the most profitable use is made of the data being generated at any particular time and in any specific project.

3.2.2 Customer (or user) interfaces with quality management

For a product of acceptable, or (better) of welcome qualities, it is essential that there is a professional and constant level of interaction between those developing the product and those for whom it is being developed. (For a general-purpose product intended for the open market, there must be one or more persons taking responsibility for representing the interests of the eventual users.)

For their own protection and for the good of the product, each customer/user should be encouraged into an active project role, consisting of:

- actively encouraging the making and following of detailed quality plans for the products and projects with which they are concerned;

- requiring access to previous quality plans and their recorded outcomes before accepting the figures and methods quoted in the new plan;
- enquiring as far as possible into the sources and validity of synthetics and formulae used in estimating and planning;
- appointing other appropriate customer personnel as needed (to attend reviews, provide test materials and test cases, arrange for access to customer staff and activities, organize trials and demonstrations, and ensure that training is given at the appropriate time), and to provide authoritative responses to queries from the developer and a managed interface between developer and customer;
- receiving and reviewing reports of significant audits, reviews, tests and demonstrations;
- making any queries and objections in detail and in writing, at the earliest possible time.

3.3 QUALITY PLANS

It is becoming more common for the better organized procurers of software to ask for a quality plan as part of the contractual package, and for suppliers — especially those working to fixed prices — to have at least some form of common quality plan for all their developments. There are thus several general-purpose, and company-specific, standards (or models) of quality plans available and it has not been thought necessary to provide another definition here, although there are two points it does seems useful to emphasize:

1 Quality plans should be made at the very earliest point in a project, preferably before a final decision is made on feasibility, and before a development contract is signed.

2 Quality plans should be devised and agreed between all the concerned parties — senior management, software development management (both administrative and technical), senior members of the software development team, customers/users (or those acting for them), and any involved general support functions such as software engineering development, resource management, maintenance management, and company-wide quality management.

The quality plan brings quality objectives together with the means by which they are to be achieved, the controls which will assure that the processes and their results are in line with objectives, and the organization and the administration which will support and relate all the activities and intentions of the plan.

Quality plans and quality records, therefore, provide the guidelines for carrying out and controlling the following:

- requirement and specification management;
- development processes;
- documentation management;
- design evaluation;
- re-use of parts;
- product testing;
- data collection and interpretation;
- acceptance and release processes.

For convenience of maintenance and use, most quality plans contain or refer to subsidiary plans, relating to topics (such as product and process control, documentation control, configuration management, data management, etc.) which are to be the specific responsibility of identified persons or functions. The two most important of these subplans are the *Test Plan* and the *Data Plan*. The two interact in many ways, providing each other with many of the mechanisms and much of the history they need. They are essential if the quality of the product is to be assured, and if that assurance is to be justified.

3.4 COORDINATION THROUGH QUALITY PLANS

3.4.1 General notes

A quality plan cannot be made without cooperation, since all the concerned parties must understand and agree the plan if it is to be effective. Points of common interest, and the appearance of useful information for one activity in the course of another, are usually noted in the joint writing and reviewing of the various sections. Thus the creation of the quality plan can be instrumental in raising project effectiveness and mutual support, as well as in preventing expensive and time-consuming misunderstandings during the project, and at release/acceptance time. In addition, the level of planning appropriate to these documents makes it simple to pick out and evaluate any needs for special training and special tooling, and to predict the effects of changes or failures during the project.

While a basic quality plan might be applied to the straightforward undertaking of a sequence of development processes, with a little more thought it may be used to ensure that all the information gathered in one instance of a process is used to help plan and control later instances of the same process, and other related processes, within the project. By similar extensions, process and product information from one project may be used in the planning and control of other projects. A third level of utilization occurs when the information is used in the evaluation of tools and methods and the setting of performance standards for several projects, or even for several separate organizations.

3.4.2 Serial and parallel coordination

'Serial' coordination has been used as the term for the application of information from one phase or process in a later and different phase or process. An example of this is the use of module or program error records, and complexity measurements from early design reviews in choosing the most appropriate testing strategies for those modules or programs. The same information can also be used to support estimates of the effort that is likely to be needed for such processes as code reviews, unit and integration testing, release/acceptance and, eventually (and with information from those later reviews and tests added to the initial records), to predict the size and resource needs of support and maintenance activities.

'Parallel' coordination is the application of information from one instance of an activity or process to other instances of the same process, whether in the same project or in others in progress at the same time. For example, if it were found that the first few module design reviews undertaken in a project used markedly more or less effort than usual, then the planned effort for the remaining design reviews might be adjusted accordingly. This should result in more accurate schedule predictions and more effective use of resources. Similarly, a quality plan can contain checks on its own assumptions — and improve the information base on which its software engineering is founded — by including a degree of experimentation. An example of this is of calling for occasional repeats of reviews by different people than those first involved, and/or using variations on the method and check-lists, and (if there are distinct differences in the number and nature of faults found in the reviews), going on to examine the potential benefit of revising review procedures and objectives for the rest of the project and for parallel and subsequent projects.

3.4.3 Coordination of quality plans between projects

In order to be effective, coordination of quality plans requires careful management, both technically and administratively. In particular, the differences between products and between projects, and the rates of change in hardware and software environments, mean that the interpretation and application of recorded information cannot become routine but must always be the subject of intensive technical scrutiny.

Although some elements of each plan must be made specific to the quality needs and other circumstances of the project in hand, conceptually and practically there will be many areas in common which can be considered together. These considerations might include the potential for shared use and acquisition of facilities, re-use of parts and plans, and the application of lessons learnt from one situation to the avoidance of problems in others.

Thus the coordination of quality plans includes the selective re-use of methods and procedures (to reduce re-invention and to benefit by experience), the harmonization of goals and measurements, the provision of support tools and services, and the extraction from project and product records of indications of what works and what should be avoided. This helps to gain local control of the development situation (environment, methods, tools, etc.), to progressively refine that control, and to promote efficiency. In time, perhaps, it also helps to contribute to the better general understanding of software products and processes.

Study of the initial specifications, quality plans and their outcomes, and in-service records of previous products, is a valuable input to:

- settling on mutually acceptable (and understood) forms of characterization in specifications;
- finding workable and effective forms of control during development;
- defining and implementing demonstrations of achievement;
- devising workable and meaningful schemes of description and measurement for use in recording and reporting both the development and its final results;
- devising workable and meaningful schemes to control, record and report in-service performance and maintenance activities.

In particular, coordination of data plans and collected data (that is, the treatment of all data activities and outcomes as one body of information) reduces the inherent risks of trying to extract truths from inadequate data sets. The improved quantity and quality of data makes more reliable:

- the estimation and planning of projects, both in administrative and technical terms;
- the re-estimation and planning of on-going projects;
- the management of the project, its products, processes and resources;

- the selective re-use of methods and procedures (to reduce re-invention, and to benefit by experience);
- the harmonization of goals and measurements across projects;
- the rationalization of the provision of support tools and services;
- the extraction from project and product records of indications of what works and what should be avoided.

3.4.4 Coordination of test plans

Test plans are created as a subsection or as an associated document of the quality plan, and become progressively more detailed and expanded during a project. Their purpose is to ensure that all testing activities (including those used for controlling the process of development, and in indicating the progress of the project) are expected, are manageable and are managed. In the literature of software testing, the emphasis is often more on the mechanics of testing the items in hand than on ensuring that all relevant items *are* identified and tested, and that the testing is purposeful and informative. For a discussion of the consequences of failing to get a tight grasp on testing, see Evans (1984).

3.4.4.1 The contents of a test plan

Each test plan defines its own objectives and scope, and the means and methods by which the objectives are expected to be met. It is concerned equally with the performance of tests and with assessing the meaning of the results of those tests. Thus a complete plan would include measuring and testing the product testing techniques themselves (to decide which are most effective), as well as looking for indications from early tests of the probable results of those which will be made later in the project.

The plan predicts the resources and means required to reach the required levels of assurance about the end products, and the scheduling of all testing, measuring and demonstration activities. It also provides a basis for identifying what to test, when to perform the tests, how to perform the tests, how to record their results and how to use those results — for example, in identifying elements which are particularly at risk or are otherwise abnormal. In addition, the plan outlines the remedial techniques associated with each process, by which faults are detected and corrected — while keeping the creation of new difficulties to a minimum.

Tests, measurements and demonstrations are used to establish that the software product satisfies the requirements document, and that each process during a development is carried out correctly and results in acceptable outcomes. Thus the test plan must be updated and refined throughout the project as information becomes available about the details of the testing yet to be performed, and the results of that which has been completed.

Examples of this updating include the addition of new items to be tested (as the result of redesign or new requirements) and the extension of test sets as items progress from their high level design to detailed design, and then to implementation and integration.

3.4.4.2 Coordination of test plans and test results within a project and between projects

Examples include:

Uses in the management and planning of resources and environments. Test plans, and their supporting plans for resources and equipment, can be based on results from earlier projects — and adjusted during the current project by considering whether the results of testing indicate that the plan is having its desired effects. For example, monitoring the ratio of rework to primary work helps to locate whether the product is better or worse than expected, and whether its quality is improving or degrading as the project goes on.

The role of test plans in ensuring the applicability and testability of the design and the code. The test plan should provide a medium for communication between the customer for a product, the designer of that product and the designer of the tests of that product, so that details of the design of the product can be controlled against both its eventual usefulness and its capacity to assist, rather than hinder, the testing of the product.

The existence of the plan, and the association of portions of that plan with the specific design elements to which it refers, helps ensure that programs and their constituents are both designed and coded in a way that is consistent with expected and achievable methods of testing those elements and the larger items into which they will be integrated. When a code item is under review, consideration must be given to the requirements, the design, the detailed implementation, and the associated test set.

Test plans used as a guide for those managing testing. Test plans should act as a guide for those controlling testing and enable individual testing activities to be seen in the context of the full test schedule. It is possible that staff carrying out testing meet with difficulties in following the specified range and sequence of tests (due to time pressures, faults in product areas on which other areas depend, equipment failure, lack of resources, lack of special facilities, etc.). In such cases, decisions on the nature and sequence of alternative paths through the testing task should only be made and justified in the light of the complete testing plan, the required qualities and functionality of the product, the qualities of the product as evident in testing and control activities to date, the possible consequences of omitting some parts of the original plan, and present project priorities.

For example, where there is insufficient time or effort to complete the full test plan, it may be decided that all available effort should go into the testing of key product items, rather than spreading the resources evenly over all the items still to be tested. The plan should help in making such a decision by providing information on the time and resource implications of alternative strategies, as well as identifying both 'key' items and ones found to be at risk from testing so far.

Test plans used as an input to quality assurance and quality control processes. Test plans and recorded results should be used as reference materials for independent quality control and quality assurance staff who will use the schedules of required actions and outcomes in order to audit a project's progress and achievements. Plans relating to the acceptance and release of a product should also include evidence of quality as shown by the testing methods and their recorded results.

The use of test results to decide on an appropriate course of action following a testing activity. The test plan should contain, for each testing activity, a statement of what specifically should be tested for, and what test outcomes should be used as guides to acceptance, rejection, or further action. That is, the test plan should supply a prescribed analysis of the test results to be made after each testing activity, with indications of both the courses of action to be taken as a result, and the justification of each course. For example, tests related to either the quality of the process being followed, or of the quality of its products, could require different actions depending on whether the actual number of errors found is lower than, equal to, or higher than some expected number. The 'expected number' could be some average value found from previous projects, or one fixed in relation to the quality requirements of this particular product. Obviously, the dynamic adjustment of expectations must be handled very carefully and openly, and its effects fully recorded.

For a further discussion of the interpretation of test results see Doerflinger & Basili (1983) and Myers (1979).

Test plans and test results used as an input to project management, including resource planning and scheduling. Two examples are given below of the serial coordination of test plans and results. By keeping a record of the testing activities and corresponding test results throughout a project, a 'test history' can be produced for each project. The test history states exactly which testing activities were performed at each stage of the project, and what results were observed. The test history can then be compared with the test plan, and as a conclusion to the test history a list of guidelines can be produced for what can reasonably be expected in terms of quality and productivity in future projects.

A joint review of the in-field use of a product and its test history can provide information to help in the refinement in future projects of similar types. In particular, the information should support policy making and procedures definition for the following areas:

- development processes;
- selection of suitable types of tests;
- test plans;
- quality plans;
- cost and resource estimates;
- testing methods;
- quality control procedures;
- choice of tools;
- project and process scheduling;
- project planning;
- product design.

The idea of 'learning lessons' from previous projects and refining working methods between individual projects can be extended to be part of an organization's working strategy. In this situation a company would set up a standard method of collection and review of results, and a means of applying the lessons learnt in any one project into all subsequent projects. This method of working helps to avoid projects suffering from problems which have already been solved: it may also avoid projects being able to obtain only those tools and services which can be justified within their individual budgets — since justification across several projects may result in better tools and better results for them all. For example, it is more effective to procure test beds, test analysers, simulators and other special testing-related tools as a resource for several projects, thereby spreading the benefits and the cost.

The re-use of the format of the test plan from one project to another. Once the format, contents list and major and minor section headings of a test plan have been designed and established for one project — and a set of proven testing procedures and supporting tools found — then the document can serve as a useful proforma for other projects.

The outline of contents and headings should provide a useful guide to what should be in the test plan, and minimize re-thinking and reorganising the plan for other projects. Some sections of the plan (for example, testing methods, test cases and test result analysis) may actually be re-usable for other, very similar, projects.

The use of test results to identify unusual modules. Product elements showing a greater-than-average level of fault occurrence are known as 'fault-prone modules'. As fault-proneness during development is almost always followed by a high failure rate in service, it is worthwhile identifying these items as soon as possible and either eliminating them (by re-design) or ensuring that they receive the most rigorous investigations and testing available. Similarly, product elements found to be of greater than average 'complexity' may be selected for special attention. ('Complexity' can be measured in several ways, one of which is by the use of coverage analysers. Elements of the product for which the test coverage is found to be low after passing through the normal testing procedures, can be diagnosed as 'of high complexity'.) See Fagan (1976) and Myers (1979).

The use of test results to assess the effectiveness of testing procedures. Test results can be used to assess the effectiveness of the standard testing procedures being used within a project, by randomly selecting a small number of modules for a period of additional intensive testing, subsequent to their 'normal' testing. Observation of the number of faults disclosed by this additional testing, interpreted relative to the number of faults found by the standard testing, gives a rough estimate of the effectiveness of the project's standard testing procedures. It can also give some indication of the wisdom of releasing the product without further testing.

3.4.5 Data plans

The data plan prescribes what should be measured and recorded during a project, how it should be checked and collated, and how it should be interpreted and applied. Data may be collected for several purposes, within the specific project and beyond it, and ideally there should be a higher level of data collection and application into which project data is fed.

In this brief summary, it will not be possible to examine what can be collected or how it can be collated and analysed, in any detail. However, data sources can be expected to include all of manual recording on hard-copy, man-machine recording into a data base or data files, and automatic recording by support software (operating systems, security systems, device handlers, and various utilities). However measurement and counting are achieved, it is important that the measurements and recording methods are defined and controlled, in order to obtain comparability within a project and between projects.

3.4.5.1 The roles of the data plan and collected data within a project

A brief list of uses for project data would include those listed below. As can be seen, some are within the immediate project while others have wider applications: however, as the same data is frequently applied both within and outside a project, they are listed together:

- administration and project management;
- progress reporting and control;
- continuous product assessment;
- continuous process assessment;
- quality reporting and control;
- process management (including process improvement);
- project planning and prediction;
- enhancing software engineering capabilities.

3.4.5.2 Coordinating data plans between projects

The data plan contains a scheme for the collection, analysis and application of project data. While the collection of information to serve management purposes is usually routine, and quality records will be kept to support statements on the character of the delivered product, more sophisticated data usages can often be found which can identify areas of risk in any project or product, as well as helping to locate reasons for deviations and predict long-term outcomes.

Data collection, analysis and review are the main means of achieving a steady improvement in the ability to engineer desired qualities into both products and the processes by which they are made. A collection of data which covers more than one project and several different development routes (including tools, procedures and controls) provides opportunities to compare and contrast the means of production (and thus supports rational choices between them), as well as allowing the selection of standard expectations for performance which can be used in project planning and project control. Where projects begin with identical entries in their data plans, any changes or enhancements to those clauses made by one project can be assessed for their relevance to the others, and introduced quickly if this is found to be justified.

3.4.5.3 Coordinating (or sharing) data between organizations

Just as the use of data plans over a group of projects is more beneficial than within a single project, there is a greatly enhanced value to data collections and applications which cover wider ranges of product, project and development types. In particular, once the similarities and differences are reasonably well understood, evaluations and experiments can be shared amongst sites, resulting in both more searching investigations and reduced costs of undertaking them.

Apart from providing a wider base for evaluation, sharing of data should lead to a more general view of what is comprised in 'good practice' and of the connections between working methods and their results. Once managers of developments and of procurement have well founded and mutual understandings of relationships between requirements, processes, costs and qualities, there will be a reduction in the scope for horrid surprises (whether commercial or technical) and a corresponding growth in trust and cooperation.

While there are several possible ways of reaching this ideal of shared and rational beliefs (including the work being done in the Alvey-funded Software Data Library Project, and by the STARTS initiative) there is little point in collecting or comparing data which is itself of unknown quality. If the rationale, definitions and procedures of the appropriate data plan (plus any records of known problems or oddities found while collecting the set in question) are standard accompaniments to any set of data, then a substantial part of the risk of misuse or misunderstanding should be removed.

3.5 SUMMARY AND FUTURE DIRECTIONS

It seems clear that there is a need for improved quality management throughout the software industry, both in terms of improving the procedures available and of implementing those procedures more widely and effectively.

The quality plan and its associated data plans and test plans should be seriously considered when striving to achieve improvements in quality management. Their value is such that it is probable that these documents will be a standard requirement for all software developments. In the future, it is likely that 'advisor' systems will be developed to assist in the production of quality plans during interactive computer guided discussions within the development team, and between them and their customers or users. The user, with the quality engineering manager and his team, will together provide relevant information throughout the life of the project, for example when changes are caused by external events or when the desirability of new directions is prompted by the system. The system in turn will ensure that the documentation set is complete and accurate within its span of information.

Required supporting work includes the research into and development of appropriate concepts, models and metrics for the controlled achievement of required qualities, as well as the overt and demonstrable inclusion of quality management concerns in the continued development and improvement of methods or techniques such as specification languages, design languages, automated pseudo-code interpretation and automated source code generation.

In conclusion, software managers, procurers, developers and researchers need to work together towards sets of data, methods, procedures and tools which will improve the quality of software products and which will be easy to use, produce the required results consistently, and be sufficiently predictable, controllable and cost-effective to meet most project management and quality management objectives.

Acknowledgements

This work was supported by the Alvey Directorate as part of the Test

Specification and Quality Management project (project reference: ALV/PRJ/SE/031).

References

Boehm B.W. (1981) *Software Engineering Economics*. Prentice-Hall.

Doerflinger C.W. & Basili V.R. (1983) Monitoring software development through dynamic variables. *Proc. COMPSAC* **83**, pp. 434–445.

Evans M.W. (1984) *Productive Software Test Management*. Wiley.

Fagan M.E. (1976) Design and code inspections to reduce errors in program development. *IBM Systems Journal* **15** (3), pp. 182–211.

Hennell M.A. & Hedley D. (1985) *Testing in Difficult Situations*. Version 1. TSQM Project Document.

Myers G.J. (1979) *The Art of Software Testing*. Wiley.

Chapter 4

Design Fault Tolerance in Practical Systems

T. ANDERSON
Centre for Software Reliability,
University of Newcastle upon Tyne, Newcastle NE1 7RU

4.1 INTRODUCTION

Traditionally, the provision of reliability in computing systems has been based on the use of *fault prevention*, which tries to avert system failure by ensuring that no faults arise when the system is in service. Fault prevention is itself based on two further approaches, namely *fault avoidance*, an attempt to ensure that no faults are introduced during the design and construction of the system, and *fault removal*, which refers to techniques used to identify and eliminate as many faults as possible before any reliance is placed on the operational system.

Despite the obvious necessity for such techniques, it has long been recognized by the builders of hardware for computing systems that fault prevention alone is inadequate for achieving systems of very high reliability. Additional *fault tolerance* techniques have therefore been extensively utilized to provide a further means of defence against the damaging effects of those residual faults which fault prevention has not succeeded in eradicating. However, the traditional approaches to fault tolerance in hardware systems have largely been based on coping with the effects of well-understood failure modes of physical components. Although this facilitates the economical provision of effective redundancy, it also limits the applicability of the techniques. Specifically, conventional hardware fault tolerance methods are rarely powerful enough to cope with deficiencies of design. Consequently, most hardware fault tolerance techniques cannot be directly applied in software, where all faults are design faults.

It is, nevertheless, feasible to provide tolerance for design faults, but for this to be successful a more general form of redundancy is required. Redundancy must be incorporated in the design itself by including replicated modules which have been independently designed. Avizienis (1982) has suggested the phrase *design diversity* for this approach, which for its success must ensure an adequate level of independence of fault behaviour.

The basic justification for the use of design fault tolerance is that perfect designs will always be extremely difficult to achieve, and furthermore, are sure to be very expensive. Despite the availability of a variety of techniques which aim to prevent the presence of design faults in systems (such as design and testing methodologies) it is clear that completely fault-free designs are rarely, if ever, developed. Confirmation of this point is evident from the current inadequacy of software development technology. Programs which do not contain any faults at all (zero-defect software) are an aspiration rather than a reality. In fact, in practical contexts where highly reliable software is demanded, the project manager is likely to rely on so-called 'exhaustive' testing techniques in the hope of reducing the incidence of faults to a satisfactory level. A strong case can be made for the adoption of a wider range of techniques simply on the grounds of diminishing returns.

Despite the apparent need for utilizing design fault tolerance in software systems, this approach has not found widespread acceptance. One reason for this may be a lack of information on the potential advantages, and of examples of systems which have already made use of the technique. The purpose of this chapter is to summarize the status of design fault tolerance techniques, to record their application in existing systems, and to review the results of evaluation studies on their effectiveness.

4.2 DESIGN FAULT TOLERANCE

To provide protection against the unpredictable effects of faults in design, a very general form of redundancy is needed to support fault tolerance. This necessarily involves the provision of modules of diverse design operating on replicated states. Two principal approaches have been described in some detail in the literature, and these are known as recovery blocks (Horning *et al.* 1974) and *N*-version programming (Chen & Avizienis 1978). Although these are often viewed as radically different and even competing approaches, they are in fact quite similar in concept. What is usually regarded as a significant difference is that the standard mode of operation for recovery blocks involves the sequential execution of a set of modules, whereas the modules in an *N*-version program are conventionally assumed to be executed in parallel. The distinction here is more apparent than real since parallel execution of a recovery block or serial execution of an *N*-version program is easily envisaged. The mode of execution should be regarded as a detail of implementation since it need not affect the semantics of the constructs. Of much greater significance is the mechanism used to select which of the results from the multiple modules should be taken as the result of the diverse computation. These issues have been discussed at greater length elsewhere (Anderson 1986).

A simple unified diagram (Fig. 4.1) illustrates both schemes; the method used to obtain the agreed result is termed the *adjudicator*. This is an additional module which adjudicates between the (potentially) multiple outputs from n different modules $M_1,\ldots,M_n$. Note that in certain circumstances the adjudicator may not be able to determine a single result R from the subset of the outputs $R_1,\ldots,R_n$ which it actually receives from the modules. In this situation it must be possible to signal an exception by giving an 'alarm' indication.

4.3 FAULT TOLERANCE TECHNIQUES

As well as the two principal notations referred to above, a number of other proposals have been made in the area of design fault tolerance. The earliest suggestions can be categorized as techniques for *defensive programming*, in which a programmer adopts relatively *ad hoc* methods in an attempt to minimize the damage which could arise from the presence of residual 'bugs' in critical software. Whenever a program contains the comment 'it won't ever get here' it can be assumed that the intention is to provide some form of safe response in the event of an unforeseen design fault. A specific system in which it has been reported that extensive use was made of defensive programming is the Safeguard ballistic missile defence system (BSTJ 1975). It has been rumoured that so many safety checks were built into the software that

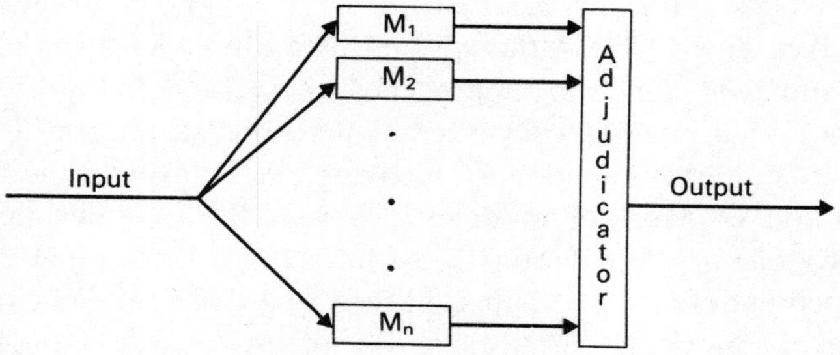

Fig. 4.1. Design diversity with adjudication.

military officers had doubts whether missiles could actually be launched in the event of a nuclear attack. Perhaps this should be a design feature for all missile systems!

A more comprehensive approach to tolerating faults in a software system is adopted in the *dual software* technique (also referred to as *distinct* or *dissimilar* software). This approach has a substantial history (Gilb 1974, Fischler *et al.* 1975) and has often been advocated as a particularly effective method of performing system-level testing (Gilb 1977) for software. As the names suggest, the approach involves the implementation of two distinct versions of the software. The intention is that these should exhibit dissimilar behaviour with respect to faults, so that by executing both versions in a dual configuration a comparator applied to the outputs will be able to detect any discrepancy and raise the alarm. Some practical systems utilizing dual software will be mentioned later.

Suggestions have been made which combine the basic recovery block and *N*-version proposals to yield hybrid schemes. In the Tandem approach (Soneru 1981) (which has no connection with the commercial organization of that name), a sequence of two-version systems attempt, in turn, to produce matching results. The consensus recovery block (Scott 1983) attempts to resolve the conflict between disparate outputs from an *N*-version program by belatedly applying an acceptance test to the results.

Considerable attention has been given to the problems of employing design fault tolerance techniques in concurrent systems, where some coordination of recovery strategies and process interactions is likely to be needed to avoid the *domino effect* of unconstrained rollback. The canonical approach is based on establishing a *conversation* (Randell 1975) whenever processes need to communicate. However, the conversation merely constitutes an appropriate structuring concept; notations and mechanisms have to be devised before it can be embodied in software. Gregory & Knight (1987) will provide an overview of work on this topic.

A further application area of relevance to design fault tolerance is that of real-time systems. Techniques have been proposed to ensure that the potential overhead in performance incurred by fault tolerance techniques is minimized and allowed for in system design, and to explicitly address the issues raised by timing faults in critical systems. The deadline mechanism suggested by Campbell *et al.* (1979) is based on a scheduling strategy which allows time for the execution of both primary and alternate versions of software modules. A restricted conversation regime, termed an *exchange* (Anderson & Knight 1983) has been advocated for real-time systems which have a cyclic mode of operation. The CRAnfield Fault Tolerance (CRAFT) proposal, sometimes called Foodtaster, is based on using algebraic transformations to produce multiple software versions which then execute in skewed time domains. Tolerance to design faults is likely to be limited, and Morris (1981) has noted difficulties with the transformation techniques involved.

4.4 ESTABLISHED MECHANISMS

There is a considerable body of experience in a wide area of supportive technology which can be exploited in making use of design fault tolerance in a practical system. The point being stressed here is that the mechanisms needed for fault tolerance are hardly novel — checking and recovery procedures have always been needed in computing systems, particularly in database applications.

Software checking for fault conditions should not be confused with conventional decision making within the program, and ideally should be supported in a similar way to run-time assertions, or more comprehensively by a generalized exception handling mechanism. Recovery strategies can exploit the wealth of experience gained in the provision of recovery in database systems, such as checkpoint/restart facilities, audit trails and compensation algorithms. Error propagation can be limited by providing support for *atomic actions*, which isolate groups of processes from the rest of a system in a similar fashion to that adopted in disciplined transaction processing systems. Work on commitment protocols and interactive consistency can be harnessed in support of design fault tolerance. Anderson & Lee (1981) discuss many of these techniques in more detail.

Specialist techniques may also be useful, so long as due account is taken of their original purpose. Work at Waterloo on robust data structures (Taylor & Black 1982), methods in the area of secure systems based on the notion of a trusted kernel (Rushby 1984) and the highly developed and well-established technology for providing hardware (physical) fault tolerance (Carter 1985) can all yield insight for coping with the more general problem of arbitrary mistakes in design.

Furthermore, current trends in computer system design are in harmony with the needs of fault tolerance. The general notions of modularity and information hiding, and the principles of hierarchical design, have as their primary aim a reduction in the complexity of computer systems. Design fault tolerance should be incorporated in a system in such a way that any consequential increase in complexity is minimized. This would appear to mandate a modular and hierarchical approach to fault tolerance as well (Anderson & Lee 1981).

The interconnection of multiple computing nodes to form distributed processing systems provides a natural pool of resources (computation, memory and peripherals) which fault tolerant designs can exploit. But the difficulties introduced by networked communications between concurrent cooperating activities pose new challenges (Cristian *et al.* 1985).

Perhaps the most beneficial trend is the continuing decline of hardware costs. This should ensure that the costs of providing redundancy in computer systems are more frequently recognized as acceptable when compared with the benefits available in increased reliability and safety from fault tolerant approaches. More specifically, special purpose hardware features, which can greatly facilitate the provision of design fault tolerance, are becoming much more feasible and attractive in cost terms. Examples are recoverable memory units, monitoring and checking devices, fine grain protection schemes, and accurate high resolution clocks.

4.5 PRACTICAL EXPERIENCE

Most of the practical systems in which design fault tolerance techniques have been used are critical systems, in which a failure of the software could lead to loss of life. For such applications the relevant regulatory authority will usually strive to ensure that the occurrence of a single fault will not lead to a failure of the system. Redundancy and fault tolerance are consequently standard practice. With the advent of embedded computer systems taking responsibility for the control of critical systems, it was argued that the software was an obvious 'single point of failure' and that a multi-version approach should reduce the risk of a single bug resulting in a system failure. Dual version software systems were therefore implemented for certain transport and power systems.

An excellent illustrative example is the slat and flap control system of the Airbus A310 civil aircraft (Martin 1982). This avionic system is completely 'fly-by-wire' in that deployment and control of the relevant wing surfaces is totally entrusted to digital electronics. There is no provision whatsoever for any alternative control via hydraulic or other mechanical linkages. Two independent channels contain separate software versions, programmed in different languages, with each version executed on a dual microprocessor. The outputs from the two channels drive the stepping motors which move the slats and flaps, but any discrepancy locks the surfaces in their current position; a warning is issued to the pilot that slat and flap adjustment is no longer available. By so doing, the system 'fails safe', since the aircraft is certified to operate without slat and flap control — so long as there is no uncommanded movement (and wing surfaces remain symmetrical). Three-version software, with voting to resolve disagreement, is being considered for avionic systems in the design of the A320. Boeing have used dual software in the flight management system for the 737/300 and in the yaw damper and stabilizer trim systems for the 757 and 767.

Perhaps the best known application of dual software is in the flight computers for the NASA Space Transportation System, the 'Space Shuttle'. Four identical primary computers (IBM AP101s) execute the normal flight software, while a fifth computer (also identical) runs a back-up version of the software. A range of error detection mechanisms are used to check for any malfunction, but reconfiguration of the system is under the control of the astronauts. In particular, an irreversible switch from the primary system to the back-up can only be performed manually. On the occasion of the first planned launch of the Shuttle, the two versions of the software failed to synchronize with each other and the launch had to be delayed (Garman 1981). This bug has been cited as indicating the penalties of redundancy in software, but what is rarely stressed is that the penalty of a delay, even an unnecessary one, is minimal compared to the cost of an accident in flight. At the first launch attempt the fault tolerance mechanisms operated flawlessly, detecting a problem and responding appropriately. With hindsight the problem can be seen to be spurious, and one that should have been identified earlier — but this does not detract from what should count as a success for design fault tolerance.

A slightly more prosaic application of dual software is the JZS interlocking and station control system originally developed for railway use in Scandinavia (see Chapter 15), but which has now been installed at a range of locations throughout Europe. Independent teams developed two complete versions of the software, which is deployed with an electronic comparator unit. In the event of a disagreement being detected, track and vehicle movements are halted, and signals are set at red, pending manual resolution. An attempt was made to increase the independence of the two versions by stipulating that one of the systems must input and manipulate all its data, including static descriptions of track layouts, in an encoded representation.

Another area where multi-version software has received considerable attention is that of safety shutdown systems for nuclear reactors.

At least three examples can be cited. Atomic Energy of Canada developed a system based on two dissimilar channels, each of which was then operated in triplex mode. In early experimental work, Gmeiner & Voges (1979) reported on the implementation of a three-version reactor safety control system where three different languages were used. This led to the design of the MIRA reactor shutdown system (Voges *et al.* 1982). A major international study called PODS (Project on Diverse Software) involved the implementation of three versions of a reactor over-power trip system. Two different languages, two different specification methods and two different major algorithms were employed by the three teams, diversely located in England, Finland and Norway (Bishop *et al.* 1986).

A research project at the University of Newcastle upon Tyne implemented a subset of the facilities of a naval command and control system, using recovery blocks and a form of conversation structure (Anderson *et al.* 1985). Approximately 8000 lines of Coral were written by experienced programmers in accordance with normal commercial software development standards. Alternative designs for diverse modules were not difficult to devise, but some adjudication modules proved less tractable. In difficult cases, a structural consistency check on primary data structures had to be adopted as a means of providing limited run-time error detection.

A further group of systems using fault tolerant software should be mentioned, and these concern military applications (Slivinski *et al.* 1984). Draper Laboratories were reported to be implementing a dissimilar back-up software system for the F8 digital fly-by-wire fighter aircraft. Boeing have developed an approach (called MOSS) based on a software kernel which supports essential functions, and have applied this in a flight control system simulation for the C-135 transport. Again in a simulation system, Milco have applied the CRAFT approach to the terrain following the software of the B1 bomber; dual hardware executed both versions of the software, with adjudication of error situations by means of an averaging voter subject to pre-set tolerances. System Development Corporation experimented with distributed recovery blocks in a real-time closed loop control system for a missile tracking application (Welch 1983).

4.6 EVALUATION STUDIES

There is little dispute that the best evidence for (or against) the effectiveness of design fault tolerance techniques would be drawn from practical systems such as those presented in the previous section, and ideally would be based on data collected on the behaviour of these systems in full operational service (rather than simulated or experimental regimes of operation). It is unfortunately the case that such data is not currently available. One reason appears to be that the data is either not recorded or not reported, but another is the obvious difficulty in obtaining a significant volume of data on failure events in systems with very high reliability targets. Any critical system experiencing more than very infrequent failures would soon be taken out of service until confidence had been restored.

In the absence of hard operational evidence, there are two alternatives. The first is to consider analytic modelling techniques for the reliability of software embodying design diversity. A surprising number of models have been proposed, covering most of the notations mentioned in this chapter (Grnarov *et al.* 1980, Bhargava 1981, Soneru 1981, Wei 1981, Migneault 1982, Scott *et al.* 1983, Laprie 1984, Eckhardt 1985). Much of this work suffers from a lack of empirical validation, and depends heavily on assumptions which may be questioned. Nevertheless, all of the models do confirm that design fault tolerance has a potential for enhancing software reliability. However, it is difficult to quantify what improvement can be expected until the models have been calibrated and their accuracy confirmed by experimentation.

Therefore, for direct evidence of reliability improvement, it is necessary to turn to the second alternative, namely the results of experimentation. One difficulty here is that measurements are usually made on relatively small scale programs which may not accurately reflect the behaviour of the more complex software likely to be needed in realistic applications.

An experiment at UCLA to investigate *N*-version programming (Chen & Avizienis 1978) employed students to produce 18 versions of an airport scheduling program. The programs were written in PL/I and contained about 400 lines each. All 816 different three-version combinations were investigated by executing a series of transactions. In 27.1% of these combinations, two correct versions successfully masked the incorrect results produced by a defective third version.

A subsequent experiment conducted jointly at UVA and UCI (Knight & Leveson 1986) generated 27 versions of a program to verify missile launch conditions. After independent development and testing, the versions were evaluated by executing each one on a million test cases. Considered as single versions, the average success rate per test case was 99.92%. Run in pairs, the two-version combinations detected a failure of one of the versions (when this occurred) in 99.5% of cases.

In three-version combinations, failure masking was achieved in 95% of the cases when a failure occurred, and a discrepancy was detected in a further 3.6% of these cases. Thus the three-version programs demonstrated a 20-fold improvement over the single version programs.

Experimental evaluation of the naval command and control system constructed at Newcastle was based on determining the effectiveness of the fault tolerant software in eliminating failures which would have occurred in the absence of diversity. Data was obtained from a series of action scenarios driving a simulated tactical environment. A detailed analysis of these runs (Anderson *et al.* 1985) showed that without fault tolerance the software would have failed on 222 occasions as a result of faults in the command and control software. But of these 222 potential failures, only 57 actually happened, the other 165 being successfully masked by the use of error detection, recovery and execution of an alternate module. A small number of new failures (eight in fact) were actually caused by deficiencies in the fault tolerance mechanisms, so the overall success ratio was 157/222, i.e. 71%.

4.7 CURRENT STATUS

The preceding sections were intended to make the following points concerning the status of design fault tolerance as a viable technique for the practising software engineer.

- The approach has had the benefit of extensive conceptual development.
- A range of notations, mechanisms and supporting technology is available.
- The technique has already been adopted for a number of practical systems used in critical applications.
- Results from evaluation experiments are highly supportive.

Any software engineer should aim to construct reliable software as economically as possible. In striving for reliability, design faults can be avoided, removed or tolerated, and techniques are available for each of these three strategies. It seems likely that the most cost-effective approach to the design of reliable software will involve a judicious selection of techniques covering all three areas. Eventually, experimental evidence on the relative merits of different methods may enable such judgements to be made on a basis of fact rather than special pleading. Until then, folklore and common sense may be the best guide — don't put all your eggs in one basket!

References

Anderson T. (1986) A structured decision mechanism for diverse software. *Proceedings of 5th Symposium on Reliability in Distributed Software and Database Systems, Los Angeles*, pp. 125–129.

Anderson T. & Knight J.C. (1983) A framework for software fault tolerance in real-time systems. *IEEE Transactions on Software Engineering* **SE-9** (3), pp. 335–364.

Anderson T. & Lee P.A. (1981) *Fault Tolerance: Principles and Practice*. Prentice-Hall.

Anderson T. *et al.* (1985) Software fault tolerance: an evaluation. *IEEE Trans. on Software Engineering* **SE-11** (12), pp. 1502–1510.

Avizienis A. (1982) Design diversity — the challenge of the eighties. *Digest of 12th International Symposium on Fault Tolerant Computing*, Santa Monica, pp. 44–45.

Bhargava B. (1981) Software reliability in real-time systems. *Proceedings of National Computer Conference*, Chicago, pp. 297–309.

Bishop P.G. *et al.* (1986) PODS — A project on diverse software. *IEEE Transactions on Software Engineering* **SE-12** (9), pp. 929–940.

BSTJ (1975) SAFEGUARD data-processing system. *Bell System Technical Journal* **54** (special supplement).

Campbell R.H. *et al.* (1979) Simulations of a fault-tolerant deadline mechanism. *Digest of 9th International Symposium on Fault Tolerant Computing*, Madison. pp. 95–101.

Carter W.C. (1985) Hardware fault tolerance. In *Resilient Computing Systems* (ed. T. Anderson), Collins, pp. 11–63.

Chen L. & Avizienis A. (1978) N-version programming: a fault-tolerance approach to reliability of software operation. *Digest of 8th International Symposium on Fault Tolerant Computing*, Toulouse, pp. 3–9.

Cristian F. *et al.* (1985) Atomic broadcast: from simple message diffusion to byzantine agreement. *Digest of 15th International Symposium on Fault Tolerant Computing*, Ann Arbor, pp. 200–206.

Eckhardt D.E. & Lee L.D. (1985) A theoretical basis for the analysis of multi-version software subject to coincident errors. *IEEE Trans on Software Engineering* **SE-11** (12), pp. 1511–1517.

Fischler M.A. *et al.* (1975) Distinct software: an approach to reliable computing. *Proceedings of Second USA-Japan Computer Conference*, Tokyo, pp. 573–579.

Garman J.R. (1981) The "bug" heard round the world. *Software Engineering Notes* **6** (5), pp. 3–10.

Gilb T. (1974) Parallel programming. *Datamation*, **20** (10), pp. 160–161.

Gilb T. (1977) Distinct software: a redundancy technique for reliable software. In *State of the Art Report on Software Reliability*, Infotech, pp. 117–133.

Gmeiner L. & Voges U. (1979) Software diversity in reactor protection systems: an experiment. *Proceedings of IFAC Workshop on Safety of Computer Control Systems*, Stuttgart. pp. 75–79.

Gregory S.T. & Knight J.C. (1987) Concurrent system recovery. To be published in *More Resilient Computing Systems* (ed. T. Anderson), Collins.

Grnarov A. *et al.* (1980) On the performance of software fault tolerance strategies. *Digest of 10th International Symposium on Fault Tolerant Computing*, Kyoto. pp. 251–253.

Horning J.J. *et al.* (1974) A program structure for error detection and recovery. In *Lecture Notes in Computer Science 16* (ed. E. Gelenbe & C. Kaiser), Springer-Verlag, pp. 171–187.

Kelly J. & Avizienis A. (1983) A specification oriented multi-version software experiment. *Digest of 13th International Symposium on Fault Tolerant Computing*, Milan. pp. 120–126.

Knight J.C. & Leveson N.G. (1986) An empirical study of failure probabilities in multiversion software. *Digest of 16th International Symposium on Fault Tolerant Computing Systems*, Vienna. pp. 165–170.

Laprie J.-C. (1984) Dependability evaluation of software systems in operation. *IEEE Transactions on Software Engineering* **SE-10** (6), pp. 701–714.

Martin D.J. (1982) Dissimilar software in high integrity applications in flight controls. *Proceedings of AGARD Symposium on Software for Avionics*, The Hague. p. 36:1.

Migneault G.E. (1982) The cost of software fault tolerance, *Proceedings of AGARD Symposium on Software for Avionics*, The Hague. pp. 37:1–37:8.

Morris M.A. (1981) *An Approach to the Design of Fault Tolerant Software*. M.Sc Thesis, Cranfield Institute of Technology.

Randell B. (1975) System structure for software fault tolerance. *IEEE Transactions on Software Engineering* **SE-1** (2), pp. 220–232.

Rushby J.M. (1984) A trusted computing base for embedded systems. *Proceedings 7th DoD/NBS Computer Security Initiative Conference*, Gaithersburg. pp. 294–311.

Scott R.K. (1983) *Data Domain Modelling of Fault Tolerant Software Reliability*. PhD Dissertation, North Carolina State University, Raleigh.

Scott R.K. *et al.* (1983) Modelling fault tolerant software reliability. *Proceedings of 3rd Symposium on Reliability in Distributed Software and Database Systems*, Clearwater Beach. pp. 15–27.

Slivinski T. *et al.* (1984) Study of fault tolerant software technology. *Mandex Inc. Report*, NASA Langley Research Center.

Soneru M.D. (1981) *A Methodology for the Design and Analysis of Fault-Tolerant Operating Systems*. PhD Dissertation, Illinois Institute of Technology, Chicago.

Taylor D.J. & Black J.P. (1982) Principles of data structure error correction. *IEEE Transactions on Computers* **C-31** (7), pp. 602–608.

Voges U. *et al.* (1982) Use of microprocessors in a safety-oriented reactor shut-down system. In *Reliability in Electrical and Electronic Components and Systems* (ed. E. Langer & J. Moltoft), North Holland. pp. 493–496.

Wei A.Y.-W. (1981) *Real-Time Programming with Fault Tolerance*. PhD Dissertation, University of Illinois, Urbana.

Welch H.O. (1983) Distributed recovery block performance in a real-time control loop. *Proceedings of Real-Time Systems Symposium*, Arlington. pp. 268–276.

Chapter 5

Software Failures are Management Failures

A. WINGROVE
*Centre for Software Reliability,
The City University, London EC1V 0HB*

5.1 INTRODUCTION

There is a direct relationship between the success of any product and the quality of management that has gone into the process of its creation. It is the task of management to plan the most economical course for reaching the required objectives in a reasonable time with available resources. The key parameters which need to be measured and controlled are performance, schedule and cost.

The title of this paper is not intended to be a condemnation of managers. It has been chosen simply to focus upon the relationship between the creation of a reliable software product and the management process which is used to develop the product, get it into service and then look after it until its useful life is finished. We call that process 'Project Management' and it might be as well that we understand what is implied by the term.

5.2 PROJECT MANAGEMENT

Figure 5.1 shows the elements which make up a project. Not all projects involve both hardware and software. However, since software has now become a common constituent of many of the more difficult projects, the comments in this paper will, for the most part, assume we are dealing with the development of systems with 'embedded' computers. Nevertheless, much of the commentary relates equally to the development of software alone.

We can divide the life-cycle of a project into six distinct phases, from its conception to its replacement or termination.

1 *Feasibility*. A user's perceived need usually starts off as some form of 'target' requirement. The target will be examined and explored for possible solutions, refined to a formal user requirement which will become the basis for a system specification. The requirement details

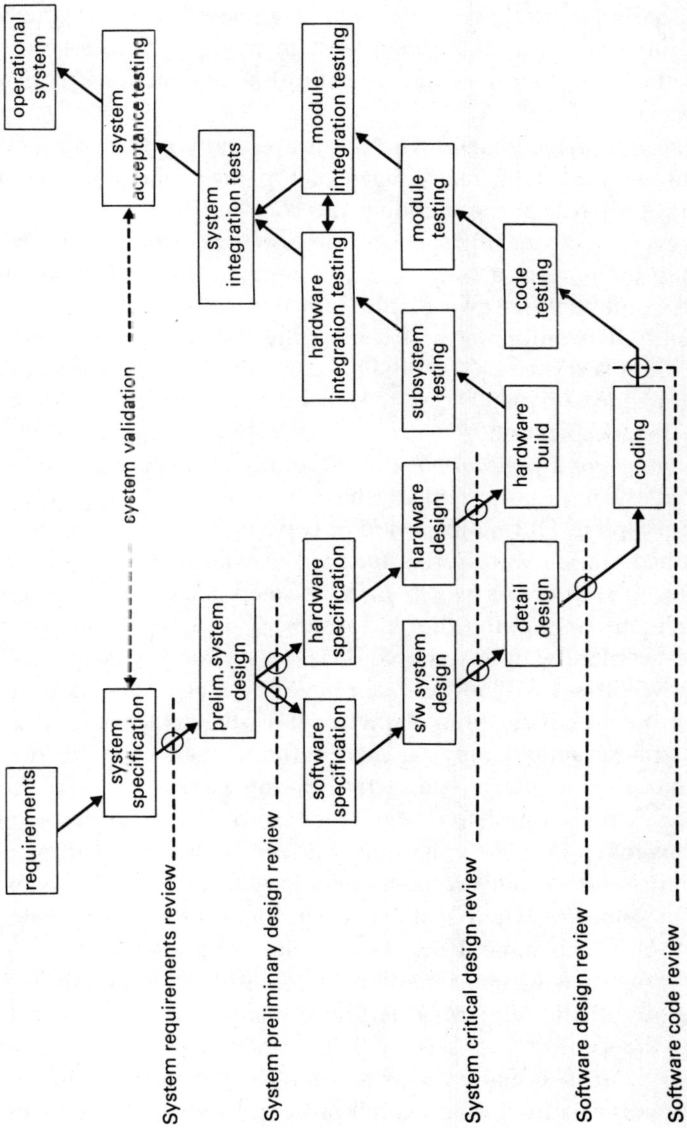

Fig. 5.1. Stages of a project.

what the user wants; the specification reflects how the system requirements will be implemented.

2 *Definition*. Using the system specification, an outline (or preliminary) system design is prepared, giving a 'high level' view of the system design implementation, the main system modules and, where appropriate, the apportionment and specification of functions to hardware and software.

3 *Design and development*. The hardware and software specifications are now expanded through stages of top level and detail design to building the hardware and coding the software.

4 *Testing*. Testing usually starts at the lowest possible functional level, gradually building in a step-by-step manner to tests of complete subsystems combining hardware and software.

5 *Integration*. Combining and testing the subsystems checked out in the previous test phase. The final part of this phase is usually a demonstration to the user that the system meets the contractual requirements set by the specification.

6 *Acceptance and operational use*. Operational testing is used to confirm that the user requirements have been met and that the system can be accepted. During its period of service the system will need to be maintained. In software terms this will usually involve a combination of repair (fixing errors which have escaped the testing process) and enhancement (improving the performance).

One problem with any simple division of the project life-cycle into descriptive phases is that there can never be a clear allocation of each of the project activities into a single phase. Ideally, progress to a subsequent phase should only be made after a review of the preceding phase has shown that all the activities and goals of that phase have been successfully completed. In practice, activities merge across phases. Decisions taken in a later phase may affect the work of earlier phases. The solution of design problems may influence previous system concepts. In some cases parts of the design may prove to be infeasible, necessitating fundamental revisions to the requirements.

A project management plan needs to be flexible enough to accommodate any of the numerous perturbations to the 'ideal' plan but yet provide the project manager with a sufficiently rigid framework to maintain control. Usually this is accomplished by using a hierarchy of control plans relating to the overall project, project phases (which may be different from the phases described here), and individual project activities. Project control is then based on feedback from lower to higher levels using various forms of assessment and review to determine progress.

But despite all that is known about the techniques of project management, it is still the case that projects which involve software seem to run a higher risk of over-running their budget, being delivered late and sometimes having a lower performance than expected. Project managers give many reasons for their difficulties — the most common are listed in Table 5.1. Encountering any of these problems is bound to have some effect on the economics of a project. The central problem with software is that it needs to be produced more economically and with greater reliability — meaning that it will perform the job expected of it every time — than can be done at present.

5.3 THE ECONOMICS OF COMPUTER-BASED SYSTEMS

There are advantages to be gained by using computers and software to replace many of the functions previously implemented in hardware. The basic costs of computing (processing unit plus memory) are now very low, especially when microprocessors are used. Costs are still falling, even though processing power is increasing. Software (programs) can replace complicated mechanisms and circuits, so reducing system complexity and offering the prospect of higher intrinsic reliability. Computers and memory are relatively lightweight — software weighs nothing! Power requirements are low and the space taken up by the hardware is small — all considerable advantages for embedded computer systems. But even in more conventional applications, the falling

Table 5.1. Management problems.

General lack of *Visibility*
Incomplete and ambiguous *Requirements*
Incomplete and imprecise *Specifications*
Lack of common *Terminology*
Uncertainties in software/hardware *Apportionment*
Rapid changes in *Technology*
Determining the suitability of *Languages*
Difficulties in modelling *Systems*
Uncertainties in cost and resource *Estimation*
Measuring and predicting *Reliability*
Difficulties with progress *Monitoring*
Complicated error and change *Control*
Lack of agreed *Metrics*
Problems with *Interfacing*
Problems with *Integration*
Difficulties in controlling '*Maintenance*'

costs of computer hardware, its good reliability and the versatility of software, make the use of computers attractive.

But, in practice, some of these advantages have proved to be illusory. Replacing conventional hardware with lower cost computing power has rarely reduced system costs. Lower basic costs are almost inevitably traded for higher functional complexity. This also means that the expected gains in system reliability are seldom realized. What has happened is that, over the past 30 years, the ratio of software costs to hardware costs has changed from 20:80 to around 80:20. The high cost associated with software development is one of the main drivers of the higher system costs.

There is some evidence that software development costs could be reduced if we were better able to control and manage software projects. In a Report to Congress in 1979, the US General Accounting Office made an analysis of software development in nine Federal Projects. The analysis showed that out of a total of about \$6.8M spent on program development, only 5% was used (Fig. 5.2). While these statistics are often disputed (some of the projects were in trouble, some of the unused software was developmental and for tests, etc.) the message would be disturbing even if the proportion of software used was an

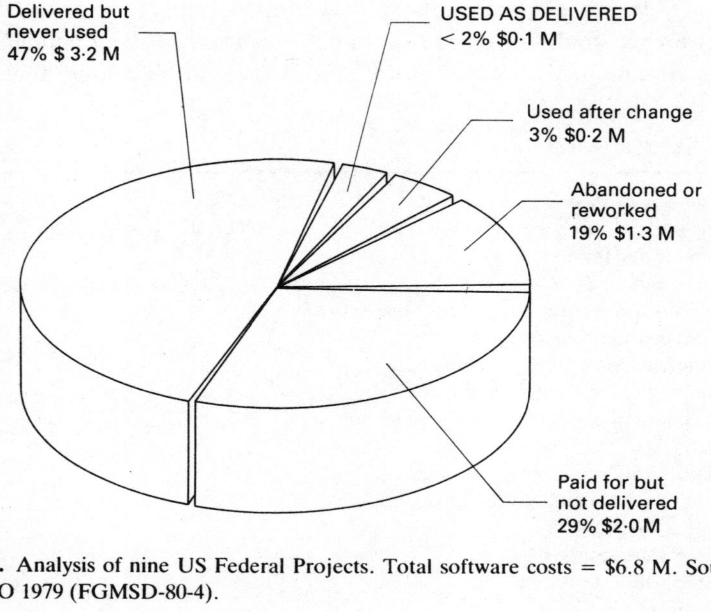

Fig. 5.2. Analysis of nine US Federal Projects. Total software costs = \$6.8 M. Source: US GAO 1979 (FGMSD-80-4).

order greater. Again, this is but one isolated piece of evidence. We have no such published authoritative evidence from European sources to compare. But anecdotal evidence and published reports of projects with software problems do suggest that 'getting the software right' is a costly business.

Clearly, any means of reducing software development costs must be worthy of attention. Figure 5.3 illustrates the pattern of the relationship between actual project expenditure and the proportion of the total project budget committed at the end of each of the major stages of a project. It can be seen that by the time the system specification has been prepared, and even before full development starts, about 80% of the total project budget has been committed. The message is that if changes are necessary, the earlier they are made the better. Figure 5.4 shows the general trend of the increasing cost of change as the project progresses.

A classification of software errors (Fig. 5.5) reinforces the point. Early errors in the specification can account for more than a quarter of all errors that will need to be corrected. When the unresolved omissions and ambiguities of the requirements are added to this it is easy to

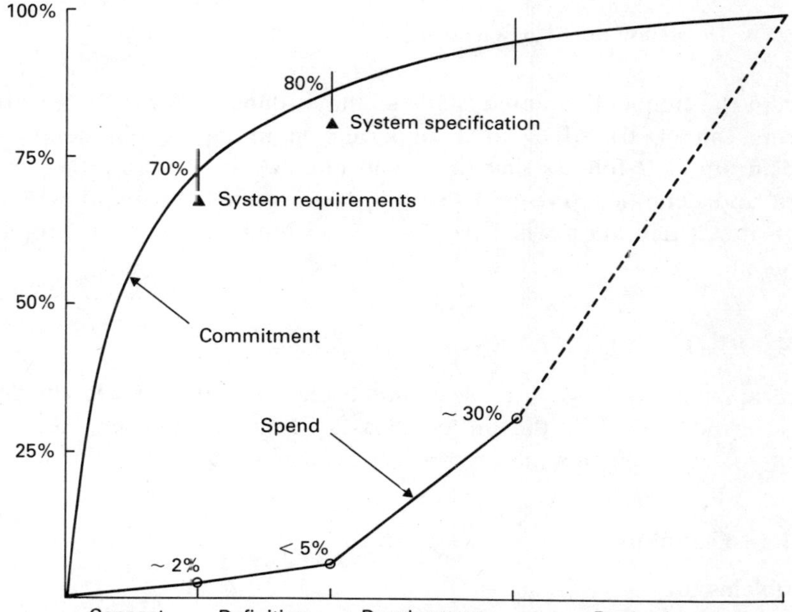

Fig. 5.3. Project spend and commitment. (Total = hardware and software.)

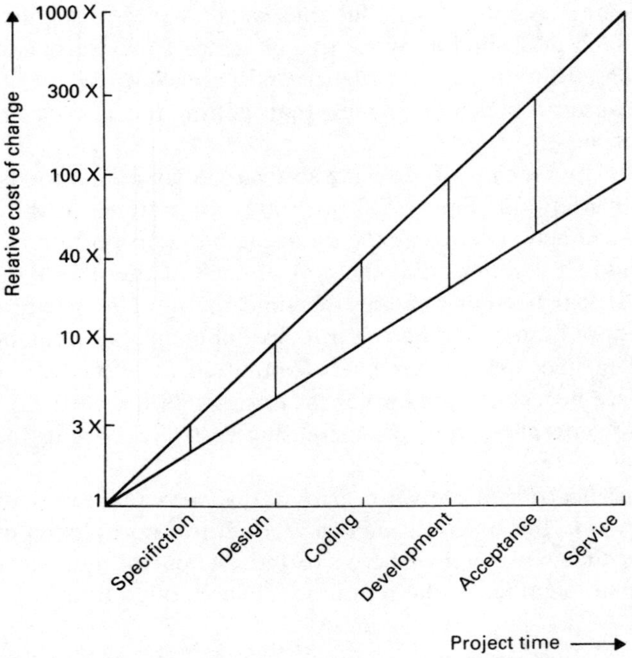

Fig. 5.4. The relative cost of software changes. Sources: TRW, GTE, IBM.

accept the frequently quoted 'statistic' that around 50% of all software errors can be traced to some imperfection in the requirements or specification. It follows that time (and money) spent during the concept and definition phases of a project reconciling the requirements with the specification will have a powerful influence on total project costs.

5.4 PROJECT PHASES

Bearing in mind the general observations that have already been made, we can now consider the project phases in more detail and identify some of the problems met by project management.

5.4.1 Feasibility

Problems are:
- incomplete and ambiguous requirements;
- incomplete and imprecise specifications;
- lack of a common terminology.

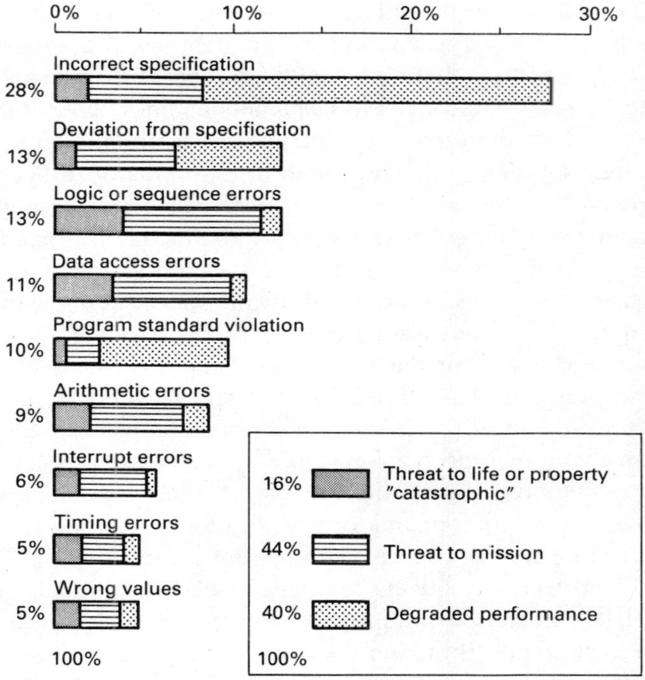

Fig. 5.5. Typical classification of software errors. Source: ED 22–7–82.

At the start of a project, it is often the case that the customer (or user), having identified a need, will have only a vague knowledge of the best way of satisfying that need in detail. The feasibility stage of a project should be the most flexible stage of all — when the expertise of the supplier (the contractor) can be brought to bear on the customer's problems with a view to a mutually agreed solution which fits the customer's initial view of costs. For larger projects this process may well be conducted upon the basis of competition between a number of contractors.

The dialogue between customer and contractor must be sufficiently detailed and searching to ensure the production of a firm set of requirements which are as complete and unambiguous as possible. The requirements should define exactly *what* is required. But, except for the most trivial of applications, there can probably never be any such thing as a 'complete and unambiguous' requirement. Specifications derived from most requirements will be imperfect and will need to be refined as the project proceeds.

User's requirements will almost certainly be written in an 'informal' language (e.g. English, possibly supported by drawings and diagrams), which includes technical terms and 'jargon' familiar to the customer. It is absolutely essential that the contractor and customer understand each other's terminology to avoid misunderstandings being written into the system specification which will detail *how* the requirements will be satisfied. For software, this may create the first major difficulty when formal methods are used for the software specifications. In many cases, the mathematically based specification will be incomprehensible to the customer so there will be a need for the system supplier to assure the customer, in some way, that the software specification with its unfamiliar notation satisfies his/her needs.

The understanding of the needs represented in the requirements and the capture of those needs by the specification is one of the factors, if not the most crucial one, of a successful project. Experience has shown that a high proportion of the 'failures' and problems subsequently encountered during the life of a project will stem from inadequacies in the requirements or specification.

The amount of effort that is needed from the customer in the early stages of a project is frequently underestimated — particularly by the customer! It is in the best interests of the customer to pay very close attention to this transformation of requirements to specification, since the acceptance of an agreed system specification will probably form the basis of the contract to develop the final system.

Errors and omissions in requirements and specifications are the largest single cause of software errors. They can be corrected or eliminated more cheaply at this stage of the project than any other. Any known omissions, which may be unavoidable when there are design uncertainties, must be noted for future action.

5.4.2 Definition

Problems are:

- uncertainties in apportioning hardware/software;
- inability to model systems;
- difficulties in estimating resources and costs;
- predicting and measuring reliability.

The system specification is analysed to provide the 'top level' view of how the system requirements will be met in the system design. The analysis will include the apportionment of system functions to hardware and software, and the resulting hardware and software specifications (which will be used as the basis for detail design). The customer should still be fully involved at this stage to ensure that the design concepts for the system are still satisfactory.

The apportionment process has its problems. Little definitive advice exists on optimizing hardware and software functions on the basis of cost or reliability. With time and experience, this advice may become available. But at present there exists an over-optimistic view of software costs, the effort needed for its development and its flexibility. For some applications there is now a growing view that it is sometimes more effective (in both cost and reliability terms) to implement a design in hardware than to use a software solution.

Even though, at this stage, little detail design will have been started, many of the decisions made in analysing the system specification will have a profound effect upon the detail design. Decomposition of the system specification to subsystems, modules or functions will inevitably reduce the freedom of design at lower levels. High level decisions on the technology and architecture of one subsystem may have the effect, hidden at the time, of imposing considerable constraint on the design of another subsystem. Unfortunately, our present ability to construct system models which can be thoroughly analysed for design interactions is very limited: for systems which combine both hardware and software functions it is all but non-existent. Consequently, many projects find the transition from system definition to design and development far from easy. Where there is good coordination between subsystem design groups, most design conflicts will show themselves quickly, providing an early opportunity to modify the high level design structure. Poor coordination inevitably increases the risk of serious design conflicts being hidden until late in development.

The remedy lies entirely with project management. If the inevitability of change is recognized, then the overall technical control exercised by the project manager within a project management plan can be suitably organized to provide a fast feedback of problems with rigorous control of resulting changes.

During the feasibility phase, the initial project management plan will have been prepared using estimates of resources, costs and time needed for completing the project. This initial plan is refined during definition as the details of the actual system design emerge. A number of estimation models are available for helping with this task but none of them are particularly easy to use. The difficulty lies not so much with the models themselves as the lack of previous project experience and data against which they must be calibrated. Similar problems exist with reliability models. A number exist, but they are all more useful for tracking reliability during a project than for making estimates of resources and effort required to achieve a particular level of reliability.

5.4.3 Design and development

Problems are:

- rapid changes of technology;
- suitability of languages;
- monitoring progress;
- error and change control.

The detailed organization of staff, working structures and methods will not normally be the concern of the project manager. The strategy, methodology and tools used during design and development should, for most contractors, be reasonably well established. For software, appropriate development techniques and standards for a particular project should be agreed with whoever is responsible for quality assurance. But there are issues which will concern the project manager and on which he/she must be consulted.

A common problem is the choice of the particular technology and architecture to implement the system design. Computer technology changes at a frightening pace and there is always great difficulty in building experience from project to project, particularly when the project time scales are more than three or four years. With these longer development times it is not uncommon for the 'latest' technology decided upon at the start of the project to be obsolescent when the project is complete. This makes it very difficult to preach a policy of 'conservative design' using technology that is familiar and for which there exists some previous experience. Nevertheless, the project manager will do well to persuade designers to treat the choice of technology with caution.

The choice of programming language is frequently a problem. The obvious principle for choosing a language is its suitability for the application to which it will be put. But there are other practical issues which may override this view — the experience of programmers with particular languages, the availability of mature compilers and development tools, or even the insistence of the customer that a certain language be used. Some of these factors by which a language is chosen are helpful, while others can cause difficulty. There is little advice available to the manager on how best to trade off advantages and disadvantages.

Monitoring progress can often be difficult, particularly on larger projects where there are a number of separate design groups or teams which may be dealing with hardware, software or even a mixture of both. Well coordinated design groups with timely intergroup design reviews will pay dividends by exposing, at an early stage, interrelated design and interfacing problems. But coordinated groups will not solve the manager's problems if there is not an efficient path for feeding back information on both progress and problems.

The usual result of a software problem is some change. Keeping track of error reports, the changes made to correct an error, and controlling the impact of a change on other parts of a design, are still considerable causes of difficulty. Even with the introduction of the IPSE it is still likely that there will be problems in integrating hardware and software error and change control.

5.4.4 Testing, integration and into service

Problems are:

- lack of agreed metrics;
- interfacing;
- integration;
- controlling 'maintenance'.

The lack of an agreed set of measures which can be used to determine the performance and quality of software can be a serious impediment to the design of an economic test program. The problem also has an impact during earlier stages of a project, in making it more difficult to relate data used for monitoring progress during development to test data obtained later.

Interfacing and integration problems are almost always the result of a failure to control properly the earlier stages of design or development. Lack of attention during design and, particularly, poor integration of development, are the usual reasons. The only solution is a rigorous attention to detail during the design reviews.

Software maintenance (the correction of errors which have not been exposed before release to service and the enhancement of performance and capability) can be a serious problem for the system supplier. The principal need is for tight error and change control. However, at this stage, the system is usually out of the direct control of the supplier and it can be a very difficult (and often expensive) task to verify that a reported problem is a real one.

5.5 CONCLUSIONS

Management of any project can be a difficult task and the larger and more complex a project becomes, the greater the difficulty for the manager. The catalogue of problems cited above merely illustrates the range of the difficulties — there are many more which are just as serious.

A considerable amount of research is currently being undertaken into tools and methods which will help to avoid some of the most serious problems in the future. Unfortunately, little is being done to integrate these various solutions in a way that can be developed for managing projects, particularly when the project involves embedded computers.

For some time to come, project managers will have to continue to use their wits to adapt established management principles to the wide variety of projects which they undertake. While this approach has been shown to be successful in practice, it is a slow process and gives little support to the uninitiated.

One fundamental point is clear. Much more attention needs to be paid to the earliest stages of a project — more time and more money — to get it off to a good start. But it is at this stage that higher management is unwilling to invest heavily and the customer is anxious to get on with the job as quickly as possible! As much as anything, we need to educate everyone to understand just how expensive our inability to manage properly has become.

We can't afford to do it right
But we have to afford to do it again,
. . . and again
. . . and again!

Chapter 6

STATENGINE — a Software Reliable Digital System for Synchronous Engineering. Task Model, Dedication Architecture and Task Language

A. STEWART
12 Woodgreen Road, Stopsley, Luton, Bedfordshire LUT 8BT

6.1 INTRODUCTION

6.1.1 Digital system architecture, software approach and software reliability. The overall system requirement as the necessary design basis

The digital system approach depends on the formulation of the overall system requirement for the class of system. The digital system architecture and the software approach should fit into successive solutions from the requirement level down. This defines the top down approach.

There is a reverse demonstration of deductive synthesis of the requirement. This is proof, or design assurance. Therein lies the approach to software reliability, conditioned by the class of system.

6.1.2 The digital system for synchronous engineering. The task model, based on the state concept, as the digital requirement

The synchronous engineering system is well understood in analogue engineering as a connected functional block diagram of signal flow; synchronism is tacitly understood as meaning that all the signals are at the same time. This is for a given system mode. Control logic switches the system from mode to mode.

The design basis of this system, when expressly stated, is the state concept, tacitly present in the convention that all the signals are at the same time; all the signals together express the dynamic state. For mode switching, state is an old and classic concept for the general digital system as a switching network; this is a functional concept and applies to any technology from relays to telephone networks to computer lines and gates; the state is the state of the switches, identifying the modes so determined.

For the digital requirement there is also a functional block diagram, which is the task model. The task model rests on an updated version of the state concept; this is to bring it into line with multiple digital processes in a synchronous engineering system. It has been found necessary to restate the state concept, in its two forms, as the synchronous digital dynamic state and the mode or logic state. The problem for multiple processes was how they synthesized to behave as one, both in the logic state and in the digital dynamic state. This is resolved in the task model. The task is a state transition process, exactly as in the formulation of the general digital system. The digital dynamic tasks connect up in a block diagram exactly like the transfer function block diagram in an analogue system, for a given mode. The logic tasks switch the system from mode to mode. Finally, communication tasks bridge the gap of physical separation.

6.1.3 The task model as the basis of an architecture of independent task processors, or dedication architecture

The synchronous task model shows that concurrent tasks in series need dedicated processors. Concurrent tasks in parallel need processor dedication, either truly so, as for tasks in series, or virtually so, on dedicated channels for the time sharing option. This dedication architecture is outlined in Fig. 6.1.

The dedication architecture allows modular task timing, to synchronize with the rest of the task system and engineering. Modular task timing is invariant with respect to dedication architecture options.

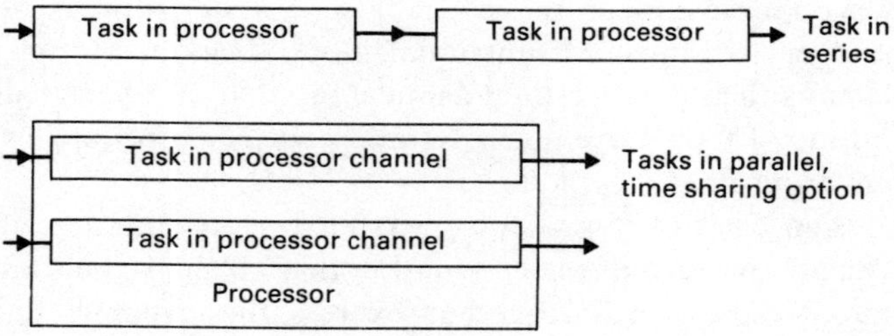

Fig. 6.1. Task processor dedication architecture.

Consistent with dedication architecture, tasks in separate non-competitive logic states may optionally share a processor, but with processor dedication in each state.

6.1.4 The task as state transition mathematics, as the basis of synthesis

This is analogous to the engineering mathematics of the analogue system, as transfer functions for dynamics and as switching network logic for mode control. This was also manifest in digital engineering, before multiple processors, in sampled data control systems.

The basic form of state transition is that the next state is a function of the last state and the input; in the dynamic case the next state is also a function of the cycle time. Proven system synthesis rests on the state transition mathematics. This is not in itself technically difficult.

6.1.5 Internal state transition as the necessary design basis of the task

The task itself synthesizes its overall result as a series of internal state transitions. This is no more than taking the mathematical algorithms underlying programs and putting them in processable form. It represents 'program thinking', but not in program language. This distinction matters for proof, as program language does not express deduction.

This completes the explicit task model.

6.1.6 The task model in concurrent task language

The language must support task synchronism and be invariant with respect to dedication architecture options. Appropriate examples are Ada and Occam.

6.1.7 STATENGINE as a 3-pass top down design approach

This is put together, from system requirement to language, as:

- Pass 1. The task model.
- Pass 2. Dedication architecture.
- Pass 3. The task model in concurrent task language.

The approach is termed STATENGINE in recognition of its dependence on the state concept for proven synthesis.

6.1.8 Repercussions on alternative design approaches

6.1.8.1 *Incompatibility with the postbox approach to software*

The postbox approach may be described as the decoupling of processes through storage in data areas with processor time scheduled.

In contrast, in the task model in dedication architecture the tasks clear at every cycle. Processes within a task, in precise order in each cycle, are simply serial, for which scheduling is irrelevant. The task model has the status of requirement; it does not lead to the postbox response.

6.1.8.2 *Task model versus formal method for software reliability*

The alternatives in this respect are compatible approaches to program proof. The task model is top down in state transition form: Formal Method is bottom up from the program. The task model is thought to have greater power, relevance and simplicity, and is in any case committed to proof as part of its construction. The task model is also a guide to structuring software reliability trials, for an error metric.

The scope of Formal Method seems limited to the internal proof of the task. The external synthesis is above the program level.

6.1.9 Repercussions on architecture

Dedication architecture is an essential principle. But within this principle, as essential for system integration, the task model shows the task types of central logic and communication as determining the connectedness of the system. These types are also common and simple, and thus ripe for design exploitation.

A communication 'black box' from anywhere to anywhere, specified simply in terms of sampling interval and delay, is probably designable on a time multiplexing basis. Control logic on the basis of a lookup table array, replicated for failure protection, seems feasible.

6.1.10 Overall aim

Positively, the principle of STATENGINE is:

- Task model, as a process synthesis of the requirement;

(a) task block diagram; each task a state transition form,
(b) task internal algorithm; series algorithm of state transition steps.

- Dedication architecture, with repercussions.
- Transcription of task model into concurrency language.

Negatively, the aim is:

- A departure from the postbox method.
- A shitt of effort from formal method to task model for proof.

The issue of the transfer from principle to application is evolutionary — except for the postbox incompatibility. The irreducible minimum is the task model and the dedication architecture. Something at a lower level than Ada or Occam would suffice, provided it had the same synchronous approach; this could be relevant, for instance, at the interface with engineering hardware, where the concurrency languages are less clear.

How far the state transition approach is pushed within the task is an issue of software reliability, i.e. whether the effort should be left at the production of program with only implicit 'program thinking', or whether explicit proof is demanded.

A complete view of software reliability, for this class of system, would be proof internal to task, proof external to task, and an error metric from software reliability trials directed from the task model. The error metric is beyond the scope of this analysis, but any statistical measure must come from the imposed statistics of trials usage, which ought to come from the task model, e.g. control logic in usage.

The task model has a certain project urgency, to be acted on in principle on project now. It has the status of requirement, not optimal method, but nothing with this degree of explicit functional synthesis — relating back to engineering — seems to exist.

The task model is presented in completely general terms, although it was initially thought through on weapon systems. This is deliberate; first, because it has to be so for general validity and power, second, because only so is it practicable to keep the scale of analysis to manageable size, which is relevant to the necessary object of understanding the model as a completely connected functional system.

6.2 THE TASK MODEL. PASS 1

6.2.1 The digital dynamic task in the synchronous engineering system

There is more than one kind of real-time system. The synchronous engineering system is identified by the coupling of its processes. At the common sense level it is easy to see examples of systems that through the looseness of process coupling do not fit the pattern of synchronous engineering. Thus there is a degree of autonomy and loose coupling in systems like road traffic, or the telephone traffic of a multitude of independent conversations, or unconnected accounts in a banking system. In synchronous engineering there is, however, a unity of mutually related order and timing of the engineering processes. This is manifested in the time dependent relation of output to input for each process, but further in the connection of these processes to each other — also time dependent — so that the total process is a time dependent unified system.

Thus, in any given mode of dynamic behaviour, synchronism is summarized as:

1 Behaviour of all the variables, together, is related to time *t*.

2 Transition to values at the next time, is a function of the input and the current values of time *t*, and the interval to next time. This is true of each individual process, and of the total process, where for the total process the input is from the external world.

It is this synchronism, thus defined, that is expressed in the usual engineering practice of system representation by block diagram of all the interconnecting engineering processes and their input/output signal flow, tacitly understood as at time *t* together.

The digital dynamic process, envisaged as interacting with engineering functions in such a way that the whole process remains determinate in time, must have its input from engineering at determinate time, and its output to engineering at determinate related times. The input to the digital process is conceived as a discrete series of values at a series of sampling instants. The output is also conceived as a discrete series but now as a complete waveform in time — typically a pulse train — presented to the engineering function. The general picture of the digital dynamic task between two engineering functions is shown in the block diagram in Fig. 6.2.

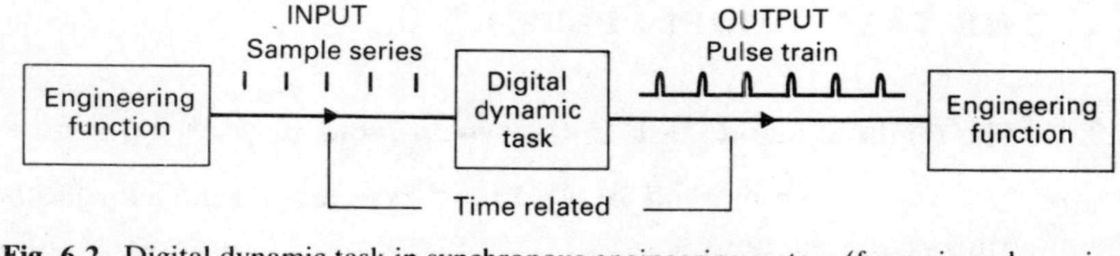

Fig. 6.2. Digital dynamic task in synchronous engineering system (for a given dynamic mode).

In many cases the time relationship between the output pulse train and the input sample series is that they both run at a constant sampling interval, with, say, the output delayed by one interval.

The digital input/output relation has the same transition form as for engineering functions: the next output is a function of input, last output and the interval to next output. This way all the variables preserve their relationship to time as a system link.

6.2.2 Communicating dynamic tasks; synchronism and modular timing

For cycling dynamic tasks, each task cycles and the whole task sequence also cycles, where the overall time between engineering functions is specified. The joint conditions of overall delay. task order, task cycling and task delay define task timing as in Fig. 6.3.

The task timing so defined, from which the overall task sequence timing between engineering functions may then be proved, specifies the time requirement for the task as a process module. This is strictly a requirement for concurrent tasks, not as yet a processor commitment: in particular each task has a stop-phase (which may or may not reduce to zero) but a processor might continue.

6.2.3 Control logic tasks in the synchronous engineering system

A functional block diagram of the system type, in its entirety now also envisaging changes of mode, can be seen in Fig. 6.4.

Engineering and dynamics together, in any mode, constitute a unified synchronous process. The speciality of the engineering functions is as sensors and motors interacting with the external world. The dynamic functions complement engineering performance; communication tasks are implied.

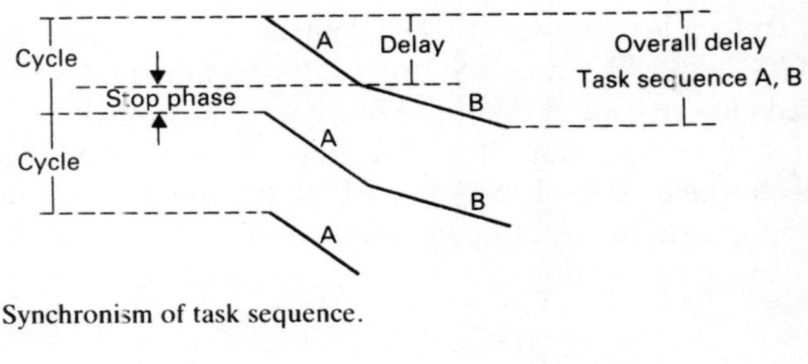

Fig. 6.3. Synchronism of task sequence.

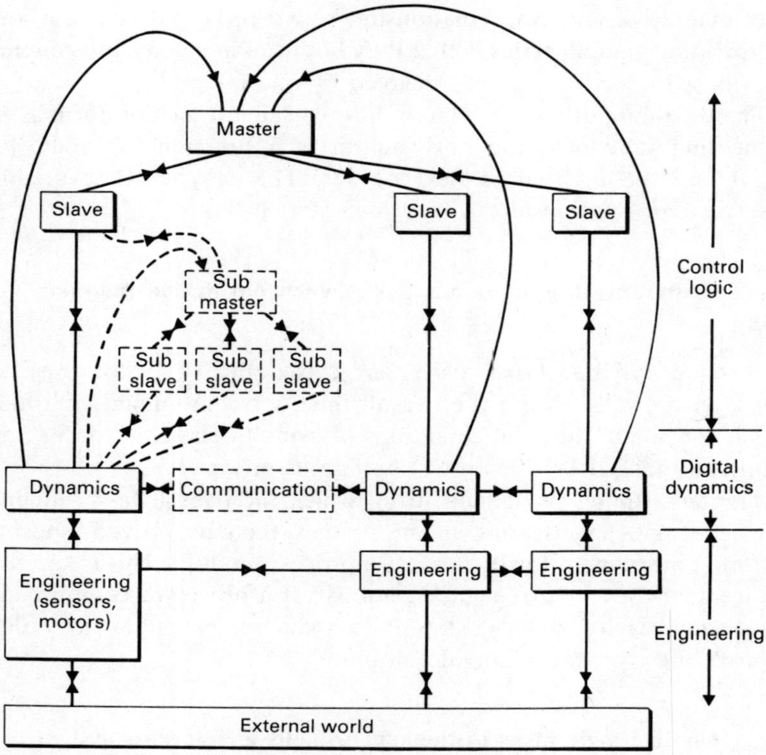

Fig. 6.4. Synchronous engineering system with control logic and dynamics.

The dynamic mode, or logic state of the system, embraces all the engineering functions as well as the digital dynamics. Typical modes, for example in a weapon system, are SEARCH, TRACK, ENGAGE.

Modes are initiated through conditions in the external world working their way through engineering functions and dynamic functions, eventually crossing some threshold in the dynamics that gives a logic signal for control logic to act on. The control logic is portrayed in Fig. 6.4 as MASTER and SLAVES, to handle coordinated switching in dispersed digital dynamics. Within this general picture of coordinated change of system logic state it is indicated that local mode variations can occur through SUBMASTER and SUBSLAVES; examples are use of a sun shutter for tracking in bright conditions, or the windscreen wiper in driving in the rain.

6.2.4 Multiple control logic task synthesis of single process of system logic

All digital processes belong to the general class of digital system, classically formulated as the state transition of a switching network. The next state is a function of the last state and the input, the function being either Boolean logic or more generally a lookup truth table. The whole concept is entirely functional, free of technology; at the level of the task model, fulfilling a requirement, the processes are relatively simple, with a finite number of states.

A quite simple representation of a simple state transition is the transition graph in Fig. 6.5.

This graph has the desirable properties of all states being reachable and no locking; there is always some input sequence to get to anywhere and get out of anywhere. These are properties which any coherent requirement must have, and easy to verify.

An equivalent form to the state transition graph in Fig. 6.5 is the feedback truth table in Fig. 6.6. (The connection back to 'truth table' is through the binary digitization of A, B, C, D, E, F, G; 1, 2, 3, 4 . . . converting the output to *True/False* combinations for joint input (input and feedback) *True/False* combinations.)

The question of what might happen, in general terms, if two or more state transition processes interacted, could be quite formidable. Instead, it is asked how they might interact to behave as a single transition process, for which there are simple solutions.

The general problem of the coordination of state transition over many subsystems is solved through one MASTER and many SLAVES. The MASTER states are copies of the required system states. The

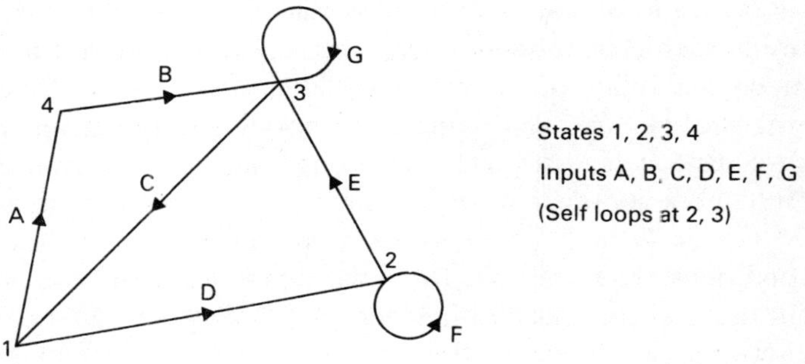

Fig. 6.5. Simple logic state transition graph.

FEEDBACK TRUTH TABLE		
Input	Feedback	Output
A	1	4
B	4	3
C	3	1
D	1	2
E	2	3
F	2	2
G	3	3

Fig. 6.6. State transition truth table.

MASTER state transition is a copy of the required system state transition. Inputs to the MASTER are logic signals generated by the external conditions which provoke the system state transition. The many SLAVES trigger the contribution to system state in each subsystem. The SLAVES having achieved, the MASTER moves on to the next state. To show how this interlocking works, a simple problem of coordinated cyclic order is worked through in detail in the Appendix to this chapter.

The further necessary concept of synthesis is the combination of independent autonomous branches of substate transition, subject to the combination remaining in the main state, as illustrated in the branching substate transitions of Fig. 6.7.

The independent branches, when they form substate combinations, form substates of the main state and so synthesize one single process of state transition. It will be observed that although there may be $(m \times n)$ combinations the complication is only of size $(m + n)$ because of the independence.

A general form of state transition graph can be used to formulate both synthesis aspects of the requirement, coordination and independent branch combination, as in Fig. 6.8.

This general picture can be further elaborated hierarchically to any degree, for instance subsubstate transitions branching out from a substate. The autonomy of branching is always constrained to the degree that it is part of the main state; entry is only through entry into main state; conditions requiring exit from the main state will also impose exit from the branch, and all branches.

6.2.5 Synchronism of logic tasks and dynamic tasks

Timed dynamic tasks loop with control logic, the logic input being

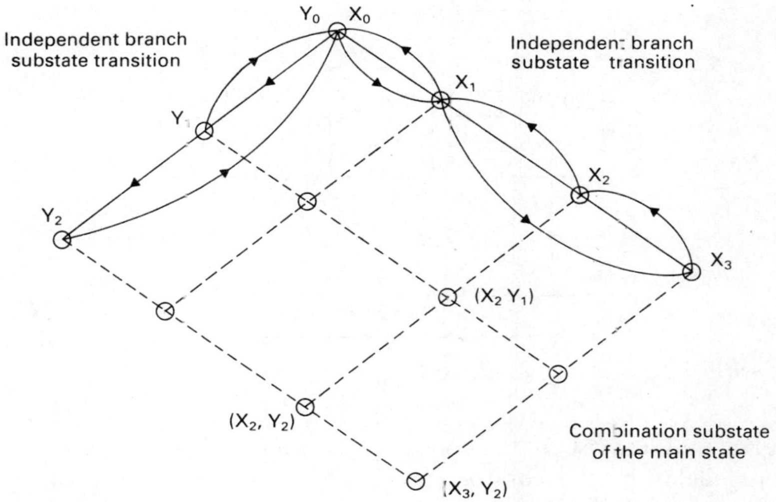

Fig. 6.7. Combination substate transition of independent branches.

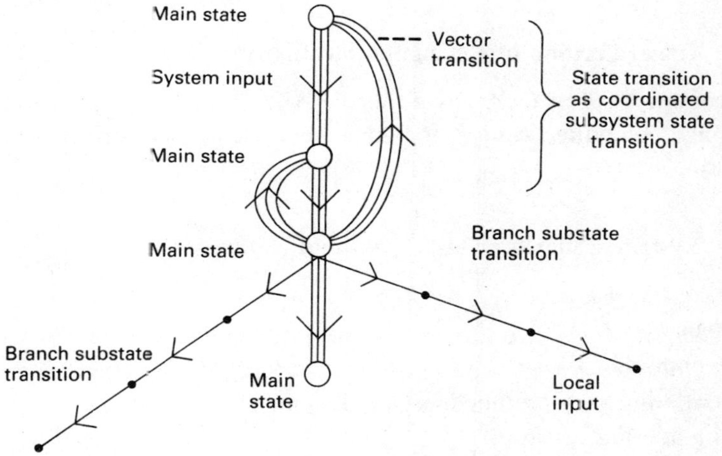

Fig. 6.8. System logic requirement as coordinated and branch transition.

generated from the dynamics, and the logic output switching the dynamics. This is shown with overall control logic broken into subordinate tasks as in Fig. 6.9.

The significance of the overall delay is that until the next system state is complete, the 'next' input is not determined. Nevertheless, intermediate 'next' inputs and outputs must operate at the sampling

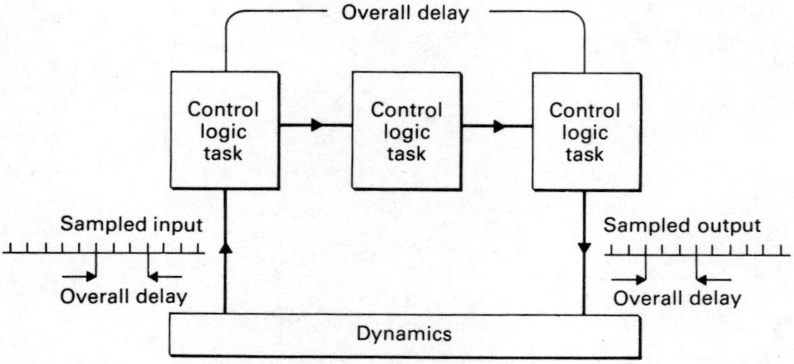

Fig. 6.9. Synchronized control logic loop.

interval and likewise all the control logic tasks. This is reconciled with overall delay by the control logic inhibiting tasks at each sampling interval until cleared by completion. The control logic carries changes spasmodically, akin to a 'modulation' of the sampling interval 'carrier', in between carrying 'no change'.

6.2.6 Generalization of the communication task

The communication task may either be part of control logic or part of dynamics. In either case it would have a delay and operate at the sampling interval.

6.2.7 System scenario of task types and connections

The task types are:
[L] Logic.
[D] Dynamics.
[C] Communication, either logic or dynamics.
(E) Engineering function.
Systems are connected through control logic and communication functions, the communication role being to bridge physical separation. Dynamic tasks and engineering functions may be specific to logic states. A typical outline task type connection is indicated in Fig. 6.10.

6.2.8 Synthesis of the serial task

Whereas tasks are concurrent, the steps in a task are in series, even

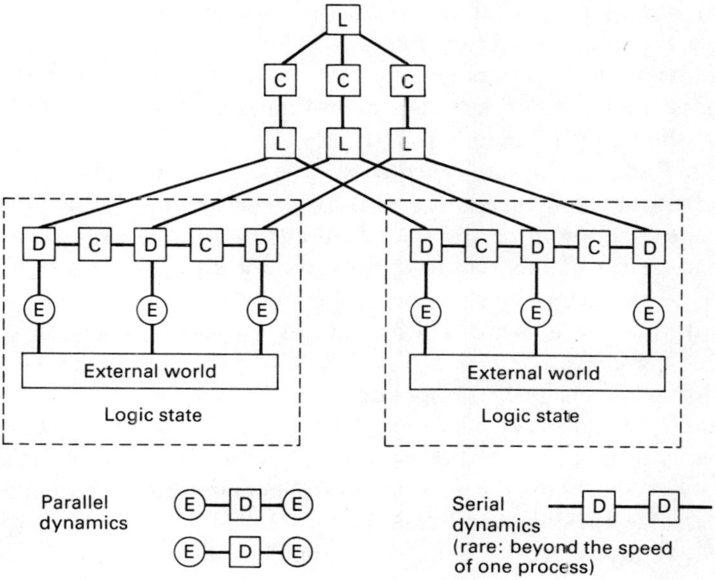

Fig. 6.10. Outline typical task connections and dynamic task cases.

though any one step might have parallel power like an array operation.

Tasks have been defined as:

1 *Dynamic tasks*. The output variable is a function of the input variable, last output, and the time to next output.

2 *Logic tasks*. The output constant is a function of the input constant and last output, i.e. a lookup table.

For any one serial step in the dynamic task, the basic concept is that:

Input of the step = Operation to be performed; say F_n
Last output = Variable output of last step, say V_{n-1}
Output = Step variable output; say V_n
whence V_n = $F_n\ (V_{n-1})$

The concept is presented in this curious way to point the equivalence to the cycle of operations in the general digital switching network, to which a digital process must eventually conform; it also shows the step as a change of state in the dynamic variable.

At the end,

$$V_n = F_n\ \{F_{n-1}\ \{F_{n-2}, \ldots, F_1\ \{V_0\}\ \ldots\}\}$$

What is required to prove is that this is equivalent to $V_n = F(V_0)$, where F is the overall function.

Clearly, such processes can call on all the usual algorithms of numerical analysis. In fact such algorithms are the usual mathematical foundation to programming. They are characterized as being in 'processable' form. The difference from program is the explicit use of the state concept and the power to prove. The analogy with program is that the 'operation' corresponds to the stored instruction.

The status of the overall interval for the dynamic task is that this value — the cycle time — affects the values of the parameters in the overall function F, which is why the task output must be delivered on time.

For the logic task the lookup table gives a one-step option, but obviously could be broken down in the serial way as a succession of Boolean processes. The presentation of serial steps as state transition merely connects up the general Von Neumann concept of the serial processor with the general concept of the digital system as a switching network; the stored program is the input to the switching network.

6.2.9 The state concept and proof for the task model

As has now been shown in principle, proof is feasible for the task model. The proof rests on the state concept but it also rests on the class of system. This is not a new class, and the state concept is not a new concept. For older engineering systems the concepts may well be intuitive and implicit without formal statement. For example, system modes are well understood and their control by hardwired logic would have been performed intuitively in a unified manner. For example analogue dynamics in the continuous time domain are naturally synchronous, like the functions of engineering hardware, as part of their physical nature.

The novelty of explicitly proven synthesis is needed for multiple digital process coupling and for proof within the process. For the class of system this has implied synchronous digital dynamics and interlocked control logic for task coupling, and step algorithms within the task. Such tight coupling defines the digital process requirement for the class of system.

Once this synthesis has been achieved, the relation with engineering function becomes what it previously was for digital processing by single process. This is well illustrated, for example, by sampled data servo control systems, where the digital recurrence equation — to take a very simple case of state transition — might be:

$$X_{n+1} = X_n + aU_n$$

where $n = n^{th}$ sampling interval of duration δ. In terms of pulse train input and output, to connect with engineering, this would have transfer function:

$$Y = a/\{e^{\delta p} - \lambda\},\ p = \text{Laplace operator}$$

This would connect with engineering function very well in the typical block diagram (Fig. 6.11).

This also illustrates very well the further point that time intervals, however small, are not to be neglected but determine the processes.

The whole thrust of the task model, as well as the objective of proof, is to move digital process thinking into the engineering area, before program language is considered.

Proof rests on state transition and the finiteness of state; in the logic case a finite number of logic states as system constants, and in the dynamic case a finite number of dynamic state variables.

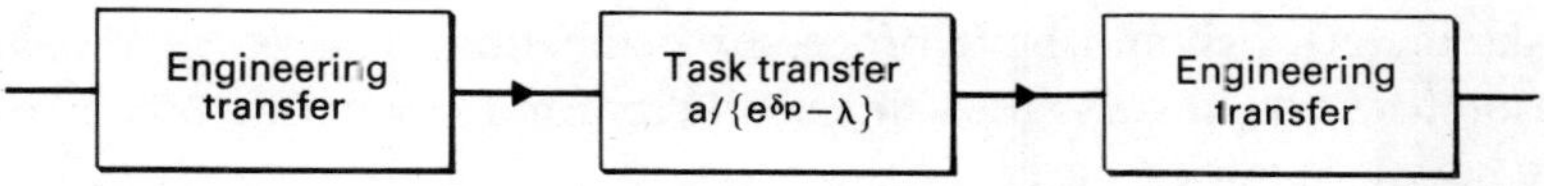

Fig. 6.11. Digital and engineering function synthesis.

6.3 THE TASK MODEL IN DEDICATION ARCHITECTURE. PASS 2

6.3.1 Time sharing channel dedication condition for modular task timing

Patterns of time multiplexing for channel dedication are, for example, simple staggered patterns, or at escalating sampling intervals, as in Fig. 6.12.

Such dedicated channels secure that for any one task both the sample interval and the delay are met for each task modularly. Looser arrangements are not sufficient as the times would overlap.

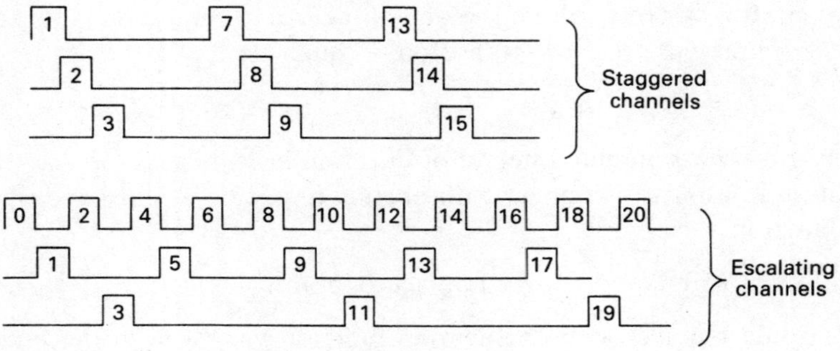

Fig. 6.12. Dedicated channels.

6.3.2 Dedication forms for modular task timing

The possible forms are:
1 the separate processor;
2 the separate channel;
3 processor use in separate logic state.

6.3.3 Task model distribution of the form of dedication

Tasks in series should have processor dedication. This is because the reason for serial tasks is the same as the reason for separate processors. The serial conditions are:
1 physical separation;
2 serial processes beyond one processor capacity, if not then there will not be two tasks;
3 control logic in series with dynamics.

In the control logic case the argument for the separate processor form of dedication is not final but rests partly on the dynamics being specific to logic state while control logic is not specific, and partly on the cardinal importance of the control logic being isolated from hardware failure outside it and being itself protected by redundancy.

For tasks in parallel the separate channel form of dedication is a possible option. The dedication cases are summarized in Fig. 6.13.

6.3.4 Processors for task types. Logic lookup table and the communication black box

The task model (see Section 6.2.4) has already identified the most

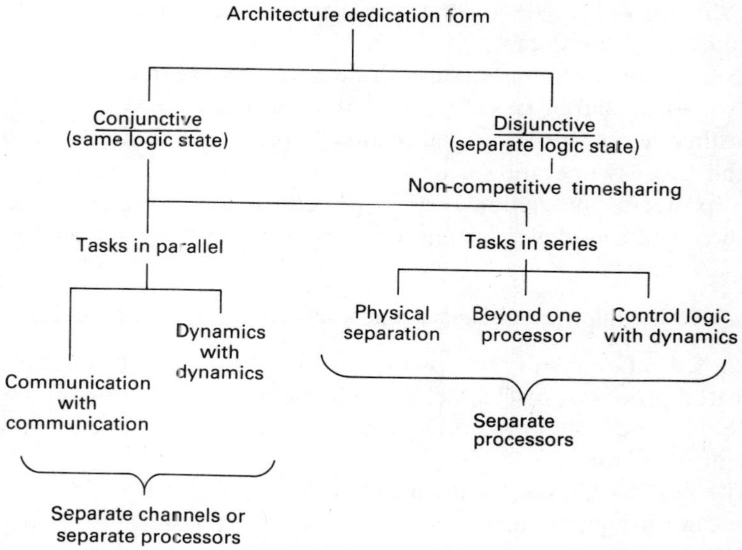

Fig. 6.13. Task model distribution of dedication form.

general formulation of control logic process as a finite truth table of output in response to input and feedback of previous output. This gives a three column table with a finite number of rows, not large. This is more general than Boolean options. This is a one-step process in response to input, the process operating on 'system constants' rather than transforming data. It is possible to think of this as direct lookup of a stored array rather than a Von Neumann stored program and still retain flexibility of loading for modification.

Channel dedication is especially simple for the provision of parallel communication, where communication is specified by sampling interval and delay. This gives a simple specification which is directly usable for the synchronous coupling of separated subsystems. In engineering terms communication from anywhere to anywhere can be conceived as a 'black box' for route, sampling interval and delay.

6.3.5 The general case for the processor true dedication option. Hardware specialism, economics and failure strategy

For dedication architecture it is always possible for hardware options to be slotted in, like the fast Fourier transform on a chip. In comparing the cost of true v. channel dedication it has to be borne in mind that time sharing only saves on the active processing, and not the stored programs, nor the data.

Dedication facilitates failure strategy, as failure repercussions do not spread to shared tasks. In the failure strategy the control logic is of cardinal importance, and can readily be protected by redundancy, as a small process operating a lookup table. For dynamic tasks, not so easily protected by redundancy, true dedication facilitates the alternative of shutting down, giving a system with reversionary modes.

6.3.6 Task timing modularity; machine dependence as modular

Given dedication it still remains true that the time requirement for that dedicated processor or channel can only be implemented on an appropriate machine. The problem is, however, modular within each task in its dedication form.

The penalty for non-modular task timing is unpredictable run-time error from pre-emptive output timing taking the last data available.

Modular task timing is an essential constituent of modular response to the next phase of concurrent task language, with modular task compilation.

6.4 THE TASK MODEL IN CONCURRENT TASK LANGUAGE. PASS 3

6.4.1 Concurrency language to match the task model

The characteristics of concurrency language necessary to match the task model are:

1 input/output statements to couple the tasks;
2 delay statements to serve modular task timing;
3 as an intermediary between the task model and the dedication architecture, the language to be the same irrespective of the options of dedication form.

Languages that appear to satisfy these characteristics are Ada and Occam. The Occam input/output statements, for example are:

Q!s	*P*?s
Output *s* to task *Q*	Input *s* from task *P*
Statement made in task *P*	Statement made in task *Q*

The necessary characteristics are semantic, not syntactic. The internal step language within the task is, in concurrency respects, immaterial. The reservations yet to be cleared concern the coupling of tasks to functions of engineering hardware, where the languages are not so forthcoming.

6.4.2 Incompatibility with the postbox data flow method

Synchronous engineering must first be distinguished from quite different classes of system with looser forms of process complexity, as for example in business and traffic problems, for which postbox models may apply as a different requirement from the synchronous task model.

For synchronous engineering, at the level of method, as in MASCOT, the postbox concept is one of storage in data areas to decouple the processes, with access procedures and queue management, and scheduling to determine the sharing of active processor time, extending to the postbox treatment of serial processes within a task.

The task model conceives serial processes within a task, occurring once only in prescribed order per cycle, as simply serial, for which the postbox method would be an unnecessary overhead. Tasks in communication clear every cycle, with no postbox relevance beyond (at most) storage within the cycle. In dedication architecture, for modular task timing, postbox scheduling is irrelevant. Thus incompatibility of the postbox method is manifold.

This means that the task model matched into the concurrency language is not compatible with the postbox method. The language does not contain scheduling, nor procedures of data area management. The language means what the task model says in dedication architecture with modular task timing, for synchronized tasks clearing every cycle, with each task a serial process.

6.4.3 Software reliability as proof; task model basis of proof v. formal method

Program bugs — a serious error issue — have stimulated explicit analysis of software reliability, the two approaches being the metric of error measurement, and prevention by explicit proof. The software based approach to proof is formal method for program verification. The alternative proof is from the task model. Both proof approaches recognized the paradox that proof cannot be conducted in program language, although the *raison d'être* of the program is to solve a problem, and solution implies deductive consequence. The paradox arises because a program statement is an executable statement but a deduced property is not. The explanation of the existence of deductive thinking is that it must be implicit. The approach to proof is to make the thinking explicit, documented and therefore verifiable.

Insight into proof is yielded by the concept of *latency* of conclusion. For example, if:

$$\sin x = x - x^3/3! + x^5/5! - \ldots$$

and

$$\cos x = 1 - 1 - x^2/2! + x^4/4! - \ldots$$

then $\cos^2 x + \sin^2 x = 1$, as a latent consequence. The extra statement is tautologous in the sense that no new fact of evidence or action is needed, but nevertheless the statement is new — even difficult to see — as a further conceptual property, latent as it were in the 'conceptual model'.

The latency of program proof resides in the concept of state transition. This is illustrated for a trivial example of store transfer, in Fig. 6.14.

This is but another example of the synthesis of the serial task as state transition algorithm already outlined in Section 6.2.8. The reason why this works is the very general fundamental property that the Von Neumann serial processor still remains as a general digital system, conceived as a switching network, and formulated thus in mathematical terms as state transition:

Formal method does not depart from the basis of state transition.

Additionally, the basis appears to be:

- A program theory language into which program language is converted and in which deduction is possible.
- An apparatus of primary concepts and first principles in binary arithmetic and formal logic.
- Formal definition of secondary concepts e.g. $m \times n = (m + m + \ldots)$, n times.

Program language	State transition
Y = X	$y_{n+1} = x_n$
Z = Y	$z_{n+2} = y_{n+1}$
No conclusion statement	Latent ∴ $z_{n+2} = x_n$ where n = n^{th} transition

Fig. 6.14. Explicit state transition: implicit program deduction.

- Proof notated by mechanical syntactical operations.
- Program verification means showing that the program falls within the scope of what can be demonstrated by such an apparatus.

The broad distinction between the two approaches is that the task model is top down from the system requirement while formal method is bottom up from existing program, with no pre-language model. A critique of formal method, as a system proof apparatus, is on three grounds of principle:

1 *Power*. The limitations of scope lie in intertask relations and in relation with engineering functions, beyond the internal mechanisms of the single task, and above program language.

Limitations of tools come from inhibitions on going beyond the formal binary apparatus, whereas in the task model all the resources of engineering mathematics and algorithms bear directly. (Gödel's Theorem — on the impossibility of proving that mathematics is a unified dependence on one set of hypotheses — might well be relevant. In practice, deductive thinking in different areas subsists with some autonomy.)

2 *Relevance*. Without direction from the task model there is a danger of solving the wrong problem, or unnecessary byproducts. On the other hand, given the proven task model, program language proof is redundant.

In contrast, the task model proof is assured of relevance through creation as a necessary phase of the solution, at the time of solution. The need for relevance, in the form of the task model, shows up very clearly when the errors have actually to be corrected, as distinct from their existence being detected.

3 *Simplicity*. Formal method appears as a complex and laborious package, and with repercussions on existing language characteristics; apparently, for example, not all languages, in respect of their syntax, are equally suitable for conversion into program theory language. The complexity is such as to raise questions of whether more errors will be created.

The task model, on the other hand, can be pushed towards explicitness as an issue of degree for proofs within the task, leaving 'program thinking' implicit to program language to a degree that matches the effort available. External to the task, i.e. above program language, nothing can be done except through the task model.

6.4.4 The software reliability metric: the task model basis

In hardware reliability the statistics are those of the environment, hopefully stable in reliability trials. Software reliability trials have their statistical stability of usage thrust upon them. The task model provides a guide to the imposed structure of trials usage.

In the task model the simplest parameters are those of the system logic state, which are a finite set of constants. Moreover, the control logic might be evaluated separately, as of special significance. On the other hand, as a finite set of constants, it is possible to test the system determinately for logic behaviour.

Whatever way this is attacked, the useful concept is to impose system structure on the metric and design trials accordingly. Besides, unless the task model is taken as standard there is no way of judging that an error has occurred.

However, the error metric is beyond the scope of this analysis.

6.5 STATENGINE AS THREE-PASS APPROACH, WITH CONCLUSIONS

6.5.1 Positive aim

The three passes are outlined in Fig. 6.15. The task is a digital transfer function. Like the analogue transfer function it is a mathematical form, only it has a transition cycle with a delay. The task transfer function gives output as a function of the input and the last output, and also of the delay for the dynamic task. (The chief simplification is the omission of independent branching substates of the system logic — which extends the system hierarchically with a large degree of sub-system design autonomy — see Section 6.2.4.)

6.5.2 Negative aims

- a departure from the postbox method, as incompatible with the task model and task timing modularity and their matched expression in concurrency language;
- a shift of effort from formal method to the task model for program proof. The task model is preferred for power, relevance and simplicity; it is essential for proof external to the task, above program level.

6.5.3 Software reliability

The problem is transformed by formulation for the class of synchronous engineering. Proof in the task model divides into:

- proof external to the task, above the program level;

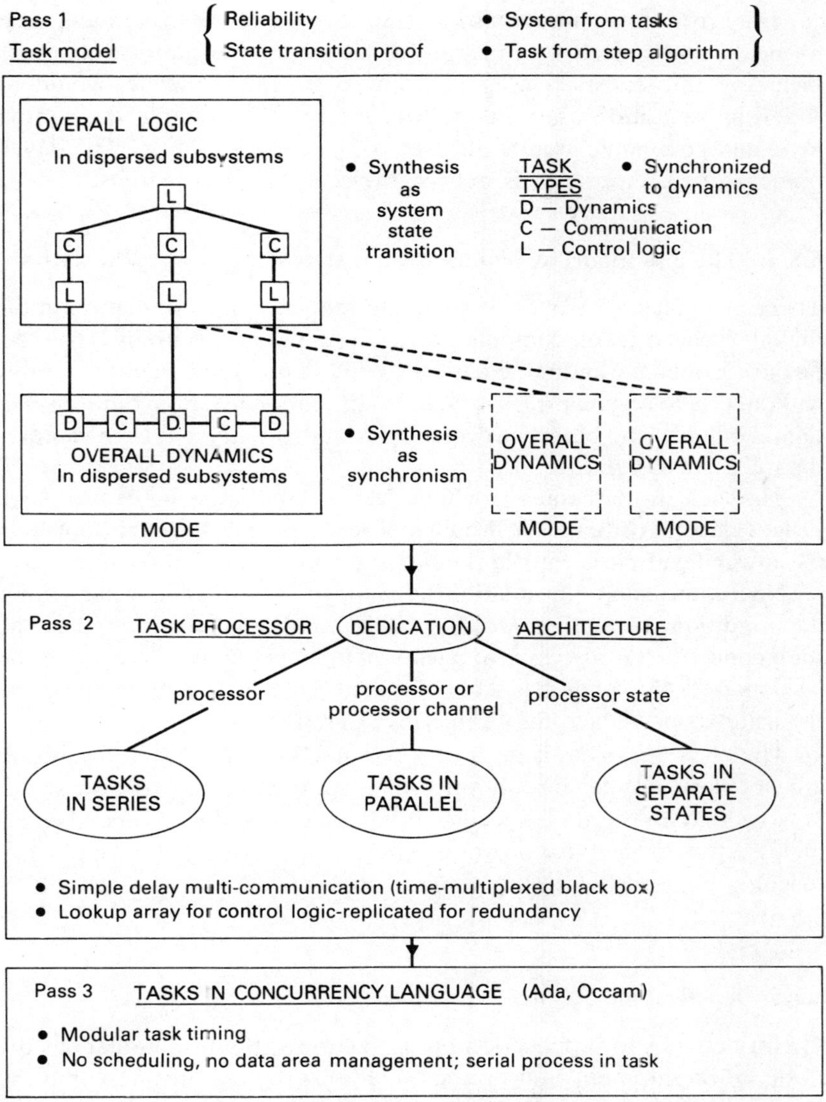

Fig. 6.15. STATENGINE. Outline three-pass approach for digital system.

• proof internal to the task.

Proof, in the state transition form, will have been a necessary function at the time of creation of the task model, as the recognition of latent implied properties; it remains to document them. For proof internal to the task, state transition gives a means of documenting 'program thinking', denied to program language.

The error metric would also be transformed by the task model, as it would be manifested by reliability trials where the pattern of usage, including the statistical usage yielding a statistical metric, would be superimposed and based on the task model, for example the control logic and communication as the key to system integration. The development of this approach is outside the scope of this analysis.

6.5.4 The task model as requirement as state transition mathematics

There is a general absence of adequate requirement formulation in the digital area, true of computer science literature generally. The deficiency is a lack of a mathematical chain. This compares unfavourably with analogue engineering systems. It also compares unfavourably with digital engineering before processing, as in the mathematics of sampled data control systems.

The lack of mathematical chain destroys the meaning of top down system decomposition. Each higher level block must contain not only the lower level parts but the latent conclusions implied by the parts.

No requirement formulation appears to be available which fulfils the conditions of mathematical synthesis, and none that attend to the state concept (for processor applications); hence the formulation of the task model. No other basis but the state concept seems to have the requisite scope, hence the term STATENGINE.

The class of system is not new. The mathematics of state transition are not new, nor technically difficult — only universal. It also seems obvious that a task model needs a task language and vice versa. Nevertheless, the explicit formulation where none existed may have far-reaching consequences (the general implications are in 6.5.1, 6.5.2, 6.5.3).

6.5.5 Application

The principle is for application on project now; the task model has the status of requirement, not optional method (the options lie within the approach).

Apart from the issue of the postbox method, development can be evolutionary. The degree of explicitness of proof internal to task can be set against cost. The issue of concurrency language is also evolutionary; a lower level language would do, provided the approach is synchronous for dedication architecture.

It is tempting to think of new research vistas, and possibly the change of mental framework will encourage this to happen. The disappearance of software management overheads and the case for extended processor dedication, with special hardware possibilities, suggests an increase of parallel processing power within the task, and a further dedication of the 'shopkeeping' software necessary to get parallel effects from serial processes; this in turn suggests the simplification of internal program proof.

6.6 APPENDIX

6.6.1 Master and slaves for coordinated cyclic order

The start is a system logic state, or a system with three modes of behaviour. For example, we can have a cyclic order of the system logic states A', B', C'. The system cycles round from A' to B' to C', etc. in response to external conditions x', y', z', according to the system state transition diagram (Fig. A1).

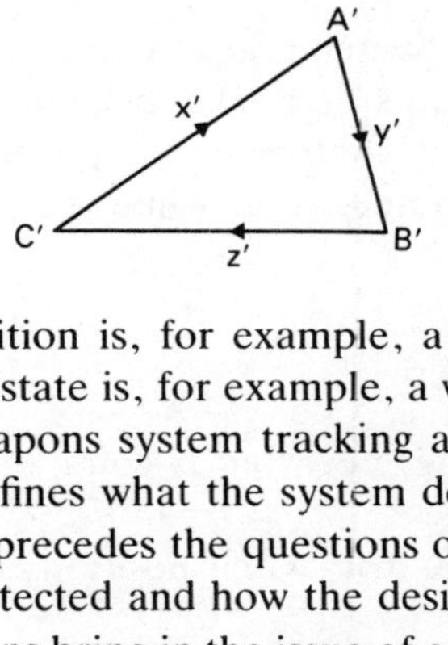

Fig. A1

An external condition is, for example, a day dawning or the rain coming on. A system state is, for example, a weapons system searching for a target, or a weapons system tracking a target. The system state transition diagram defines what the system designer wishes the system to do; this definition precedes the questions of how the external condition is going to be detected and how the designed system is to be controlled. These questions bring in the issue of control logic, which means:

- A set of switches operated on by the external conditions x', y', z' to give logic signals x, y, z (Fig. A2).

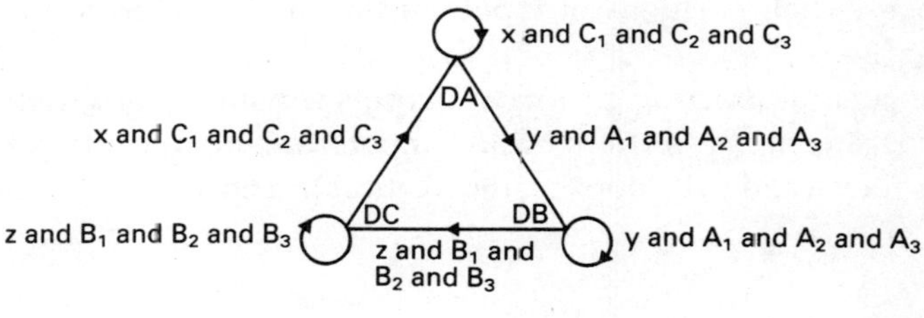

Fig. A2

• A set of switches to determine the systems states, in this case *DA*, *DB*, *DC* as control logic switch positions set by the master (Fig. A2) which will govern the system modes (or logic states) A', B', C'.

However, the switch positions *DA*, *DB*, *DC* belong to MASTER control logic, which governs three slaves known as SLAVE 1, SLAVE 2, SLAVE 3. For SLAVE 1 the corresponding switch positions are A_1, B_1, C_1 and for SLAVE 2 the switch positions are A_2, B_2, C_2, etc. (Fig. A3).

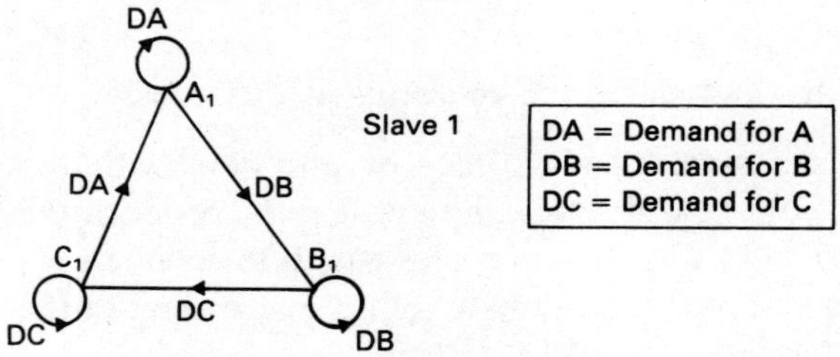

Fig. A3

Thus, when the master switch is at *DA*, the slaves are at A_1, A_2, A_3 and the MASTER output switch *DA* becomes the SLAVE input. When all the slaves are at control switch positions A_1, A_2, A_3, this group (A_1, A_2, A_3) is denoted as *A*, while the actual system state so determined is A^1.

Summary

A' = system state or mode, i.e. what is going on — searching, tracking, etc.
A = group of SLAVE control switch positions putting the system in mode A'.
DA = MASTER switch position as an output, which is also an input to each of the three slaves.
x', y', z' = external conditions.
x, y, z = switch positions of inputs to the MASTER as a measure of x', y', z'.

The general practice is to have outputs (or states) of a state transition diagram at its vertices, while inputs are on the arrows of the joining lines (and self loops at the vertices). The notation:

$$x + C_1 + C_2 + C_3$$

means:

$$x \text{ and } C_1 \text{ and } C_2 \text{ and } C_3$$

The 'and' is to ensure that all slave actions are complete before the MASTER will respond to its next input.

Further reading

For concurrent digital processes, two major areas can be considered: the state concept, and program languages.

The state concept breaks down into:

1 The physical or analogue state.

2 The state of the digital machine, or switching network.

3 The engineering system mode, or logic state.

4 The engineering system dynamic digital state, applying to the use of digital machines for dynamic purposes.

The digital machine state is covered in the following references:

Chang H.Y., Manning E. & Metze G. (1970) *Fault diagnosis of digital systems*. Wiley Interscience (John Wiley Lib. Congress 74–93487). This has an excellent historical survey and bibliography. The early chapters on system models are the important ones in this context.

Huffman D.A. (March, April 1954) The synthesis of sequential circuits. Part I and II. *Journal of the Franklin Institute*. This is on relays but very clear on state concept fundamentals. Moore E.F. (1956) *Gedanken-Experiments on sequential machines auto-mata studies. Ann. Math. Study* **34**, pp. 129–153.

The use of digital machines for dynamic purposes is well exemplified by:

Ragazzini J.R. & Franklin G.F. (1958) *Sampled data control systems*. McGraw-Hill.

The physical or analogue state is an old and universal concept running through all the differential equations of mathematical physics, and in analogue computers. No literature search or history of the concept in the abstract has been attempted. The engineering system mode is common in engineering practice but does not seem to have a literature.

Program languages for concurrent digital processes using the rendezvous concept are covered by:

(a) *Preliminary Ada Reference Manual* (June 1979), ACM (Association for Computing Machinery), Sigplan notices, Vol. 14, No. 6, Part A.

(b) *Rationale for the Design of the Ada Programming Language* (June 1979), ACM, Sigplan notices, Vol. 14, No. 6, Part B.

(c) Hoare C.A.R. (August 1978), Communicating sequential processes ACM (Communications), Vol. 21, No. 8. This language is referred to by Ada as CSP. This is the precursor to Occam and contains its rationale.

Chapter 7

Diversity by Design — Reliability Aspects of Systems with Embedded Software

P. HUMPHREYS
National Centre of Systems Reliability, UKAEA, Wigshaw Lane, Culcheth, Warrington WA3 4NE

7.1 INTRODUCTION

The objective of this paper is to provide an overview of the subject of software reliability, with particular reference to the design, justification and assessment of software. The subject will be covered under the following broad headings:

- reliability;
- development;
- justification and assessment;
- testing.

The discussion will provide some indication of the state of the art, giving consideration to the application of software, the current problems associated with the qualification of software and the tools available to aid the creation of quality software.

Software is of little value unless it is associated with a system which provides an environment wherein the software can function; consequently it will be necessary to consider the interaction of software with its associated hardware in order to obtain some estimate of how well such a system has met its objectives.

Over the last two decades, the primarily hardware-dominated electronics market has been involved in a technological revolution. Thermionic valve technology was slowly replaced by semiconductor technology, followed closely by a plethora of solid state logic devices. Then as the solid state scientist developed his art, such 'chips' were able to carry an increasingly complex set of function. Rapidly, the technology progressed through small scale integrated circuit design (SSI) up to, at the present time, very large scale integrated circuits (VLSI). So, you may ask, how is this influencing computer usage?

Whereas early computer usage was limited to large research organizations, the advent of the solid state technology has provided immense computing power at a cost well within the reach of even the smallest organization, and is even available to the hobbyist.

Computers are now being applied in a wide range of applications ranging from washing machines in the home, through robot manipulators in factories, to sophisticated protection, control and instrumentation systems in nuclear power plants.

However, this rapid growth of microprocessor-based technology brings with it problems which affect both the manufacturer and user of such systems. Briefly, two areas of concern are:

1 The rapid development of new designs of processor can be a headache to a manager of a large project, where project times of five and ten years are not uncommon. The microprocessor family selected at the outset of the project may well be obsolete before the project is completed. So there is a need to consider the feasibility of designing portable software which is system-independent.

2 Wherever a system with embedded software is capable of some form of interaction, either directly or indirectly with people, there is a paramount requirement to show that such systems will only perform their required functions, and will do so correctly, without presenting a threat to life. The problem with most software based systems is that we have not yet devised a technique which will prove the correctness of software under all foreseeable conditions. Worse than that, we are only able to show correctness in a limited number of cases.

Therefore, designers and assessors need to address the following topics:

(a) How can a system with embedded software be designed to safely achieve any required objective using the current technology?

(b) How can we demonstrate that the objections have been achieved?

(c) What weaknesses are present in the current design, justification and assessment methodologies which require further research?

Having briefly outlined the nature of the paper and highlighted some of the areas of concern, let us now consider what constitutes software.

7.2 WHAT IS SOFTWARE?

That component of a system which is most often regarded as software is the listing of the set of instructions which constitute a computer program. However, while this may have been sufficient for mainframe computer usage, the advent of embedded software such as is to be found in read-only-memories (ROMs) and the availability of programmable logic arrays causes us to question that narrow view of software. Should the micro-instructions of a processor be considered as software, or should software be seen to be all that part of the design process which leads to the creation of a set of instructions to perform the desired task?

There are a number of definitions of software, but for the purposes of this paper, software is taken to be all the design documents, listings, instructions, data, operations and maintenance manuals which are input to a programmable system to enable it to function. In practice, we are principally interested in the ability of a system, with embedded software, to perform its required function(s) correctly. More precisely, we are interested in the reliability of the product.

If we were dealing only with a hardware system then we could confidently expect to employ one of the accepted reliability derivation techniques to obtain a quantified reliability figure for our system. However, when we come to consider software reliability, there is no clear route we can take which will lead to a precise quantified reliability figure for the software, or for the system containing the embedded software. This is the dilemma currently facing the software designer and assessor. It is therefore necessary to consider what is meant by software reliability, and how we may achieve and measure it.

7.3 SOFTWARE RELIABILITY

7.3.1 Reliability

The most general form of the definition of reliability is the probability that an item will perform a required function under stated conditions for a stated period of time. This definition is equally applicable to both hardware systems and those which contain embedded software, since it is a description of the chance of achieving a desired objective, irrespective of the means by which the objective is achieved.

Taking first a system containing only hardware, a quantified probability of achieving the objective can be derived using a conventional probability analysis. Excluded from this is any equipment containing LSI and VLSI components, where there is a need to review the adequacy of conventional analysis for the purposes of determining failure probability or system unavailability. This is because complex logic designs have a non-zero probability of containing design faults.

Consider now a system containing software. With such systems there is still considerable debate regarding the viability of producing a trustworthy, quantified probability of failure. One of the sources of disagreement is the manner in which hardware and software failures are assumed to arise. Hardware failures during system operation are attributed to:

- early life failures — infant mortality;
- end of life failures — wearout;
- random failures (excluding design faults).

Providing that a sensible selection and replacement policy is adopted, the majority of component failures during use are attributed to random failure. In consequence, conventional probabilistic analysis may be used, although the effects of common mode failures of hardware need to be taken into account.

The failure mechanism of software is arguably somewhat different. Any ambiguity, omission or incorrect requirement in a specification, and any incorrect implementation of the specification by the designer which is not detected and corrected, generates software which contains embedded faults (bugs).

An error occurs when system inputs cause the faults to be executed. These errors are erroneous internal states of the software, such that if processing continues and there are inadequate fault tolerant elements in the system, system failure will occur.

The software fault resides in the software at all times unless repaired. This contrasts with hardware, where the system is assumed initially to be perfect with system failures, then becoming manifest at random. The manifestation of the software fault giving rise to a system failure is not necessarily a random event. Consequently, hardware reliability models are not, as a general rule, applicable.

Before considering how to determine the software reliability, let us consider the sources of error.

7.3.2 Sources of error

Figures 7.1 and 7.2 show typical allocations of error sources and costs to phases. One inference to be drawn from this data is that all too often the software fault prevention and removal process is inadequate, allowing faults to propagate through to the operational phase. The cost of maintenance is usually borne by the system user and is a function of the reliability of the software.

It is obviously advantageous to a user to improve reliability if it will reduce his maintenance bill. This may mean paying more for the

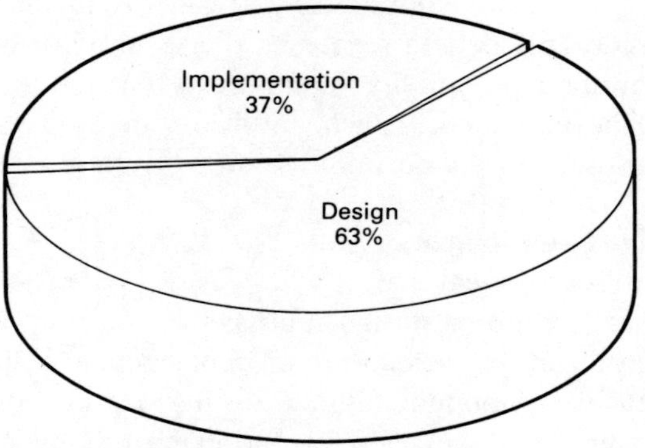

Fig. 7.1. Software life-cycle: error sources per phase.

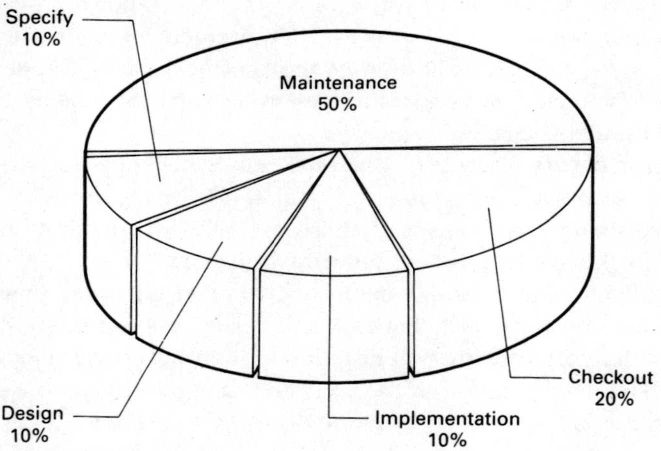

Fig. 7.2. Software life-cycle: costs per phase.

product initially, and some optimization process is needed to determine cost/benefit relationship. Such optimization processes will not be dealt with here, but the paper will consider one of the factors needed in such a process (that of determining the achieved reliability of the software) and will also review the processes required to produce reliable software.

7.3.3 The achievement of software reliability

One objective of a designer is to create a reliable product. This can only be achieved by building reliability into the product as the design proceeds. A survey (Table 7.1) of industry practices relating to the achievement of reliable software indicated that the following items were essential features of any development process intended to produce reliable software:

- use of well defined standards;
- application of rigorous project management controls;
- application of independent quality assurance (QA) and control processes;
- use of a structured development process;
- extensive use of development documentation;
- application of well defined test processes;
- implementation of a formal chance control process to record all changes to documents and code.

Two aspects were assigned particular importance in the survey; standards and QA. Although the need for these activities was recognized, there was no uniform implementation of either activity. The need for national standards has also been recognized by other bodies, and some standards are given in Ministry of Defence (1984), BSI (1979). Additionally, some guidelines for QA are given in EEA (1978, 1981).

The implementation of standards, QA and codes of practice will be discussed further in the section on the development process. In addition to the application of management controls, or fault avoidance techniques, as a means of achieving reliable software, certain techniques can be embodied in the structure of the software to make it robust. These are classed as fault tolerant techniques.

7.3.4 Fault tolerance

A system is said to be fault tolerant if that system is able to react to a fault in such a manner as to either enable the system to continue to function correctly in the presence of the fault, or correct the fault. The implementation of fault tolerance can be considered in four stages. These are given below, with some examples of the techniques.

1 Error detection.

This is the initial step along the path to fault recovery. It is often advantageous to place this trap as near to the output stage of the system as possible, to ensure that the greater part of the system has been checked. Some typical checking techniques are:

Table 7.1. A list of the main activities employed by eight companies to achieve reliable software.

Technique	Number of the company using the technique							
	1	2	3	4	5	6	7	8
Management configuration control	Y	Y	Y	Y	Y	Y	N	Y
Specification optimization	Y	Y	Y	Y	Y	Y	N	Y
Structured programming techniques	Y	Y	Y	Y	Y	Y	Y	Y
Use of QA/QC procedures to qualify the software reliability	Y	Y	Y	Y	Y	Y	Y	Y
Segmented or modular program development	Y	Y	Y	Y	Y	Y	Y	Y
Design reviews and 'walk-throughs'	N	Y	Y	Y	Y	Y	N	Y
Application of:								
MASCOT	Y	Y	Y	Y	N	Y	N	Y
JSP 188	N	N	Y	Y	N	N	N	Y
BSI	N	Y	N	Y	Y	Y	N	Y
DEF	N	Y	N	Y	N	Y	N	Y
companies own standard	Y	N	Y	N	N	N	N	N
Use of:								
flowcharts	N	Y	N	Y	Y	N	Y	Y
HIPO* diagrams	N	Y	N	Y	Y	Y	N	N
ACP** diagrams	Y	N	Y	Y	N	N	N	Y
Pseudo code	N	Y	N	Y	N	N	N	N
to describe the software prior to coding								
Top down development	N	Y	Y	Y	N	Y	N	Y
Visibility of software by documentation and in-code comments	Y	Y	Y	Y	Y	Y	Y	Y
Testing by designers	Y	Y	Y	Y	Y	Y	Y	Y
Validation testing	N	Y	Y	Y	Y	Y	N	Y
Testing in a working environment prior to active use	Y	Y	Y	Y	Y	N	N	Y
Classification of errors	N	Y	Y	N	N	N	N	Y
Use of fail-safe, fault tolerant software development practices	N	Y	Y	N	Y	Y	Y	Y
Software diversity	N	Y	N	Y	N	Y	N	Y
Hardware diversity	N	N	N	N	Y	N	N	Y

Table 7.1. (con't)

Technique	Number of the company using the technique							
	1	2	3	4	5	6	7	8
Verification and validation, of all processes used to produce the software and of the software	Y	Y	Y	Y	Y	Y	Y	Y
Use of an independent assessor and validator	N	Y	Y	Y	N	N	N	Y
Use of numerical techniques to quantify the software reliability:								
(a) none	Y	N	Y	Y	Y	Y	Y	N
(b) some	N	Y	N	N	N	N	N	Y
Language usage:								
high level language	Y	Y	Y	Y	Y	Y	Y	Y
low level language	N	N	N	Y	N	Y	N	N

*HIPO Hierarchical — Input — Process — Output diagrams.
**ACP Activity — Channel — Pool diagram.

(a) Replication — involves repeating some part of the system activities, within the system, to give sensibility checks.
(b) Reversal — involves unwinding a process from the output signal to determine what the input should be, then comparing the actual and calculated inputs for equivalence.
(c) Interface checks — provide checks on the transfer or translation of information across a system or module boundary.
(d) Coding — traps for corruption of code using techniques such as, parity, Hamming codes and cyclic redundancy checks (CRC).
(e) Diagnostics — test data is input for which the required output is known and the system response is then compared with the anticipated response. This is one form of on-line testing.

2 Damage assessment.

If there is some delay between an error occurring and its detection, it is often indicative of a more extensive underlying error state within the system. Providing that the structure of the system design is understood, it is possible for a set of tests to be defined which interrogate the system to determine the extent of the damage. Such testing is often applied by using equipment external to the system under test, but to make the best use of fault tolerance techniques, it is advantageous to integrate the testing system with the main system during the development. In this way it is possible to provide diagnostics down to printed electronic circuit (PEC) board level.

3 Error recovery.

Two complementary techniques will be considered.

(a) Backward error recovery — if the system state is recorded at regular intervals, then in the event of an error occurring, it is often possible to reset the system to a previously recorded state. This only functions well providing that the process controlled by the system is capable of being restarted at what amounts to an earlier time in the process.

(b) Forward error recovery — this technique is best applied when the consequences of a system error can be predicted by using techniques such as failure modes and effects analysis. In such cases, it may be possible to redirect the system to a new working state on detection of an error, while at the same time nullifying any interactive effects of the original error.

4 Fault treatment.

If a system is analyzed to determine the failure states which could arise, then it is possible to categorize the faults and take action to treat each type of fault. Some typical fault categories are:

(a) fail-safe-revealed;
(b) fail-safe-unrevealed;
(c) fail-danger-revealed;
(d) fail-danger-unrevealed.

Obviously, the number of categories selected will depend upon the system complexity and consequence of failure. The actions to be taken may be just to do nothing, or to incorporate features into the design to counteract, mask or negate a fault. Techniques in use today include:

- implementing voting logic, locally within software modules, and on a global or channel basis;
- *N*-version programming, where the system functions are replicated using different algorithms, different languages and processors and even using different technologies. This process is often termed diversity.

The previous notes have outlined some of the processes whereby reliability may be built into a system containing embedded software. The feasibility of measuring software reliability will now be considered.

7.3.5 Software reliability measurement

We will first deal with methods which attempt to quantify software reliability, providing a number much in the same manner as hardware reliability.

There are several models available, e.g. Jelinski & Moranda, Musa, Littlewood, Duane. These models are in general concerned with reliability growth, i.e., making some estimate of the number of errors remaining in a piece of software and predicting the time to next failure of the software. The models are adequately described in the literature. (Littlewood 1979, Dale & Harris 1982, Keiller *et al.* 1983, Gavil 1984). How good are these models? Surveys of the models reveal that:

- they require further development;
- they often give a poor fit to real data;
- reliability growth prediction can be erratic;
- generally they are still inadequate tools for evaluation of reliability in software systems where high reliability is a requirement.

In consequence, the reliability engineer is faced with a dilemma; can he make use of software when the tools available for the quantification of software reliability are still in their infancy?

Several courses of action are currently proposed. The first is to apply further research into developing quantitative modelling to a stage where the predictions can be trusted. A further course of action is to sidestep the problem altogether and provide some form of independent hardwired system or subsystem which will take over in the event of software failure, and whose reliability can be calculated using trusted techniques. If the designer cannot provide some independent hardwired backup, then he must investigate methods of qualitatively evaluating the acceptability of the software, or discard software altogether.

The hardwired alternative is a useful expedient where the customer can bear the cost. Research also continues on the quantitative modelling processes and work is being undertaken to evaluate techniques which assess the quality aspects of software.

7.3.6 Qualification of software reliability

Essentially, the qualification of software involves reviewing the design processes in an attempt to evaluate the adequacy of both the controls applied to the design process, and of the design methodology itself. It is a form of verification and validation. That process is normally performed by some group within the design organisation, but it may be preferable to have the qualification process performed by some independent group, who are not directly related to the design team and who are less affected by the financial and political climate within the design organization. Current research is directed towards the collection of data, which can be used to evaluate:

- The effectiveness of design methodologies.
- The merits of various standards and quality assurance processes.
- The viability of a merit system of marking the attributes of a design process on a sliding scale, say one to ten. For example, the application of a good change control process would be given a high mark, while the use of unstructured programming techniques would be given a low mark.
- Error classification techniques.

The qualitative processes are closely linked to the design, justification and assessment processes and will be discussed further in subsequent sections of the paper.

7.4 THE DEVELOPMENT PROCESS

The development process is the source of most software errors (Fig. 7.1). Also, because of their origin, software errors can be considered as a source of common mode system failures. This is true, because, whenever software is replicated, all the errors in the original are to be found in any copy, i.e. systems which use replicated software are not truly independent, whereas systems using replicated hardware can claim to be independent because the hardware failures are assumed to occur at random.

This should be a great incentive to attempt to eradicate sources of software error in the design phase. However, all too often the demands of project timescale, and the desire by some managers to see code at an early stage of a project, in the belief that this signifies the approaching end of the project, act as mechanisms for the introduction of errors. Perhaps this paints too dark a view of the typical software development, for there is now a greater acceptance of the opinion that code production in the early phases of a project is not necessarily beneficial.

The weaknesses in the development process, which give rise to software errors, are being attacked on three fronts:

1 standards;
2 quality assurance (QA);
3 verification/validation techniques (V/V).

The first two items are in aid to building in reliability, while item **3** is a means of checking that **1** and **2** have been implemented.

7.4.1 Standards

Initially, because there were no software-specific standards, the existing standards for hardware were employed. It is now recognized that there is a need for separate standards, or at least for extensions to hardware standards to cater for software. Typically, European (Daniels & Humphreys 1982) and British (BSI 1979, Ministry of Defence 1984) standards are being produced. The objective of the standards is to eradicate haphazard development and introduce the elements of structure, control and documentation into the design process.

7.4.2 Quality assurance

Throughout all the standards reviewed, there is a strong emphasis on the application of quality assurance and control procedures. The quality assurance activity is essentially that of assessing whether the standards and codes of practice are suitable for the job, and also whether they are applied in an effective and efficient manner, and whether the individual responsibilities designated to team members within a project team are exercised. This activity is mainly achieved by conducting audits and reviews of the development process. A useful description of the functions of both software quality assurance personnel and software designers is to be found in EEA (1981).

7.4.3 Verification and validation

These two activities are linked to the quality assurance activities. If a project is viewed as a series of phases, then the verification process is that activity which checks that the work requirements specified at the beginning of a phase have been completed at the end of the phase. The process should also confirm that the interphase links provide continuity of the development process. The validation activity provides a global check that all the functional safety and contractual requirements, laid out in the specification, have been completed at the end of the project.

All the above activities are designed to remove ambiguity, to counteract the effects of unstructured development and to instil a measure of discipline into the software development process.

There are some limitations in the implementation of such processes as standards, QA and V/V. Notably, there is a real danger of the project becoming overwhelmed with paperwork, since on anything other than a small project, the documentation can be extensive. Experience on a project on diverse software, 'PODS' (Barnes & Humphreys 1983), demonstrated that the computer provided an excellent medium for the transmission, control and production of all the project documentation. In fact, the electronic mail system was found to be essential for rapid communications between related groups on a project.

7.5 JUSTIFICATION AND ASSESSMENT

In many industries, in addition to performing the activities previously discussed, there is a legal requirement to demonstrate the adequacy of the design. This is usually in relation to the possible risk to human life, and is particularly true of the chemical and nuclear industries. The procedure usually involves two groups: the justifying organization and the assessing organization. The justifying team is usually part of the manufacturer's organization, and is responsible for providing proof of adequacy. The assessor normally represents the licensing authority and is responsible for reviewing the evidence provided by the justifier.

The process of justification and assessment has been developed over a number of years to cope with hardware systems. However, it is recognized that the hardware justification and assessment techniques are insufficient for software. Work is in progress by several organizations, including the Health and Safety Executive and SRD, to formulate new procedures. This is an area of considerable research and the procedures will continue to evolve over a period of some years. However the following is an example of a possible approval procedure for software, which is based upon work done at SRD, combined with opinions expressed in the quoted references.

The plan is summarized in the form of a milestone chart which outlines the activities and documentation required.

7.5.1 Preliminary assessment phase

1 Assessors to receive the following documents from the justifiers at an early stage in the project:

- Initial concepts document for each section of the project.
- Statements of design aims.
- Test philosophy documents.
- Manufacturers formal specification.

- A description of the project management processes.
- The standards to be used during the project.
- The software quality assurance/quality control (QA/QC) procedures.
- A description of the change control procedures.
- A statement on how it is proposed to demonstrate that the as-built system fulfills the stated system requirements.

2 Assessors and justifiers to form agreement on:

- Software life-cycle phases.
- Work content of each phase.
- The documentation to be issued at the completion of each phase.
- Error recording format.

3 Assessors to issue comment on the documentation presented in the preliminary phase.

7.5.2 Main assessment phase

1 Assessors to receive the following documents from the justifier:

- A description of the work completed in each of the software life-cycle phase, as each phase is completed.
- A copy of any formal changes implemented in each phase.
- Formal test procedures.
- Test results.
- Definition of the acceptance criteria.
- Program listings and support documentation.
- Hardware and software integration procedures.
- A description of the verification undertaken on each phase of the development.

2 Assessors to issue comments on the adequacy of the processes employed in each phase of the development.

7.5.3 Final assessment phase

1 Assessors to receive:

- The formal safety justification.
- Copies of the as-fitted programs plus program descriptions.
- Details of the maintenance and modifications processes to be employed to support the use of the software based systems.
- Operating manuals.

2 Assessors to issue final comments on the acceptability of the software based systems.

7.6 TESTING

The testing of software is an essential part of the process of producing reliable software. Often great reliance is placed upon testing as an arbitor of the quality of software, and it has been used as the sole means of proving the software fit for purpose.

It is, however, unwise to place total reliance on the outcome of testing as a guarantor of software adequacy. For example, consider an eight bit processor with two digital eight bit inputs. Assume each test takes 100 microseconds, then to test each possible bit pattern will take some 119 hours. With a twelve bit input, to test all bit pattern would take about 829 years. This is obviously an intolerable situation, but worse is to come, for to check all sequences of inputs and perform path based analysis, presents an impossible task. In practice it is not possible to test more than a small percentage of all the possible conditions. In spite of these limitations, testing is still necessary. Consequently, some form of testing strategy is needed if testing is to be of value. Typically, a testing strategy should consider:

- the number of testing stages to be used;
- the means by which testing will be implemented, i.e. will the software be tested first in a simulator before being tested with its associate hardware;
- an outline of any test harness used to model interfaces between the software and peripheral devices during breadboard and prototype testing;
- the forms of testing to be employed, i.e. path based testing — where the route through the software for any particular set of input conditions is traced, or input/output testing — where the output status of the software is monitored for a range of input conditions;
- how the test inputs will be selected, i.e., on a random basis, or selective testing to check range, limits and trip values;
- a description of any acceptance tests to be used to demonstrate that the as-built system has fulfilled the specification requirements.

It would be unwise to think that the processes of testing are well understood. In fact, the subject of software testing is a developing art, and some examples of testing methodologies are contained in Myers (1979) while additional forms of path based testing and graph analysis are contained in Woodward *et al.* (1980) and Carre (1979).

In order to overcome the inability to exhaustively test a system, selective testing is necessary. Such testing may take several forms depending upon the extent of the project. Typically, tests can be derived to evaluate the software in many ways, for example:

- during development;

- acceptance testing;
- extended post delivery testing;
- proof testing.

Tests need to be defined to exercise the software in order to prove program correctness and adequacy for purpose. This can usually only be done on a sampling basis, by employing some of the following techniques:

- design review;
- walk-through of code;
- equivalence partitioning;
- boundary value analysis;
- cause–effect graphing;
- statement coverage;
- decision coverage;
- condition coverage;
- module testing;
- top down testing/bottom up testing;
- function testing;
- hardware/software integration testing;
- system testing;
- performance testing.

Whatever methods are chosen, it is essential that the test strategy is defined prior to the testing process being invoked. This action forces the tester to consider the consequences of each test type and the benefits gained from each form of testing. The test strategy should be structured to enable the input and result of each test to be recorded, so that repeat testing can be performed after any modifications. This is of some value in attempting to check that the repair process has not introduced further errors.

The debugging process invoked when an error is revealed by testing, should be a controlled process. The cause, remedy and system response after repair should all be documented and the actual change to the software should be via an authorization process. This requires that a peer review of the proposed change is first invoked and where signed approval is given by the project managers representative before the change is implemented.

References

Barnes M. & Humphreys P. (1983) A project on diverse software. *Enlarged OECD Halden Programme Groups Meeting*.

British Standards Institution (1979) *Guide to Reliability Programme Management*. (BS 5760, pt. 1, amended).

Carre B. (1979) *Graphs and Networks*. Clarendon Press.

Dale C.J. & Harris L.N. (1982) Approaches to software reliability prediction. *Proc. Annual Reliability and Maintainability Symp.*, pp. 167–175.

Daniels B.K. (1981) Software reliability. *2nd European Space Agency Product Assurance Symp.*

Daniels B.K. & Humphreys P. (1982) Software reliability assessment. *IEE Colloquium on Design and Testing of Software for Instrumentation*, pp. 1:1–1:3.

Electronic Engineering Association (1978) *Guide to the Quality Assurance of Software*. EEA.

Electronic Engineering Association (1981) *Establishing a Quality Assurance Function for Software*. EEA.

European Workshop on Industrial Computer Systems (1981) *Development of Safety Related Software*. TC7, System Reliability, Safety and Security. EWICS (Working Paper 233).

Govil K.K. (1984) Incorporation of execution time concept in several software reliability models. *Reliability Engineering* **7** (4), pp. 235–249.

Keiller P.A. *et al.* (1983) Comparison of software reliability predictions. *13th Annual Int. Symp. on Fault Tolerant Computing*, pp. 128–134.

Littlewood B. (1979) How to measure software reliability and how not to. *IEEE Trans. on Reliability* **R-28** (2), pp. 103–110.

Ministry of Defence (1984) *Software Design Standard*. (DEF STN 00–16.)

Myers J.G. (1979) *The Art of Software Testing*. Wiley.

Woodward M.R., Hedley D. & Hennell M.A. (1980) Experience with path analysis and testing of programs. *IEEE Trans. on Software Engineering* **SE-6** (3), pp. 278–286.

Chapter 8

Management Metrics

B. KITCHENHAM

SETC Centre for Software Reliability, The City University, London EC1V 0HB

8.1 INTRODUCTION

The purpose of this paper is to discuss the ways in which metrics might be utilized to assist the management of software development. The paper will discuss the types of metrics useful to managers and will give examples of the ways in which these metrics are used within ICL. It will finish with a description of the practical problems involved in data collection.

The majority of the results in this paper are based on measurements of the VME Operating System and the production group who maintain and enhance it. VME is ICL's general purpose operating system for the 2900 series computers. Work on VME started in the late 1960s and incorporated such features as top down design, structured programming and implementation in a high level language (a varient of Algol 68). In addition, the development process has been controlled since the start of development by the CADES system (McGuffin *et al.* 1980). CADES is a database system which records the design of VME, maintains interface, data and mode information, and provides configuration control features.

VME as a whole comprises about 7000 modules. Enhancements, improvements and the introduction of new facilities to the system run at an overall rate of approximately 30 000 lines of code per month.

About 200 people work on VME including high level strategists, technical clerks, designers, programmers, testers and quality evaluation staff. The production process, however, is based on small teams (two or three people) who work on a relatively small subsection of VME.

8.2 USEFUL METRICS

Before discussing particular software metrics, it is important to consider the three types of metrics which are useful to managers. The three basic types are targets, predictions and actuals. Targets identify the basic constraints within which a manager must work. The actual achievements at the end of a project are necessary to determine whether or not targets have been met, but actuals measured throughout the development process may be used as a basis for predicting final achievements. The comparison of predictions against targets permits progress towards the targets to be monitored.

The circle is completed with the recognition that targets are usually set on a basis of previous experience, i.e. the 'actuals' observed on other projects. Thus targets, actuals and predictions have different but related uses throughout the software development process.

Returning to the actual software metrics that are of interest to managers, the measures of primary importance are cost and schedule. However, rather than monetary cost, the metric adopted in most software cost models is total effort in months or years, or a related measure such as staffing level (Putnam 1978, Boehm 1981).

In addition to cost and schedule metrics, there is also considerable interest in what are known as 'cost drivers' (Boehm 1981). Cost drivers are factors that influence or can be used to predict the cost and timescales of a particular software product. The most commonly used cost driver is the size of the product, usually counted in lines of source code excluding comments and blank lines.

Alternative metrics have been suggested which are intended to emphasize the complexity of the product (McCabe 1976, Halsted 1977) but few of the metrics appear to offer much additional information beyond that provided by lines of code (Kitchenham 1981, Gremillion 1984). Other investigators have suggested the need for size measurements which can be estimated at an early stage in the development process. Albrecht (1979) has suggested the concept of function points which are counts of the numbers of various user perceived features of a development such as inputs, outputs and master files. In addition, a number of metrics relating to design complexity have been proposed (Kafura & Henry 1981, Troy & Zweben 1981).

Nonetheless, lines of code remain a useful metric when used carefully, in spite of various criticisms (Jones 1978), and do have the considerable advantage in the VME environment that they are equally applicable to new programs and modifications to existing programs.

Other cost drivers are either lumped together as some environment specific 'constant' (Putnam 1978) or identified as a series of adjustments to a basic line of code/effort equation (Walston & Felix 1977, Boehm 1981). In general, such cost drivers consider the quality and experience of the product staff, the complexity of the product, the requirements for reliability or performance, constraints on product size, and the techniques and tools used during the production process.

In addition to costs and cost drivers, it is useful to have some measures of product quality that can be monitored throughout the development process. There are two approaches to quality metrics; quality characterization and error tracking. Quality characterization is the idea of gradually refining a number of high level quality factors into component attributes or criteria which may relate to a number of the higher level factors, and then attempting to identify various metrics which relate to the quality attributes (Fig. 8.1). Error tracking is the idea of collecting information about the number, type and method of detection of errors found during software production. Error tracking can take place throughout the entire software development cycle, starting with errors found during design inspections (Fagan 1976), and throughout coding and testing (Basili & Weiss 1982, Kitchenham 1984).

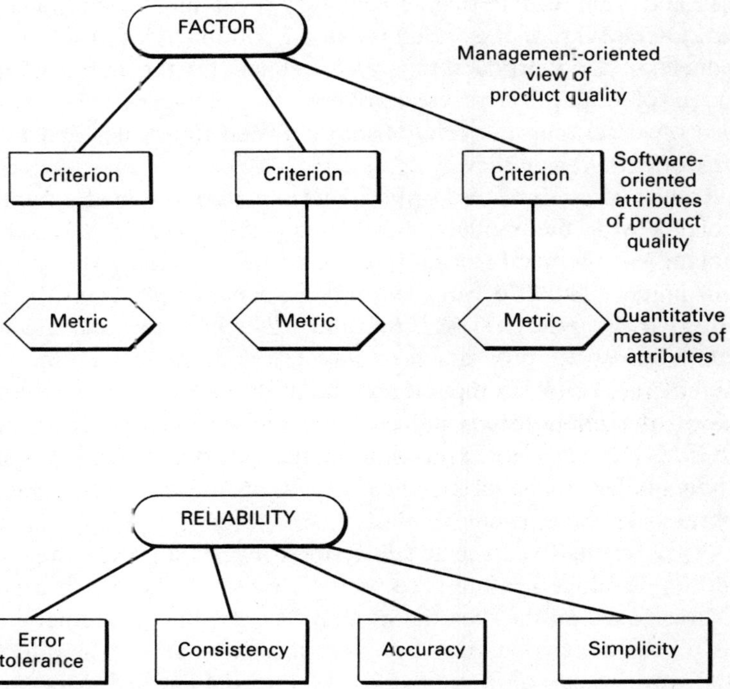

Fig. 8.1. Quality characterization.

The method of quality evaluation currently used within the VME production group is error tracking.

8.3 HOW METRICS ARE USED

Metrics may be used to assist project managers in three ways: by improving project costings and planning, by providing criteria which allow projects to be monitored during development, and by permitting the development process to be evaluated and managed. In the following sections, some methods of using metrics to assist software project management will be discussed, with examples from the VME production group.

8.4 USE OF COST METRICS

The main method of utilizing metrics to assist the costing and planning of projects is the use of a cost estimation model. Two of the most widely advocated models are Barry Boehm's COCOMO model (Boehm 1981) and Laurence Putnam's Reyleigh curve model (Putman 1978). The COCOMO model is based on an algorithmic relationship between product size and production effort, refined by the application of a number of multiplicative cost drivers. The Rayleigh curve model is based on describing the relationship between timescales and effort in terms of a Rayleigh curve.

Results of a joint ICL, British Telecom study showed a number of problems with the models (Kitchenham & Taylor 1984). A major problem was the need to calibrate the model selected to the particular environment. The effect of environment can be seen from the results of the ICL/BT study in Figs. 8.2 and 8.3, where the regression lines relating effort to program size and schedule to effort were quite different for the two companies. In addition, in neither case were they close to the relationships indicated by the default parameters of the COCOMO model or the Rayleigh curve model. Thus for cost estimation models to be of practical use to managers, they need to be calibrated to the particular environment.

Other results from the ICL/BT study investigated whether models could be developed to improve prediction during the life of a project. This was based on the idea that it might be possible to predict effort in later phases of development based on measurement of the effort used in the early phases of development. Figures 8.4 and 8.5 show the relationships between design effort and code and test effort, and between

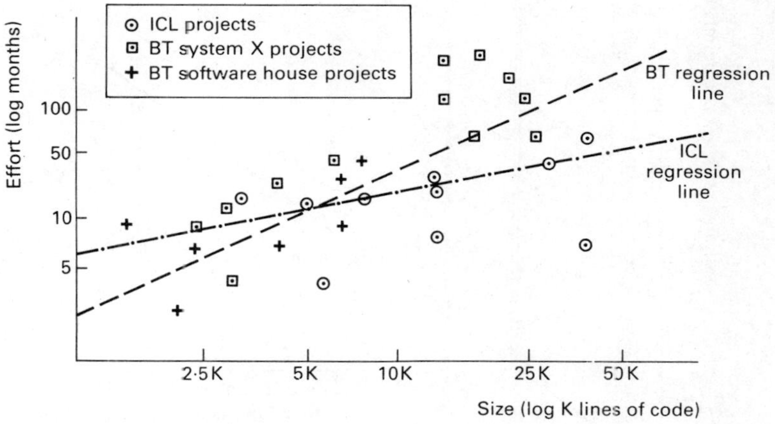

Fig. 8.2. Effort/size relationship.

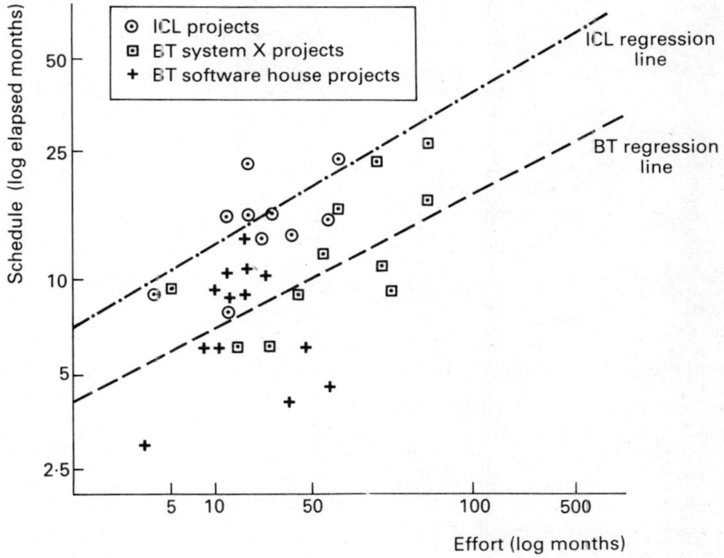

Fig. 8.3. Schedule/effort relationship.

design and code effort and test effort. From these results it does appear that there are relationships between the effort expended during the various phases of the development process, and interestingly, the relationships appear to be consistent across the different environments.

However, there are difficulties in using these results to predict

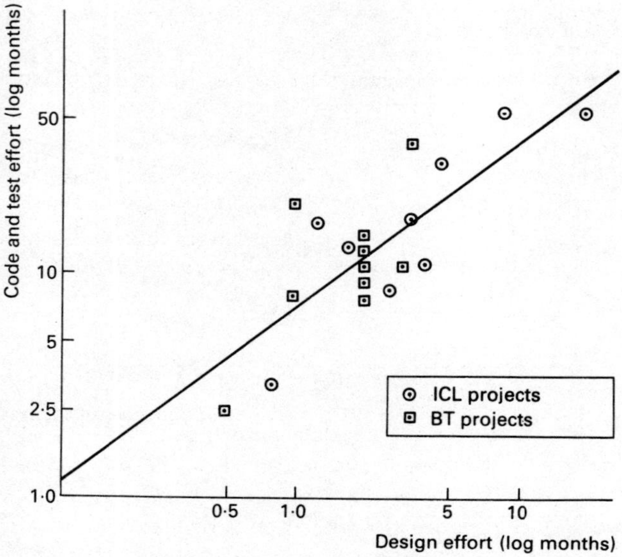

Fig. 8.4. Relationship between design effort and code and test effort.

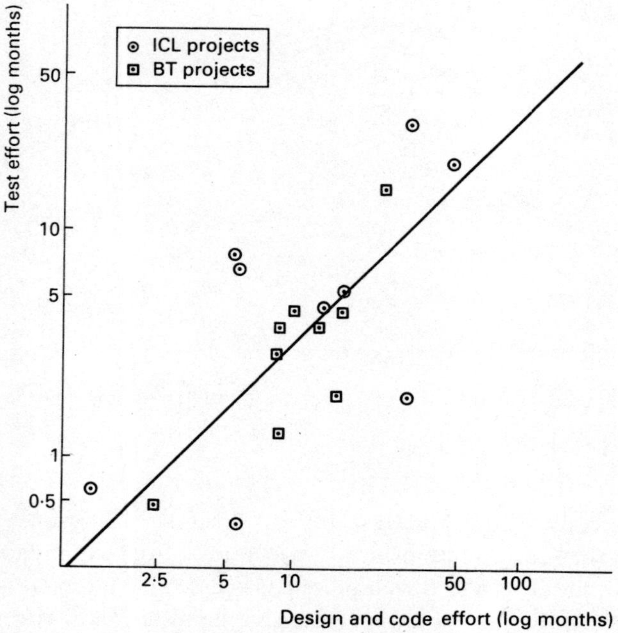

Fig. 8.5. Relationship between design and code effort and test effort.

remaining effort after each phase of project development. Investigation of the ICL data showing the distribution of effort for each phase over time demonstrated that in practice the phases overlapped one another in very complex and unpredictable ways. Thus the total design effort for a particular product was often not known until a large amount of coding and testing had already taken place (Fig. 8.6). Nonetheless, the strength of the relationship between the effort per project at various phases and its apparent independence from environmental factors suggests that investigation of this type of relationship might prove useful.

8.5 USE OF ERROR TRACKING METRICS

The results of analysis of development costs are often usefully supplemented by error tracking information. Records of the proportion of errors found during design inspection and early code checking can provide gross estimates of the number of errors expected during subsequent phases of development. For example, results in VME show that when design inspections are used conscientiously they account for

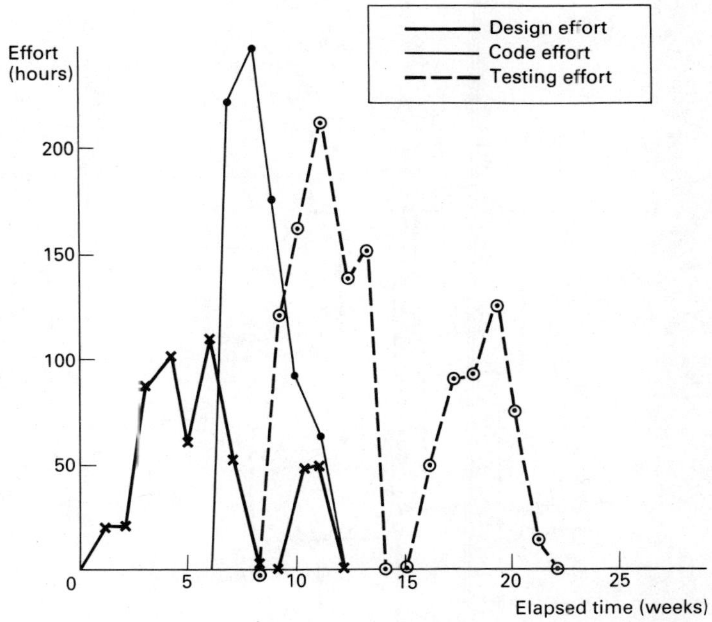

Fig. 8.6. Distribution of effort per phase over time for an ICL project.

between 40 and 50% of the total errors found before release, with early code checking accounting for a further 20–35% of total errors (Kitchenham *et al.* 1984).

Remus & Zilles (1979) have incorporated these considerations into a defect removal model (Fig. 8.7), aimed at predicting the number of errors remaining in a product at various stages in the subsequent product development process. Remus & Zilles developed a number of predictions from their basic model:
If

$$\mu = MP/PTM$$

where

MP = major defects found during inspections and reviews

and

PTM = number of defects found during testing

then

$$TD = MP * \mu/(\mu-1)$$
$$Q_2 = MP/\mu(\mu-1)$$

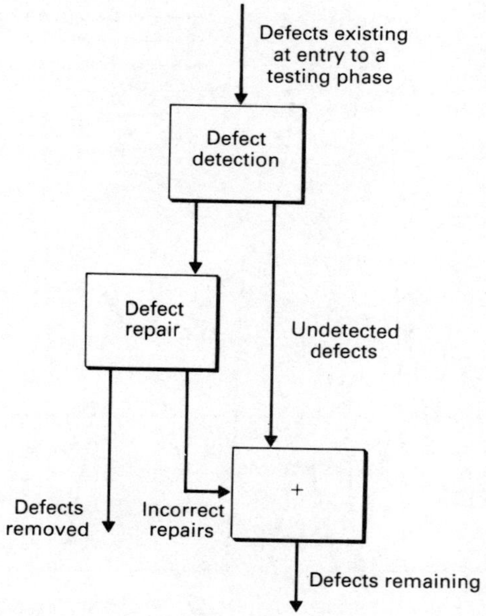

Fig. 8.7. Remus & Zilles defect removal model.

where

TD = total defects over life of product
Q_2 = remaining errors over life of product

The Remus & Zilles model, therefore, provides a quality assessment of a product during its development. However, it is a fairly simple model and can be very inaccurate (Table 8.1). One obvious problem is that it provides no error bounds on its predictions.

It also takes a fairly simplistic view of product development, since it assumes that the development process proceeds smoothly from one phase of testing to the next, whereas in practice this is not usually the case.

Drychecking may be used to detect errors during error correction activities at the same time that the major error detection method is testing by code execution. Similarly, detection of a number of errors in a particular group of programs at any stage of testing may result in a temporary reversion to static error checking methods.

In addition, the Remus & Zilles model should not be confused with a model of reliability; it only predicts error counts and does not predict the timescales within which errors will be found.

The model does, however, allow estimates of error frequencies, based on historical records, to be updated in the light of the data for a particular product. It can thus be used to improve the ability of managers to monitor product quality.

8.6 METRICS FOR ASSESSMENT

Measurements may be used to evaluate the software development process (Kitchenham & Kitchenham 1984), but may also be used to assess the results of management decisions. Tables 8.2 and 8.3 show

Table 8.1. Predictions from Remus & Zilles model.

	D1	D2
Predictions of errors remaining after testing (Q_2)	34	175
Errors found during use in-house	30	39
Prediction of errors remaining at release (Q_3)	13	6
Errors found after release (release time)	3	27
	(6 months)	(7 months)
Product size (lines of code)	13 334	39 000

Table 8.2. Comparison of two VME developments.

	Development 1	Development 2
Programs involved	117	85
Lines of code	11 241	5118
Programs with errors	26	46
Error rate/100 lines	0.5	2.1
Cost in months per 1000 lines	1.31	1.55
Design errors found during testing	2	17
Elapsed time (weeks)	37	48

Table 8.3. Breakdown of costs for two VME developments.

	Cost in hours per 100 lines	
	Development 1	Development 2
Design cost	93	70.5
Code cost	93	115.5
Test cost	11	46.5

the results of an attempt to 'speed up' the development process. Developments 1 and 2 were joint developments aimed at producing one overall facility performed by two teams who on other occasions have produced software of very similar quality. However, the work content of development 2 was identified late in the overall product planning and it was considered necessary to produce the software as quickly as possible. To this end, an attempt was made to compress the design time for the development and begin coding at an early stage.

The result of this procedure was to produce code of lower quality at a higher cost and over a longer elapsed time than the other development, which was permitted to proceed with adequate time for design inspections. This result not only indicates that managers need more information about the implications of adjusting various elements in the overall development process, it also demonstrates the crucial importance of the design phase, and provides some evidence of the potential gains to be obtained from improved design methods.

8.7 DATA COLLECTION

Throughout this paper it has been assumed that measurements of the development process are readily available to project managers. However, the process of data collection is in itself not a trivial procedure.

Since 1981 there has been an error tracking system used by the VME production staff. The system has been described in detail elsewhere (Kitchenham 1984), so the final section of this paper will discuss the main problems which have been encountered with the system.

In addition to problems with the design of the system (Kitchenham 1984), the main practical problem has been the amount of incorrect and misleading data. In order to gather information on the type of errors and how they were discovered, it is necessary for the production staff to keep detailed records. Although extraction of the data from the records and analysis of the data is automated, the self-recording element of the system induces a large number of errors. The problem of incorrect and/or missing data can be a result of unintentional errors in data recording or deliberate misrecording. Unintentional errors can be addressed by introducing systems that perform immediate data validation.

The problem of deliberate misrecording is not that it is difficult to identify but that its solution cannot be a solely technical one. The element of self-recording in any useful error tracking system may be regarded as an unwarranted intrusion or an unnecessary overhead. Ideally, the misgivings of staff involved in such a system may be overcome if the system is used constructively and they obtain useful feedback themselves. However, in the final analysis, although this paper has concentrated on the use of metrics by software project managers, it should not be forgotten that the collection of data may itself involve additional managerial problems.

References

Albrecht A.J. (1979) Measuring application development productivity. *Proc. IBM Application Development Symp.* pp. 83–92.

Basili V.R. & Weiss D.M. (1982) *A Methodology for Collecting Valid Software Engineering Data*. University of Maryland (TR–1234).

Boehm B.W. (1981) *Software Engineering Economics*. Prentice-Hall.

Fagan M.E. (1976) Design and code inspections to reduce errors in program development. *IBM Systems Journal* **15** (3), pp. 182–211.

Gremillion L.L. (1984) Determinants of program repair maintenance requirements. *CACM* **27** (8), pp. 826–832.

Halstead M.H. (1977) *Elements of Software Science*. Elsevier.

Jones T.C. (1978) Measuring programming quality and productivity. *IBM Systems Journal* **17** (1), pp. 39–63.

Kafura D. & Henry S. (1981) Software quality metrics based on interconnectivity. *Journal of Systems and Software* **2** (2), pp. 121–131.

Kitchenham B.A. (1981) Measures of programming complexity. *ICL Technical Journal* **2** (3), pp. 298–316.

Kitchenham B.A. (1984) Program history records: a system of software data collection and analysis. *ICL Technical Journal* **4** (1), pp. 103–114.

Kitchenham B.A., Fellows J.P. & Kitchenham A.P. (1984) *The Effects of Inspections on Software Quality and Productivity*. Unpublished MS.

Kitchenham B.A. & Kitchenham A.P. (1984) The use of measurement to evaluate software production methods. *Proc. Seminar — 'Approches Quantative en Génie Logiciel'*. AFCET.

Kitchenham B.A. & Taylor N.R. (1984) Software cost models. *ICL Technical Journal* **4** (1), pp. 73–102.

McCabe T.J. (1976) A complexity measure. *IEEE Trans. on Software Engineering* **SE-2** (4), pp. 308–320.

McGuffin R.W; Elliston A.E; Tranter B.R. & Westmacott P.N. (1980) CADES — Software engineering in practice. *ICL Technical Journal* **2** (1), pp. 13–28.

Putnam L.H. (1978) A general empirical solution to the macro software sizing and estimating problem. *IEEE Trans. on Software Engineering* **SE-4** (4), pp. 345–361.

Remus H. & Zilles S. (1979) Prediction and management of program quality. *Proc. 4th Int. Conf. on Software Engineering*, pp. 341–350.

Troy D.A. & Zweben S.H. (1981) Measuring the quality of structured designs. *Journal of Systems and Software* **2** (2), pp. 113–120.

Walston C.E. & Felix C.P. (1977) A method of programming measurement and estimation. *IBM Systems Journal* **16** (1), pp. 54–73.

Chapter 9

Systematic versus Probabilistic Verification Efforts — Some Examples

W. EHRENBERGER
Fachhochschule, D-6400 Fulda, Federal Republic of Germany

9.1 INTRODUCTION

The practical experience to be reported in this contribution comes mainly from nuclear applications. It has been gathered through many years in different projects on software for German power plants, mainly of the boiling water reactor type. The first of these projects dealt with the attempt to use third generation computers in the protection system of a nuclear plant; the last one dealt with the investigation of the operating experience and the performance of a computer controlling the reactor control rods. Both user programs and operating systems were considered, and both simple and complex programs or program parts were the object of the investigations. Most of the higher level programs were in FORTRAN; most of the assembler programs were in AKRA, a special language for AEG computers during the 1970s. The degree of success varied within a large range. Sometimes the systematic methods were more successful, while in other circumstances the probabilistic ones proved to be more applicable. The level of intended detail of investigation varied largely: sometimes a statement about correctness was intended, in other cases a probability distribution of the failures during operation was aimed at, or just something about whether or not a systematic verification seemed to be possible with reasonable effort.

The experiences about software verification that are reported here have contributed to some recommendations on how to make software as easy to verify as possible during its development stage. Such recommendations have recently been published by EWICS TC 7 (European Workshop on Industrial Computer Systems 1985).

9.2 INTUITIVE UNDERSTANDING

If any program should be verified by systematic means, at least some intuitive understanding about the way it achieves its functions is necessary. The problem that is to be solved by the software needs to be understood as well. Only if both types of understanding exist is a formal proof feasible. The effort that is necessary to understand any piece of software varies widely according to the following parameters:

- *a priori* familiarity of the assesor with the problem to be solved and the solution taken;
- program size;
- programming style adopted.

Figure 9.1 gives an example of a program control flow graph that is not too difficult to comprehend. The number of loops is not too high; loops do not embrace large parts of code. Several failure exits exist, as well as several subroutine calls. Since the data movements used in the related code are not very complex either, this subroutine is considered to be verifiable completely by systematic means.

Figure 9.2, on the other hand, shows a control flow graph and the related accesses to tables of a program part that is extremely difficult to understand, or rather incomprehensible. The example is taken from an operating system of a third generation computer. The operating system had been programmed with many tricks in order to save both execution time and memory space. It was infeasible to analyse this system within the limited time available in the project for the investigation of the software of that computer.

Based on the experience of numerous examples, the author has the opinion that the effort for understanding of programs increases quadratically or faster with the number of the program lines (Fig. 9.3). As a rule it is quite easy to understand simple programs and extremely difficult to comprehend long ones. The effort for program development on the other hand does not increase so quickly with the number of code lines. As a result, it is easier to understand small programs than to develop them, and easier to develop large programs than to understand them. The position of the break-even point varies from case to case according to the items mentioned earlier.

9.3 PROGRAM ANALYSIS

If the structure of a program or program part is not too complex, formal analysis may be tried. The results of the analysis are the test cases that are necessary in order to show which different types of program behaviour are feasible. It is not necessary that the analyzing

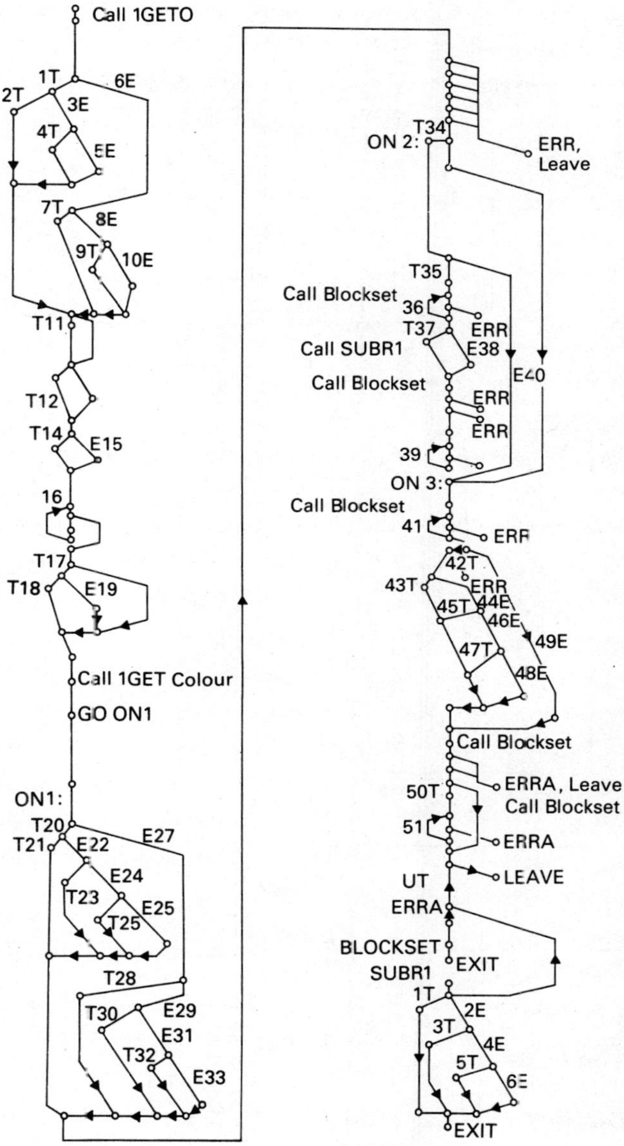

Fig. 9.1. Control flow graph of a subroutine, analysable. Call: subroutine calls; T: true branch; EPR, ERRA: failure exits. E: else branch.

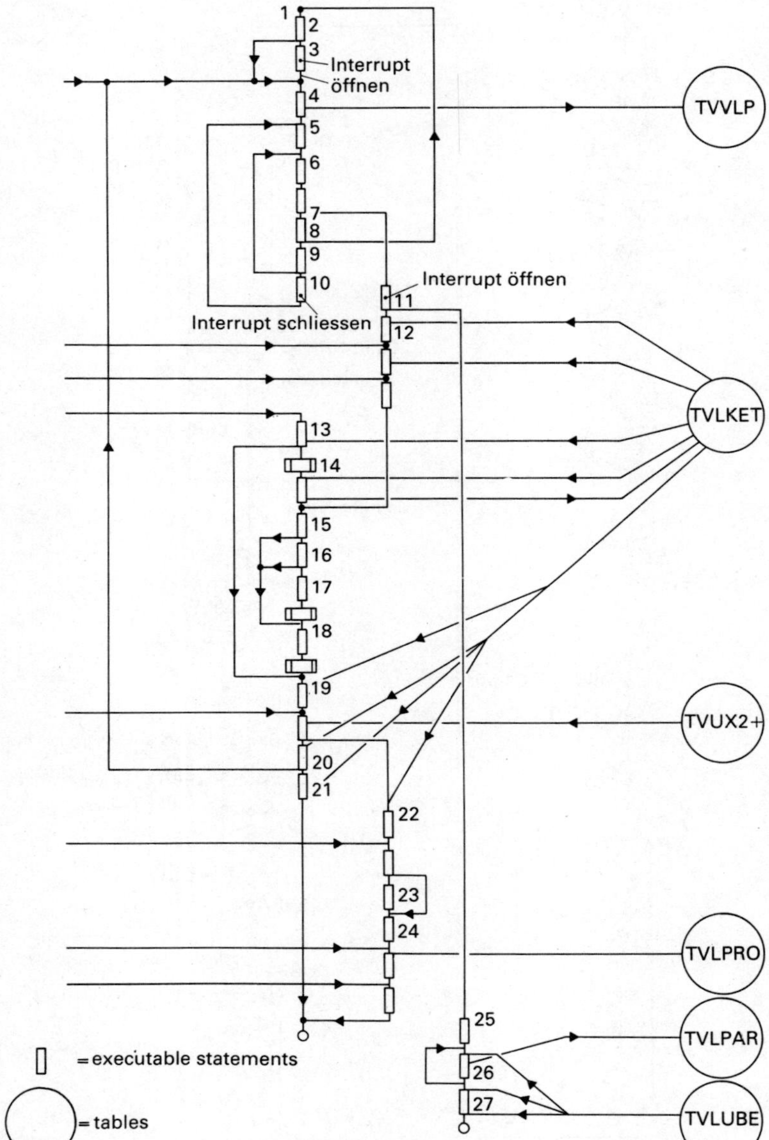

Fig. 9.2. Control flow and array access graph of a part of an operating system; not analysable.

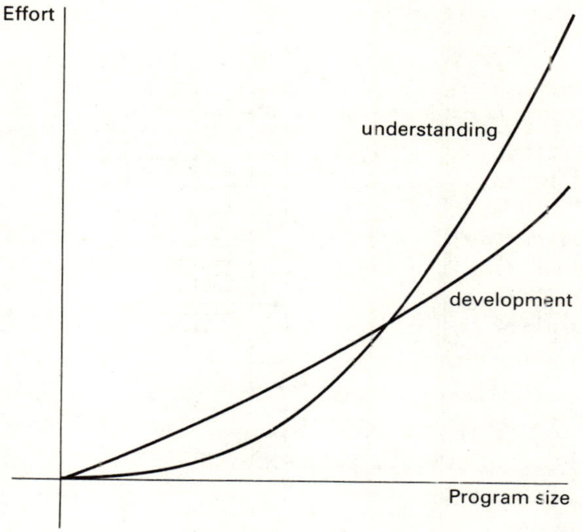

Fig. 9.3. Relationship between program size in lines of code and effort involved for development and understanding.

person fully understands what the code does; some comprehension, however, is required.

The method of program analysis is outlined on the example of Fig. 9.4. A piece of FORTRAN code is enlarged by some drawings that represent both the control flow graph and the data flow graph. From that drawing the structure plan can be derived, and hence one can come to the logic diagrams and tables of Fig. 9.6 by purely logical reasoning. Each line of a table represents the input data for one test case. Figure 9.5 gives a comprehensive view of all of the data movements of the analysed routine. Although these seem to be very complex at first glance, formal verification proved to be feasible. The method is outlined in more detail in Ehrenberger & Puhr-Westerheide (1979).

9.4 LARGE STATISTICAL TEST

Some years ago the task existed to test the software for a prototype reactor protection system. The block diagram of that system is outlined in Fig. 9.7. A large statistical test was developed which followed the scheme of Fig. 9.8. The test was driven by a hybrid computer which had a model (or a second version) of the programs to be tested.

```
     80 IF(REANO(2)-TAGWA(25)) 100,81,81
     81 CALL SETBIT (W1,2)
        IF(REANO(2)-TAGWA(24)) 100,82,82
     82 IF(REANO(7)-TAGWA(20)) 100,83,83
     83 CONTINUE
     90 IF(REANO(2)-TAGWA(23)) 100,91,91
     91 CONTINUE
     92 ISNAB=1
C
    100 IF(REANU(1)-TAGWA(28)) 101,101,110
    101 CALL SETBIT (W1,3)
        IF(REANU(1)-TAGWA(27)) 102,102,110
    102 ISNAB = 1
        IF(REANU(1)-TAGWA(26)) 103,103,110
    103 CALL SETBIT (WO,3)
        CALL SETBIT (WO,4)
C
C       FD01 BIS FD04
C
    110 DO 111 I=3,6
    110 IF(REANO(1)-TAGWA(30))111,113,113
    111 CONTINUE
        GOTO 120
    113 CALL SETBIT (W1,4)
        GOTO 120
C       KOMMT NICHT DRAN WEGEN VERZOEGERUNG
        DO 114 1=3,6
        IF(REANO(I)-TAGWA(29)) 114,115,115
    114 CONTINUE
        GOTO 120
    115 CALL SETBIT (WO,8)
        CALL SETBIT (WO,3)
        ISNAB=1
C
C
C       SBDR
C
    120 IF(REANO(8)-TAGWA(32)) 130,121,121
    121 CALL SETBIT (W1,5)
        IF(REANO(8)-TAGWA(31)) 130,122,122
    122 ISNAB=1
        CALL SETBIT (WO,4)
C
C       KDR1,2
C
    130 DO 139 I = 9,10
        IF(IDRUTI) 131,131,135
    131 IF(REANO(1)-TAGWA(34)) 139,132,132
    132 CALL SETBIT (W2,0).
        IF(REANO(1)-TAGWA(33)) 139,133,133
    133 ISNAB=1
    135 IF(REANO(1)-TAGWA(35)) 139,136,136
    136 CALL SETBIT (WO,3)
    139 CONTINUE
C
```

```
    900 IF(ISNAB)950,950,920
C
C       SCHNELLABSCHAETUNG
C
    920 CALL SETBIT (WO,0)
        CALL SETBIT (WO,1)
        CALL SETBIT (WO,2)
        CALL SETBIT (W2,5)
        CALL SETBIT (WO,11)
    950 RETURN
        END
```

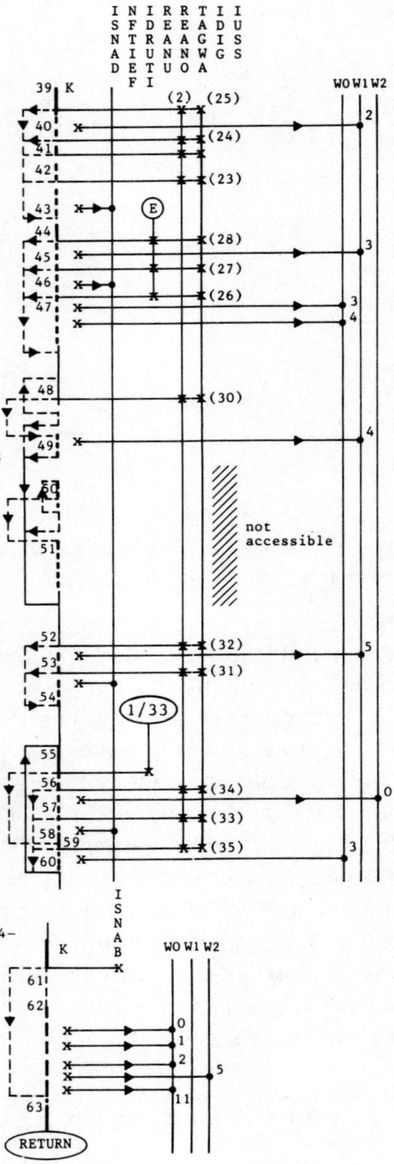

Fig. 9.4. Code and program plan of a part of FORTRAN subroutine.

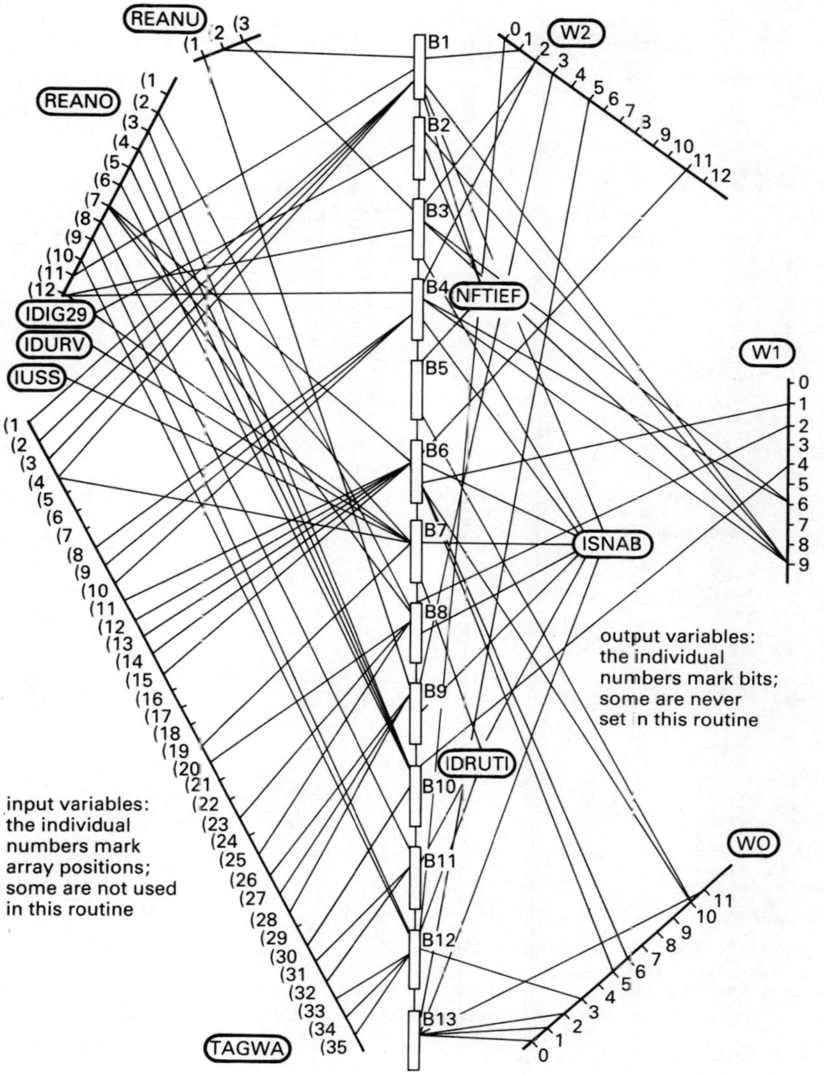

Fig. 9.5. Module plan of the example from Fig. 9.4.

Building block 8

From structure plan

S39→S40|S39 → S44 = S39 (REANO2, TAGWA25)
S40→S41|S40 → S44 = S40 (REANO2, TAGWA24)
S41→S42|S41 → S44 = S41 (REANO7, TAGWA20)
S42→S43|S42 → S44 = S42 (REANO2, TAGWA23)
S43→S44

S40↑, W1,2
S43↑, ISNAB

From this and program list

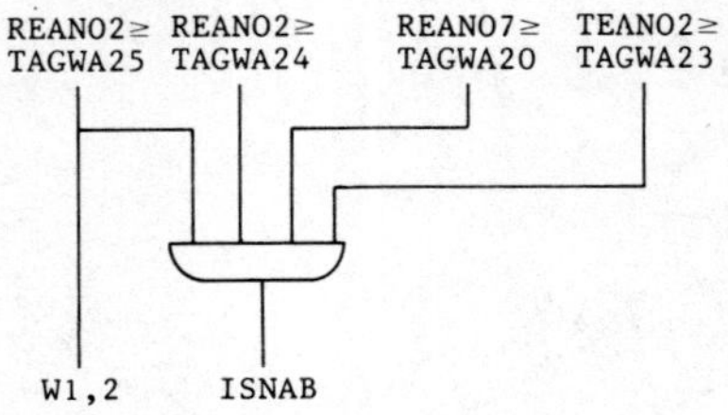

REANO2≥ TAGWA25	REANO2≥ TAGWA24	REANO2≥ TAGWA20	REANO2≥ TAGWA23
0			
1	0		
1	1	0	
1	1	1	0
1	1	1	1

Table 8.1

Logic plan 8.1

Building block 9

From structure plan

S44→S45|S44→S48 = S44 (REANU1, TAGWA28)
S45→S46|S45→S48 = S45 (REANU1, TAGWA25)
S46→S47|S46→S48 = S46 (REANU1, TAGWA26)
S47→S48

S45↑, W2,3
S46↑, ISNAB
S47↑, W0,3,4

From this and program list

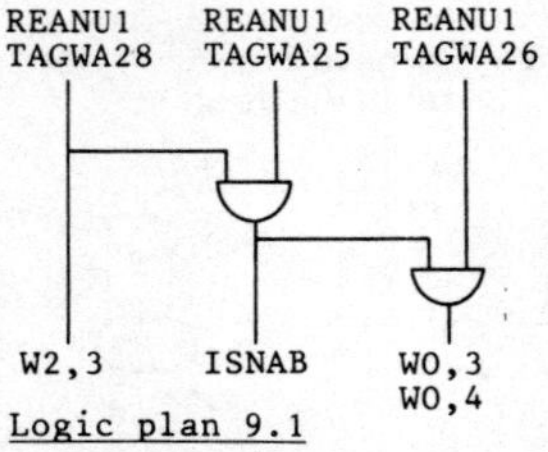

REANU1≤ TAGWA28	REANU1≤ TAGWA25	REANU1≤ TAGWA26
0		
1	0	
1	1	0
1	1	1

Table 9.1

Logic plan 9.1

Building block 10

From structure plan and program list:

loop over S48, number of runs 1,2,3 or 4
during the loop REANO3, REANO4, REANO5, REANO6 are read.

S48→S49|S48→S52|S48 S48 = S43 (REANO3, REANO4, REANO5, REANO6, TAGWA30)
S49→S52

S49↑, W1,4 S49↑↑, depending on decision in repetition 1, or 2, or 3, or 4.

Fig. 9.6a. Example of logic plans and test cases as a result of an analysis; building blocks 8, 9, 10 (partly).

From this and program list

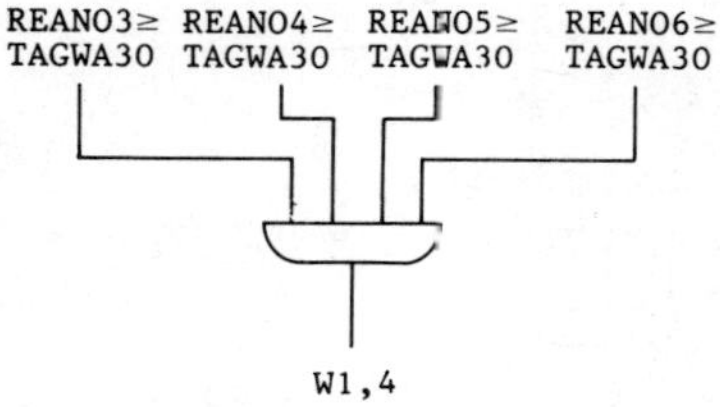

REANO3≥ TAGWA30	REANO4≥ TAGWA30	REANO5≥ TAGWA30	REANO6≥ TAGWA30
0	0	0	0
1	0	0	0
0	1	0	0
0	0	1	0
0	0	0	1

Table 10.1

Logic plan 10.1

Building block 11

From structure plan:

S52→S53|S52→S55 = S52 (REANO8, TAGWA32)
S53→S54|S53→S55 = S53 (REANO8, TAGWA31)
S54→S55

S54↑, ISNAB

From this and program list:

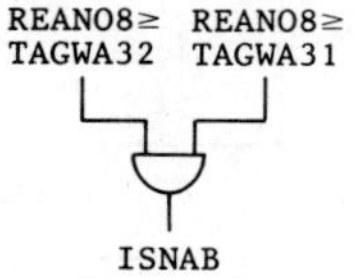

REANO8≥ TAGWA32	REANO8≥ TAGWA31
0	
1	0
1	1

Table 11.1

Logic plan 11.1

Building block 12

From structure plan and program list

Loop from S60 to S55, 2 repetitions constantly.
1st repetition ≙ I = 9 concerns REANO9
2nd repetition ≙ I = 10 concerns REANO10

Inner part of the loop:

S55→S56|S55→S59 = S55(IDRUTI)
S56→S57|S56→loopend = S56(REANO9, REANO10, TAGWA34)
S57→S58|S57→loopend = S57(REANO9, REANO10, TAGWA33)
S58→S59
S59→S60|S59→loopend = S59(REANO9, REANO10, TAGWA35)

S57↑, W2,0
S58↑, ISNAB
S60↑, WO,3

From this

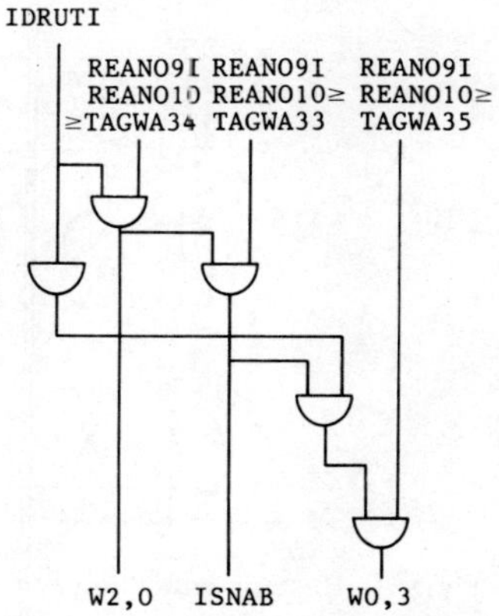

Logic plan 12.1

Fig. 9.6b. Example of logic plans and test cases; building blocks 10 (partly), 11, 12 (partly).

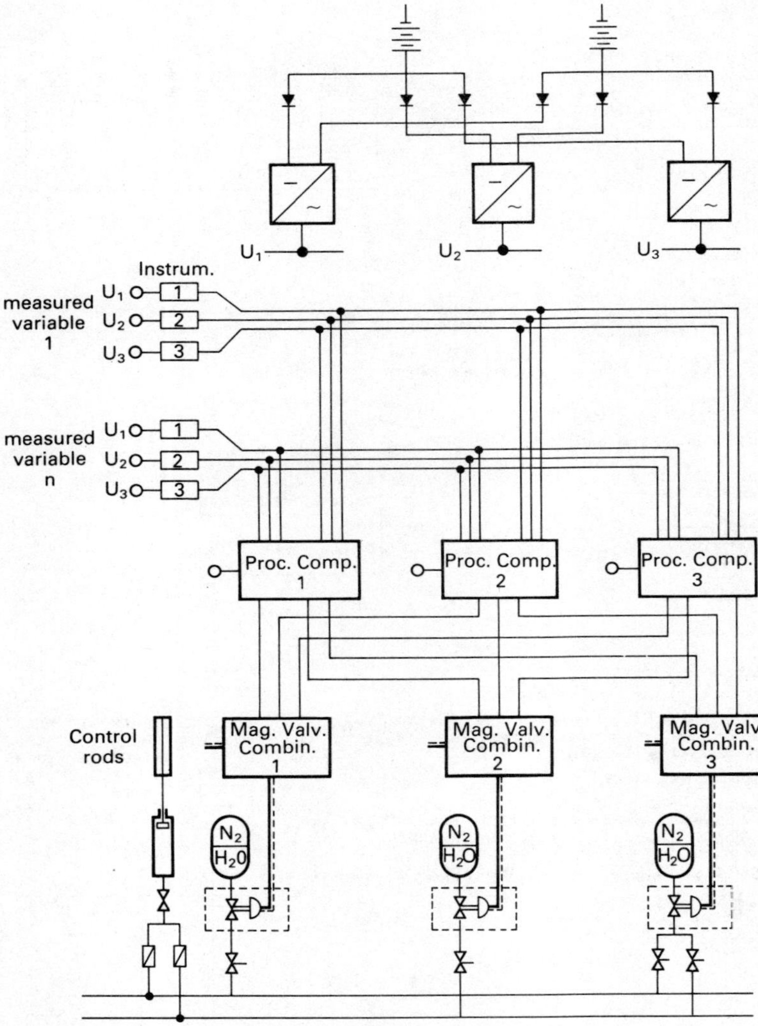

Fig. 9.7. Reactor protection system; block diagram.

Details of the test are given in Fig. 9.9. The test could run totally automatically. More than 500 000 test cases were executed, on the basis of random and systematic selections. No programming error in the test object was found. Many difficulties came from the unreliability of the analog computer involved, and from the differences of the models of the two computers with regard to one supervision criterion.

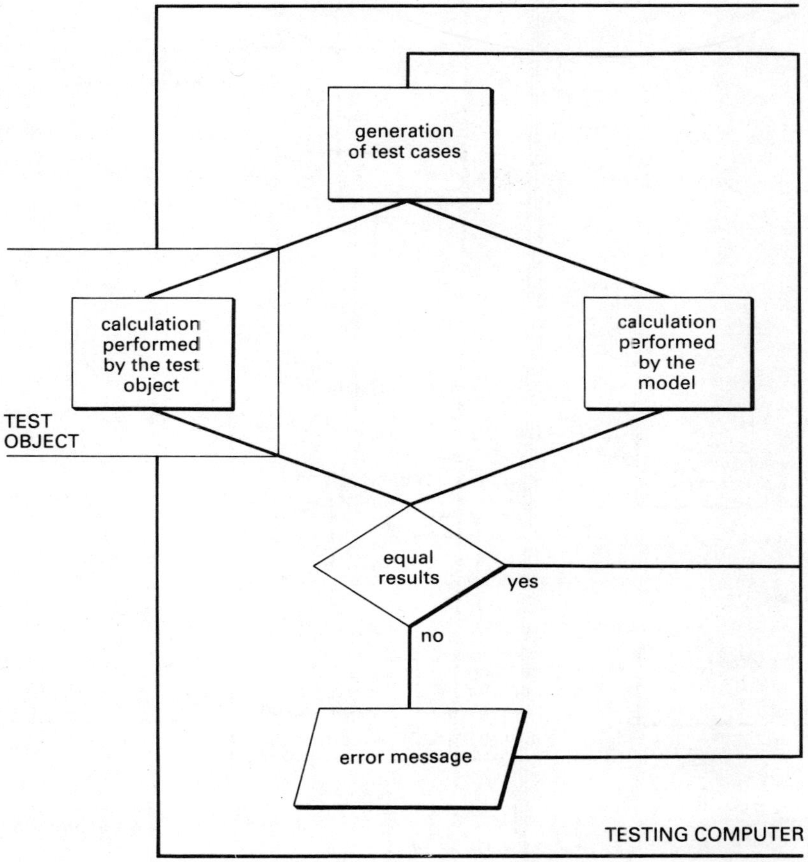

Fig. 9.8. Control of the test.

Due to different sequences of processing and two-out-of-three-selections in the two computers employed, many discrepancies were observed if the changes of input data were rapid with regard to the reactor pressure signals. The only change that came about as a result of the test was a closer supervision of the analog to digital converter of the test object (Fig. 9.10).

The test mock-up and the involved diverse programming took much more effort than the development of the original software whose reliability was to be evaluated (Fig. 9.11). The theoretical background for this section and the following ones is provided in Quirk (1985).

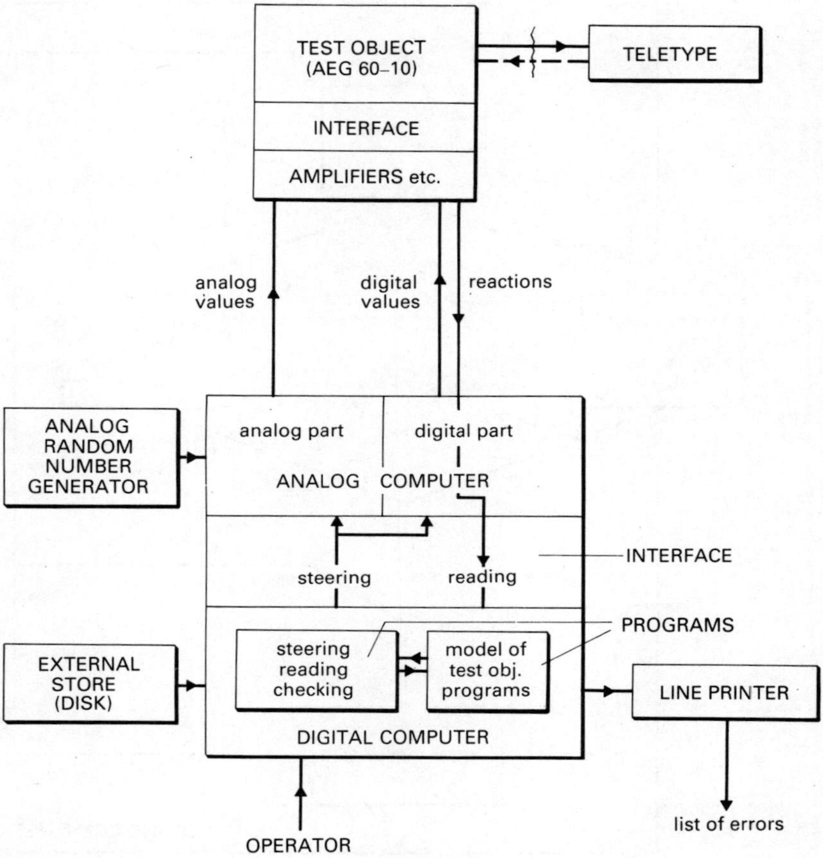

Fig. 9.9. Test configuration at the Laboratorium für Reaktorregelung und Anlagensicherung, Technische Universität, München.

9.5 OPERATING EXPERIENCE

The operating system whose central part is shown in Fig. 9.2 was investigated, with statistical means as well, because it had been shown to be not verifiable on a systematic basis. Questionnaires were sent out to several long term users of the same type of computer and operating system. The evaluation of the results was made on the basis of Bayesian statistics. The results are outlined in Tables 9.1, 9.2 and 9.3. One difficulty came from two faults that were detected and removed at two users' sites. One possibility would have been to take only the operating experience that came about after fault removal. The other would have

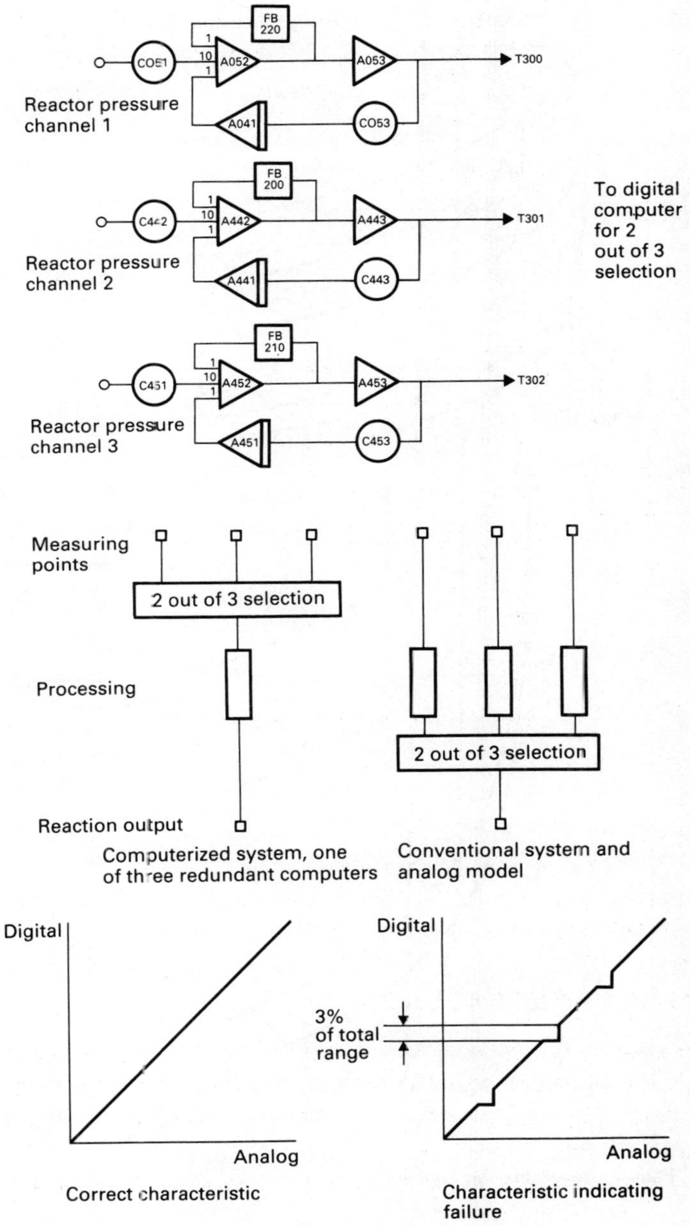

Fig. 9.10. Analog model of reactor pressure change supervision; differences in processing of the reactor pressure change supervision of the hybrid computer and the test object; failure in the analog to digital converter.

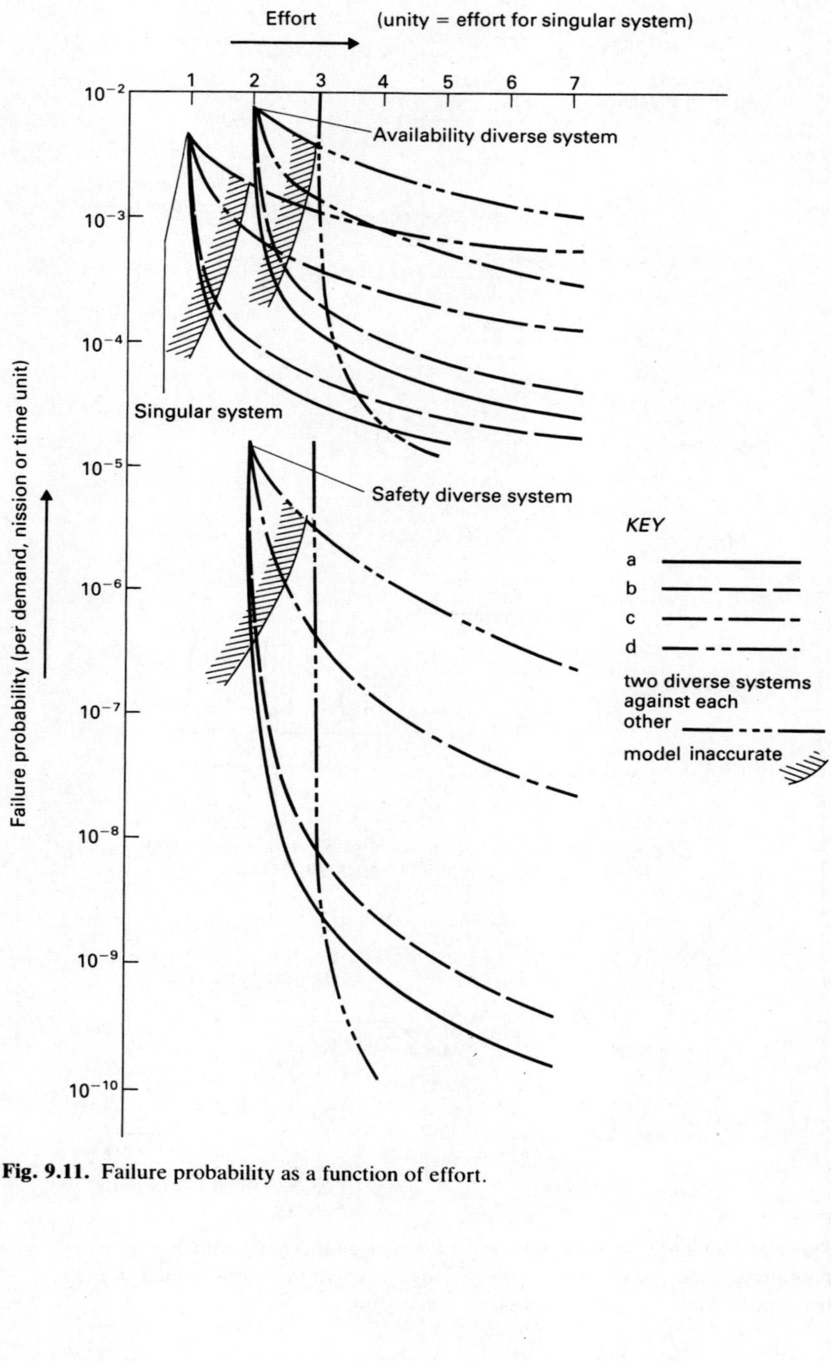

Fig. 9.11. Failure probability as a function of effort.

Table 9.1. Characteristic values for the failure rate of an operating system due to experience outside of nuclear power plants (with kind permission of Mr J. Märtz).

	Time of operating experience (h)								
Gamma distribution of the failure rate λ (1/h)	A1 92 000	A2 92 000	A3 92 000	A4 50 000	A5 90 290	A6 85 000	A7 69 000	A1, A2, A3* 74 500	A5* 77 290
Observed errors	1	1	1	0	1	0	0	0	0
95% Quantil (10^{-5})	5.16	5.16	5.16	5.99	5.26	3.53	4.35	4.02	3.88
Expectation (10^{-5})	2.17	2.17	2.17	2.00	2.22	1.18	1.45	1.34	1.30
Median (10^{-5})	1.82	1.82	1.82	1.39	1.86	0.82	1.00	0.93	0.90
Modal value (10^{-5})	1.09	1.09	1.09	0	1.11	0	0	0	0
Variance (10^{-10})	2.36	2.36	2.36	4.00	2.45	1.38	2.10	1.80	1.67
Probabilities for MTBF intervals									
$0 \leqq \text{MTBF} < 10^4$	0	0	0	0.01	0 1/3	0	0	0	0
$10^4 \leqq \text{MTBF} < 2 \times 10^4$	0.06	0.06	0.06	0.08	0.07 1/3	0.02	0.03	0.03	0.02
$2 \times 10^4 \leqq \text{MTBF} < \infty$	0.94	0.94	0.94	0.91	0.93 1/3	0.98	0.97	0.97	0.98

*Characteristic values of the changed versions; values after error removal.

Table 9.2. Characteristic values for the failure rate of an operating system due to experience inside nuclear power plants (with kind permission of Mr J. Märtz).

Gamma distribution of the failure rate λ(1/h)	Time of operating experience (h) SSFR 1 31 000	SSFR 2 25 000	SSFR 3 33 600	SSFR 4 63 000
Observed errors	0	0	0	0
95% Quantile (10^{-5})	9.67	11.99	8.92	4.76
Expectation (10^{-5})	3.23	4.00	2.98	1.59
Median (10^{-5})	2.24	2.77	2.06	1.10
Modal value (10^{-5})	0	0	0	0
Variance (10^{-10})	10.41	16.00	8.86	2.52
Probabilities for MTBF intervals				
$0 \leqq \text{MTBF} < 10^4$	0.05	0.08	0.03	0 0.1
$10^4 \leqq \text{MTBF} < 2 \times 10^4$	0.17	0.21	0.16	0.05 0.8
$2 \times 10^4 \leqq \text{MTBF} < \infty$	0.78	0.71	0.81	0.95 0.1

Table 9.3. Characteristic values for the failure rate of an operating system, combination of the experiences (with kind permission of Mr J. Märtz).

Gamma distribution of the failure rate λ(1/h)	Time of operating experience (h) BS S 10-02 Not in power plants 570 290	BS S 10-02 In power plants 152 600	BS S 10-02 Total 722 890
Observed errors	4	0	4
95% Quantile (10^{-5})	1.61	1.96	1.27
Expectation (10^{-5})	0.88	0.66	0.69
Median (10^{-5})	0.82	0.45	0.65
Model value (10^{-5})	0.70	0	0.55
Variance (10^{-10})	0.15	0.43	0.10
Probabilities for MTBF intervals			
$0 \leqq \text{MTBF} < 10^4$	0	0	0
$10^4 \leqq \text{MTBF} < 2 \times 10^4$	0	0	0
$2 \times 10^4 \leqq \text{MTBF} < \infty$	1	1	1

been to consider the failures caused by these faults as individual program failures during the calculations, which would have lead to very pessimistic results. Finally, the faults were treated as one failure per each installation, which lead to results that were slightly more pessimistic than under the first possibility.

The effort involved with that investigation was far less than the effort for a large scale statistical test or the effort for program analysis. (Contact authors for details of this investigation.)

9.6 DIVERSITY

Since the question has been widely discussed as to whether or not diversity should be used for high reliability computer software, some calculations were performed about the usefulness of diverse software. The assumptions used were idealized; in particular, independence was assumed between the programming errors or faults of the two solutions.

The question of system safety was especially carefully investigated. It was assumed that safety action was performed in case of any disagreement between versions. Calculations were performed for a singular program, two diverse programs and three diverse programs. The calculations concerned the number of necessary test cases in order to show a certain low probability of simultaneous failures. Table 9.4 shows that the savings may be substantial.

Any diverse solution does certainly require a much larger amount of *a priori* investment, due to the additional development for the

Table 9.4. Examples of numbers of test runs (K), required to achieve a confidence (P), that total system probability of failure is less than 10^{-6} per test case.*

	K =	If P = (%)
Three diverse programs	300	95
	480	99
Two diverse programs	3000	95
	4800	99
One version (no diversity)	3 000 000	95
	4 800 000	99

*These results incidentally imply that diverse programming can be cheaper than a test.

second or third diverse subsystem. This may, however, be compensated by smaller expenditure during the program test phase: Some model calculations are given in Table 9.5 for the relationship between failure probability and effort.

It must, however, be pointed out that these ideal considerations do not fit in many practical cases. Although the hybrid computer test mentioned in Section 9.4 did not reveal any contradiction to the above assumptions and results, more recent investigations from Knight & Leveson (1986) show that the independency hypothesis is not always true. Therefore the results given in this chapter should be treated with great care and should be considered as rules of thumb only.

It may be possible to get some feeling for the applicability of the independency assumption by using a reliability growth model for the estimation of the software faults and their distribution during the debugging phase. Such a model has been presented in Littlewood (1986).

Table 9.5. Mode assumptions for the curves of Fig. 9.11; model calculations of the effort for development, testing, commissioning and maintenance.

Man years	Tests	Total
3	10 per hour	50 000
6	3 per hour	30 000
10	2 per hour	3750
20	1 per 4 days	1000

9.7 CONCLUSIONS

People should be encouraged to make use of computers, not only in 'normal' applications, but in high reliability-demanding applications as well. The means to guarantee the fulfilment of the reliability requirements exist. The cost involved, however, is still high at present. This is partly due to the more rigorous methods used in the computer area as compared to conventional engineering. On the other hand, computers allow problems to be solved which are much more complex than those of other areas of engineering.

References

Ehrenberger W. & Puhr-Westerheide P. (1979) Analytical software verification. *Proc.*

Avionics Reliability: its Techniques and Related Disciplines. AGARD Conf. Proceedings C261.

European Workshop on Industrial Computer Systems (1985) *Safety Related Computers: Software Development and Systems Documentation*. TUV Report.

IFAC (1985) Reliability evaluation of a safety related operating system. In *Proc. IFAC Workshop Safecomp 85*, Pergamon Press.

Knight J.C. & Leveson N.G. (1986) An experimental evaluation of the assumption of independence in multiversion programming. *IEEE Trans. on Software Engineering* **SE-12** (1), pp. 96–109.

Littlewood B. (1987) Software Reliability and Assessment. Chapter 11, this volume.

Quirk W.J. (ed.) (1985) *Verification and Validation of Real-Time Software*. Springer.

TUV (1984) *Sicherheitsanalyse der Programme der Steuerstabfahrrechner*. TUV Report.

Chapter 10

Data Requirements for Software Reliability Prediction

C. DALE

National Centre of Systems Reliability, UKAEA, Wigshaw Lane, Culcheth, Warrington WA3 4NE

10.1 INTRODUCTION

Since the early 1970s a great deal of research has been carried out which has addressed the problem of software reliability assessment. The result has been the development of a large number of methods of assessing software reliability — the author has encountered in excess of 40 such methods (Dale 1982). The sheer number of these methods is in itself an indication that the research effort has not been as successful as one would have wished: no method has emerged as being superior to the others, and no method can be trusted to give results which are sufficiently accurate for most purposes (Schick & Wolverton 1978, Angus 1984).

The methods described in the literature split into two categories, according to the kind of data they make use of. By far the larger group utilizes data on observed failures of the software in question, usually collected during the testing phase of the software development (Littlewood & Verrall 1973, Musa 1975, Rudner 1977, Jelinski & Moranda 1982). A much smaller group uses data concerning the software itself and the way it was developed (Lipow & Thayer 1977, Motley & Brooks 1977, Walters & McCall 1978). A few methods utilize data of both sorts (Shooman 1976, Littlewood 1979).

The questions which the various models address include the following:

- What is the failure rate of this software?
- How will the failure rate improve if I carry on testing?
- How many bugs are there in the software?

Let us consider these questions in turn. Clearly, it is useful to have an estimate of the failure rate of a given piece of software, or of some other relevant measure of its reliability. It enables judgements to be made as to the adequacy of the software to its given task, and provides information on whether or not target levels of reliability have been met. It also permits the planning of contingency measures to be brought into play in the event of a system failure caused by software.

The second question is of relevance to software project managers who have to decide the point at which products are ready for release, and plan the testing and debugging effort to be applied to achieve given targets.

The third question is probably of greatest relevance to those concerned with software maintenance. A knowledge of the number of remaining bugs is an indication of the debugging effort which will be required during product life. Failure rate is of less importance from a maintenance viewpoint: a large number of bugs implies a large amount of debugging effort, and a single bug a relatively small amount, irrespective of the frequency with which users encounter the bugs.

The methods currently available for software reliability assessment have been only moderately successful in answering questions of this sort as will be discussed below. There is also a number of important issues which these methods hardly address; some examples follow:

- What are the consequences to the user of the faults remaining in this software?
- How should we go about developing this software in order to meet this target of reliability?
- How should we apportion the system reliability target to software and hardware?
- How do we predict the reliability of this system, which contains a great deal of software?

It is becoming increasingly important to have sound methods for answering such questions as these, since modern electronic systems contain significant amounts of software, which is ever more often being used for system-critical and even life-critical functions.

The current state of the art leaves a great deal to be desired in this respect. Availability of appropriate data is crucial, both for the purposes of research into assessment methods and to the application of such methods.

10.2 SOFTWARE RELIABILITY ASSESSMENT METHODS — A BRIEF SURVEY

There have been numerous approaches to the problem of evaluating software reliability by means of inferences drawn from available data on a piece of software. Most of the methods developed have been formulated by making assumptions about the nature of the failure process. These assumptions are in many cases transparently invalid, but since any model should be regarded as an approximation to reality, its quality should be judged by performance of its assessment function. Thus, if a model is claimed to estimate and predict software reliability, then it should be judged by its ability to do so.

One of the earliest software reliability models, and one of the best known, is that due to Jelinski & Moranda (1972). The assumptions underlying this model are as follows:

- The failure rate at any time is proportional to the current fault content.
- All remaining faults are equally likely to cause failure.
- Faults which are detected are instantly and perfectly removed, with the introduction of no new faults.

Thus, denoting by N the initial fault content of the software, the failure rate between the occurrences of the $(i-1)$th and ith failures is given by:

$$\lambda_i = (N - i + 1)\phi$$

where ϕ is a proportionality constant which represents the contribution of any one fault to the program failure rate.

Application of this model is by applying statistical analysis to collected failure data to estimate the parameters N and ϕ, thus giving the failure rate. Despite the relatively simple structure of this model, there are great problems of parameter estimation (Forman & Singpurwalla 1977, Sukert 1977, Littlewood & Verrall 1981).

A number of other models are very similar to the Jelinski–Moranda model (Shooman 1973, Musa 1975), and others again attempt to generalize some of the assumptions (Rushforth *et al.* 1979, Angus *et al.* 1980).

A very different approach is taken by Littlewood & Verrall (1973) who consider the software failure process to be the result of two sources of uncertainty, one concerning the selection of input and the other with the state of the program. For given software, there is a set of inputs which will cause failure, and it is assumed that this set will be encountered randomly. The second source of uncertainty is the fault-fixing operation. If fault-fixing were perfect, the software failure rate would decrease after each failure. This model assumes instead that the failure rate probably decreases each time: more formally, the failure rate λ_i prior to the ith failure is assumed to have a gamma distribution with parameters α and $\phi(i)$, where $\phi(i)$ is an increasing function of i.

This formulation ensures that the growth in reliability is probabilistic rather than deterministic.

Some attempts have been made to assess software reliability based not upon failure data, but upon other data concerning the software itself and its development history (Lipow & Thayer 1977, Motley & Brooks 1977, Walters & McCall 1978). These methods tend to be based upon collection and analysis of data concerning such things as the structure of software products, the ways in which they have been developed, and the resultant reliability. The success of the methods is dependent upon the relevance of the data on which the models are based to the particular development in question: since each of these methods has in fact used data from a single organization, the models are useful only within these organizations. Anyone wishing to apply these techniques would have to derive the necessary relationships based upon data collected by themselves; this involves a great deal of effort, and thus expense. An alternative is for some central data collection activity to take place, followed by the development of more generally applicable methods. This point will be discussed later.

Despite the amount of work which has been carried out in this area, and the number of software reliability assessment methods which have evolved, it has to be stated that the current ability to assess software reliability is disappointingly poor. Whilst it is possible to estimate current failure rates in fixed usage environments with a fair degree of accuracy on the basis of failure data, it is not possible to relate such estimates to different usage environments. The data requirements of these methods are rather stringent, as will be discussed below.

Methods which do not use failure data are not nearly as well developed as those which do, and it is these methods which offer the only hope to those who wish to estimate relatively early in the lifecycle how reliable the software in question is likely to be. There is a clear need for more work in this area.

10.3 DATA REQUIREMENTS OF EXISTING METHODS

A large number of existing software reliability assessment methods require data consisting of times at which failures have occurred on a single piece of software, in order to estimate and predict such quantities as the failure rate of the software. By and large, the methods can be generalized to take into account the existence of multiple copies of the software, and to make use of data in the form of numbers of failures during given periods of testing, with the precise times of failure unknown.

Some of the methods are capable of giving reasonable estimates of current failure rates (Keiller *et al.* 1983), but all of them are subject to the inherent assumption that the pattern of software usage during testing is representative of the usage in the environment of interest. If this assumption were strictly valid in a particular instance, then the failure rate in the hands of a user would be the same as the failure rate during testing. There are a number of problems with the implicit assumption.

The first problem is that the testing of computer software tends to be anything but representative of real use of the software. There are a variety of techniques which can be used for testing a piece of software (Myers 1979), the aim of which is to maximize the effectiveness of the exercise in terms of identifying faults in the software. None of these techniques permits the test environment to be considered as in any way equivalent to the use environment. There is very little guidance in the software reliability assessment literature on how this problem should be overcome. Musa (1975) does introduce a testing compression factor which is essentially a multiplicative constant, the interpretation of which is that testing is so many times as severe as use. It is, however, difficult to believe that the relationship between testing and use is as simple as this, and there has been very little research into the effects of different modes of software usage on the frequency with which failures are observed.

The second problem is that the software use environment cannot in most cases be determined in sufficient detail until well after the software has been in use. Almost by definition, most software products are novel in some respect and the pattern of usage develops with time as users become increasingly familiar with the capabilities of the product. If the software is destined to be used in some real-time application such as plant control, the behaviour of the plant in question may not be understood in sufficient detail before the plant is constructed and used. So even if a software developer were to make the unusual decision to test the software in conditions which were representative of real use, the carrying out of the decision would be a major challenge in itself.

Given that the application of these assessment methods requires the use of unconventional testing methods which are in themselves difficult to carry out, it is reasonable to conclude that the only software developers who would be likely to go to the trouble are those who have particularly stringent requirements as far as reliability is concerned. This implies a need to estimate failure rates which are very close to zero, and no method has emerged which has been shown to be capable of doing so.

It seems fair to conclude that this, the largest group of software reliability assessment methods, has data requirements which mitigate against the use of these methods.

There is a small group of methods which aim at estimating the number of bugs present in a piece of software (Rudner 1977). Although this quantity is clearly relevant to the failure rate of the software, the relationship between the quantities is not known at this time, so the use of these methods for software reliability assessment is not strictly possible. It is worth noting, however, that a number of software reliability models are parameterized in such a way that one of the parameters has the interpretation 'number of bugs initially present'. To take as an example the Jelinski–Moranda model described earlier, the failure rate is modelled as the product of the parameter N (= number of bugs initially present) and a constant of proportionality. This has led a number of authors (Forman & Singpurwalla 1977, Sukert 1977) to apply the model to estimate N, rather than the failure rate; this practice can be extremely misleading, as the parameter N is usually found to indicate lower numbers of bugs than are actually present, even when the failure rate itself has been estimated with reasonable accuracy. This should act as a warning against using models for a purpose other than that intended.

Moving now to methods which make use of information about the software and its development process, these are generally based upon applying relationships, observed to exist in the past, to current software developments in the belief that the relationships will continue to hold true. This leads the authors of such work (Lipow & Thayer 1977, Walters & McCall 1978) to point out that because they collected data only within their own organizations, then the derived relationships will hold only within that same software development environment. Thus the methods are not generally applicable.

Methods which make use of both failure data and other information have data requirements which are at least as severe as the combined data requirements of representative models from the two broader categories: as an example, the Littlewood structural model has of the order of $3n^2$ parameters which must be estimated, where n is the number of modules. Methods of this sort are clearly of limited utility.

In summary, the topic of data requirements is a major stumbling block to the practical application of most published work on quantitative software reliability assessment.

10.4 DATA REQUIREMENTS FOR THE FUTURE

There are a number of ways in which the current abilities in this area can be improved. On the one hand, there is a real need to improve the applicability of currently available methods, so that the full benefits can be reaped of the work which went into their development. On the other hand, it is necessary to address the development of new methods giving a software reliability assessment capability at an early stage of the software development cycle, and enabling sensible and useful answers to be given to questions such as:

- Is this reliability requirement achievable if we develop the software in this way?
- What techniques should we use to stand a good chance of achieving this target reliability?
- What will be the reliability of this system, taking account of both hardware and software?

The applicability of currently available software reliability assessment methods can be enhanced only by arriving at a better understanding of how usage patterns affect software failure rates, etc., and using this improved understanding to draw inferences about failure rate in one environment (e.g. customer use) from data gathered in a different environment (e.g. testing). There seem to be two approaches which may prove profitable. The collection of failure data from testing and usage environments for a number of products will enable direct analysis of the relationship between the two sets of data for each product. An alternative approach is to investigate the relationship between measures of testedness (of which there are a number, see, for example, Woodward *et al.* 1980) and reliability in use.

The data requirements of the first approach may seem fairly straightforward, involving the collection of failure times during both testing and use. This is indeed the minimum data required, but more valuable information might be obtained by analysing the behaviour of each of a succession of versions (produced during testing) in a user environment. Collection of data of this sort will be difficult, if not impossible. The main problem emanates not from the amount of data which would have to be collected, but from persuading users to accept early versions which contain known bugs: this may be possible only under relatively artificial conditions, which would prejudice the validity of any conclusions drawn.

The second approach may prove more beneficial. The data requirements are less daunting, since measures of testedness, etc., can be obtained at various stages of testing, and potentially during use also, as well as the usual failure time data. Relationships between measures of testedness and measures of reliability can then be investigated, under a variety of testing strategies.

The development of general methods enabling the early prediction of software reliability is a more daunting task, but probably a more important one. Only in the presence of such methods can targets be set and progress towards these targets be planned, monitored and controlled. The current position of software reliability prediction is a reflection of the situation of software development some years ago — all the emphasis is on the testing phase. Software engineering has reached the point where it is widely accepted that reliability should be designed in, not tested in; this fact should be reflected in software reliability prediction methods. Since it is acknowledged that events early in the software life-cycle have a strong bearing on the reliability of the final product, it is sensible to make predictions of product reliability in the light of events early in the life-cycle; the stumbling block is that the current knowledge of the relationship between early events and product reliability is insufficient. This realization is the key to progress in this important area.

A prerequisite to the development of such method is, then, the collection of data concerning the way in which given software products have been developed, together with data on the resulting reliability. This is the basic idea which was used by authors such as Walters & McCall (1978) and Lipow & Thayer (1977), but if the methods are to be generally applicable then the data must be generally collected. Listed below are some items of data which could usefully be collected, all of which have been claimed to have an effect on the reliability of the final software product.

- Design methods used.
- Programming languages used.
- Testing methodology employed.
- Application type.
- Size of the project:

(a) in terms of cost, apportioned to phases;
(b) in terms of effort employed, apportioned to phases;
(c) in terms of final product size.

It is also necessary to collect reliability data *per se*, both during and after development, to enable the relationships between development events and product reliability to be investigated.

A further very valuable kind of data which should be collected concerns the consequences of software failures. These can range from extremely minor irritation to death. Since software failures are important chiefly because of their consequences, it is clearly important to collect information of this sort to permit the development of models capable of taking failure consequences into account.

The above outline of data requirements addresses no more than the research need. If research along the lines suggested is successful in developing the required software reliability assessment methods, then it is likely that this outline also encompasses the data requirements for application of the methods developed. A consequence of this is that those organizations which have the vision to participate early in any data collection activity will also be in the best position to exploit the results of the research.

10.5 CONCLUSIONS

This paper has considered software reliability assessment from the viewpoint of the data required. First, the limitations of the current state of the art methods, largely due to their stringent data requirements, have been identified. In the latter part of the paper, the data required for the enhancement of old methods and the development of new ones have been outlined.

It is clear that the development of software reliability prediction methods which can be used at a relatively early stage of the life-cycle is necessary. It is equally clear that this will entail a great deal of data collection and analysis, concerning the methods used for software development and the reliability of the resulting software products.

The author is currently involved in the Software Data Library project, the ultimate aim of which is to set up a central data bank containing the kinds of information identified above. This would provide a facility useful not only from the reliability viewpoint, but also for those interested in other aspects such as cost, quality, productivity, and management of software development.

References

Angus J.E. (1984) The application of software reliability models to a major C^3I system. *Proc. Annual Reliability and Maintainability Symp.*, pp. 268–274.

Angus J.E., Schafer R.E. & Sukert A.N. (1980) Software reliability model validation. *Proc. Annual Reliability and Maintainability Symp.*, pp. 191–199.

Dale C.J. (1982) *Software Reliability Evaluation Methods*. Dynamics Group, British Aerospace (Report ST26750).

Forman E.H. & Singpurwalla N.D. (1977) An empirical stopping rule for debugging and testing computer software. *Journal of the American Statistical Association* **72** (360), pp. 750–757.

Jelinski Z. & Moranda P. (1972) Software reliability research. In Freiberger W. (ed.) *Statistical Computer Performance Evaluation*, pp. 465–484. Academic Press.

Keiller P.A. *et al.* (1983) Comparison of software reliability predictions. *13th Annual Int. Symp. on Fault-Tolerant Computing*, pp. 128–134.

Lipow M. & Thayer T.A. (1977) Prediction of software failures. *Proc. Annual Reliability and Maintainability Symp.*, pp. 489–494.

Littlewood B. (1979) Software reliability model for modular program structure. *IEEE Trans. on Reliability* **R-28** (3), pp. 241–246.

Littlewood B. & Verrall J.L. (1973) A Bayesian reliability growth model for computer software. *Applied Stratistics* **22** (3), pp. 332–346.

Littlewood B. & Verrall J.L. (1981) Likelihood function of a debugging model for computer software reliability. *IEEE Trans. on Reliability* **R-30** (2), pp. 145–148.

Motley R.W. & Brooks W.D. (1977) *Statistical Prediction of Programming Errors*. US Air Force (Report RADC-TR-77-175).

Musa J.D. (1975) A theory of software reliability and its application. *IEEE Trans. on Software Engineering* **SE-1** (3), pp. 312–327.

Myers G.J. (1979) *The Art of Software Testing*. Wiley.

Rudner B. (1977) *Seeding/Tagging Estimation of Software Errors: Models and Estimates*. US Air Force (Report RADC-TR-77-15).

Rushforth C.K., Staffanson F.L. & Crawford A.E. (1979) *Software Reliability Estimation under Conditions of Incomplete Information*. US Air Force (Report RADC-TR-79-230).

Schick G.J. & Wolverton R.W. (1978) An analysis of competing software reliability models. *IEEE Trans. on Software Engineering* **SE-4** (2), pp. 104–120.

Shooman M.L. (1973) Operational testing and software reliability estimation during program development. *Record IEEE Symp. on Computer Software Reliability*, pp. 51–57.

Shooman M.L. (1976) Structural models for software reliability prediction. *Proc. 2nd Int. Conf. on Software Engineering*, pp. 268–280.

Sukert A.N. (1977) A multi-project comparison of software reliability models. *Proc. Computers in Aerospace Conf.* pp. 413–421.

Walters G.F. & McCall J.A. (1978) The development of metrics for software R & M. *Proc. Annual Reliability and Maintainability Symp.*, pp. 79–85.

Woodward M.R., Hedley D. & Hennell M.A. (1980) Experience with path analysis and testing of programs. *IEEE Trans. on Software Engineering*, **SE-6** (3), pp. 278–286.

Chapter 11

How Good are Software Reliability Predictions?

B. Littlewood
Centre for Software Reliability, The City University, London EC1V 0HB

11.1 INTRODUCTION

When software reliability models first appeared in the literature, about 15 years ago (Jelinski & Moranda 1972, Littlewood & Verrall 1973, Shooman 1973, Musa 1975), it was felt that it would soon be possible to recommend a definitive model to potential users. This has not turned out to be the case, for many reasons. Most important, perhaps, is the great variety of software: it now looks unlikely that a single, relatively simple, mathematical model could describe this diversity.

If there is no universally 'best' model, a user might reasonably ask which model is the best for their particular problem. It is this question which is addressed in our current research, and some useful tools will be described in the present paper to help arrive at an answer.

For simplicity of exposition, we shall restrict ourselves to the *continuous time software reliability growth* context. The raw data available to the user will be a sequence $t_1, t_2, \ldots, t_{i-1}$ of execution times between successive failures. As failures take place, attempts will be made to fix the underlying faults in the software. Various fixing strategies could be adopted, but all should result in at least long-term growth in the reliability of the program.

The observed times can be regarded as realizations of random variables $T_1, T_2, \ldots, T_{i-1}$. The problem is to predict the *unobserved* $T_i, T_{i+1}, \ldots$, using the observed data. We might, for example, be interested in estimating when the program will have achieved a prespecified target reliability; or how reliable it will be at some specified time (projected completion date?) in the future.

The important point is that users are interested in using the available data for *prediction*. Even the simplest problem of measuring the current reliability of the product is a prediction: it involves questions about the random variable T_i when the available data are $t_1, t_2, \ldots,$

t_{i-1}. More generally, we shall be interested in predicting the entire future T_i, T_{i+1}, ...

Readers familiar with the conventional statistical literature will know that the prediction problem has been somewhat neglected. Mathematical statistics tends to concentrate on inference, with the exception of recent, mainly Bayesian, work (Aitchison & Dunsmore 1975). In fact, prediction involves three strands. For the notation of our problem this 'prediction system' comprises:

1 the *stochastic model* which specifies the distribution of any subset of the T_j's conditional on an unknown parameter, usually a vector, α;
2 *the statistical inference* procedure for α based on the available data;
3 the *prediction procedure* which combines **1** and **2** to allow probability statements to be made about future T_j's.

It can be seen that the problem is wider than finding the best model: disaster can strike at any of three stages. Of course, the model is an important part of the triad and it seems unlikely that good predictions will be ultimately attainable unless the model is close to reality. However, a good model is not sufficient. Some recent work of ours suggests, indeed, that certain modelling deficiencies can be overcome by the use of the tools described in following sections.

A conventional statistical approach might suggest that each of **1** to **3** above should be examined separately in each context. Thus, if all stages were trustworthy we might reasonably place trust in the predictions. Unfortunately this approach has several drawbacks. Conventional goodness-of-fit testing for stage **1** is impossibly hard for most of the software reliability models. Properties of maximum likelihood estimators, which are a common solution at stage **2**, are usually not obtainable. Perhaps most importantly, it is not easy to determine the relative contributions of stages **1**, **2** and **3** to 'good prediction'.

Accordingly, the approach adopted here will be *direct analysis* of the predictions themselves and, in particular, a comparison of prediction with eventually observed real behaviour. This approach has the intuitively appealing property of mimicking the behaviour of an actual user, who is likely to judge predictions as adequate only if they are reasonably close to what he/she subsequently observes.

11.2 AN EXAMPLE

In this section a single data set (see Table 11.1) will be analysed. We shall use only two software reliability models (really, in our terminology, prediction systems): Jelinski–Moranda and Littlewood–Verrall.

Table 11.1. Execution times in seconds between successive failures. Table reads left to right in rows.

3.	30.	113.	81.	115.
9.	2.	91.	112.	15.
138.	50.	77.	24.	108.
88.	670.	120.	26.	114.
325.	55.	242.	68.	422.
180.	10.	1146.	600.	15.
36.	4.	0.	8.	227.
65.	176.	58.	457.	300.
97.	263.	452.	255.	197.
193.	6.	79.	816.	1351.
148.	21.	233.	134.	357.
193.	236.	31.	369.	748.
0.	232.	330.	365.	1222.
543.	10.	16.	529.	379.
44.	129.	810.	290.	300.
529.	281.	160.	828.	1011.
445.	296.	1755.	1064.	1783.
860.	983.	707.	33.	868.
724.	2323.	2930.	1461.	843.
12.	261.	1800.	865.	1435.
30.	143.	108.	0.	3110.
1247.	943.	700.	875.	245.
729.	1897.	447.	386.	446.
122.	990.	948.	1082.	22.
75.	482.	5509.	100.	10.
1071.	371.	790.	6150.	3321.
1045.	648.	5485.	1160.	1864.
4116.				

Our intention is merely to show the disparate results that can be obtained and to show, in the next section, ways in which a user might make an intelligent choice between the available predictions.

We begin with a brief description of the two prediction systems to be used.

Jelinski–Moranda (JM)

This model (Jelinski & Moranda 1972) is justifiably credited with being the first reliability growth model specifically created for software. The model due to Musa (1975), which is essentially identical, has obtained wider currency because of the extra refinements built on the JM basis.

The JM model assumes that $T_1, T_2, \ldots,$ are independent random variables with exponential distributions:

$$p(t_i|\lambda_i) = \lambda_i e^{-\lambda_i t_i} \; t_i > 0$$

where:

$$\lambda_i = (N - i + 1)\phi$$

Here N is the initial number of faults in the program, each of which contributes an amount ϕ to the rate of occurrence of failures (ROCOF). As a failure occurs, it is assumed that the underlying fault is removed instantaneously and with certainty, causing the ROCOF to diminish by an amount ϕ.

At any stage, the available data $t_1, t_2, \ldots, t_{i-1}$ is used to obtain estimates of the unknown parameters, $\hat{N}$ and $\hat{\phi}$, by the method of maximum likelihood (ML). These are then used, via the 'plug-in rule', to make predictions. Thus, for example, the predicted current reliability is:

$$\tilde{R}_i(t) = e^{-(\hat{N}-i+1)\hat{\phi}t}$$

which is an estimate of: $R_i(t) \equiv P(T_i < t) = e^{-(N-i+1)\phi t}$

A serious criticism of this model is that it assumes all faults contribute equally to the unreliability of the program. This seems highly implausible, and recent empirical studies (Adams 1980, Nagel & Skrivan 1981) suggest that, on the contrary, the contributions from different faults vary by orders of magnitude. In Littlewood & Sofer (1986), it is shown that the data of Table 11.1, among others, appear to cast doubt on this fundamental assumption of JM.

Littlewood–Verrall

As in JM, this model (Littlewood & Verrall 1973) treats the successive times between failures as conditionally exponential:

$$p(t_i \mid \Lambda_i = \lambda_i) = \lambda_i e^{-\lambda_i t_i} \; (t_i > 0) \qquad (11.2.1)$$

However, the sequence of rates $\{\Lambda_i\}$ is treated as a sequence of independent stochastically decreasing *random variables*. This doubly stochastic model attempts to capture the uncertainty of the fixing operation (Littlewood 1979, Laprie 1984): fixes are not certain to improve the reliability of the program, and even when they do there is uncertainty about the magnitude of the improvement.

Specifically, it is assumed that

$$p(\lambda_i) = \frac{[\psi(i)]^{\alpha}\lambda_i^{\alpha-1}e^{-\psi(i)\lambda_i}}{\Gamma(\alpha)} \tag{11.2.2}$$

i.e. the Λ_i are independently gamma distributed.

The function $\psi(i)$ determines the reliability growth. If $\psi(i)$ is increasing in i, the $\{\Lambda_i\}$ form a stochastically decreasing sequence and the $\{T_i\}$ are stochastically increasing.

The choice of parametric family for $\psi(i)$ is under the control of the user of the model. Here we shall take:

$$\psi(i) \equiv \psi(i, \beta) = \beta_1 + \beta_2 i \tag{11.2.3}$$

Again, predictions are made by using the data $t_1, t_2, \ldots, t_{i-1}$ to obtain ML estimates, $\hat{\alpha}$, $\hat{\beta}_1$ and $\hat{\beta}_2$, of the unknown parameters, followed by the 'plug-in' rule. Thus, for example, the predicted current reliability is:

$$\tilde{R}_i(t) = \left[\frac{\psi(i, \hat{\beta})}{t + \psi(i, \hat{\beta})}\right]^{\hat{\alpha}} \tag{11.2.4}$$

We shall consider only the above two prediction systems in this paper. However, there are now some 40 different approaches to this problem, according to a recent review paper by Dale (1982). A potential user, faced with this bewildering choice, might reasonably ask which is going to be best for his/her purposes.

In Fig. 11.1 we show the median plots for JM and LV using Table 11.1 data. Because of the long-tailed distributions which seem common for software failure times, the predicted mean time to failure can be misleading or non-existent (Littlewood 1979). A simple alternative is the predicted median of the failure time distribution. For current reliability, when $t_1, \ldots, t_{i-1}$ have been observed, this is the solution, m, of:

$$\tilde{R}_i(m) = 0.5$$

Thus in Fig. 11.1 the median of T_i is plotted against i for the two different prediction systems. Such plots, although simple, might be useful in tracking progress as debugging takes place.

The results are not encouraging. Apart from the early predictions, there is startling disagreement between the two methods. From about observation 90, JM gives much more optimistic answers than LV. In addition, at these later stages, the JM predictions seem to be more noisy than those of LV.

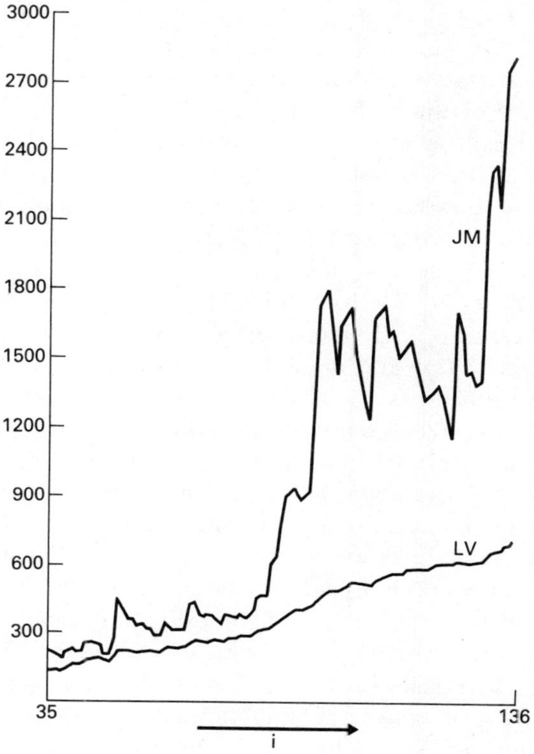

Fig. 11.1. Median plots for JM and LV, data from Table 11.1. Plotted are predicted median of T_i (based on $t_1, t_2, \ldots, t_{i-1}$) against i.

A user might reasonably enquire as to whether either of these prediction systems is close to the truth. If he/she were to use more prediction systems to analyse the same data, the confusion would increase (see Abdel Ghaly *et al.* 1985 for an analysis of ten methods on this data). What is needed is a technique which allows a user to decide which is the best prediction system *for a particular context*.

11.3 SOME TOOLS FOR THE ANALYSIS OF PREDICTIVE PERFORMANCE

First we need to understand the ways in which prediction systems can be inadequate. For simplicity we shall only consider here the problem of predicting *current* reliability, but the techniques we shall describe are also applicable to certain types of longer term prediction.

Given that we have observed data $t_1, t_2, \ldots, t_{i-1}$, a total description of current reliability would be knowledge of $F_i(t) \equiv 1 - R_i(t)$, the cdf of the next, unobserved, random variable T_i. A prediction system will give an estimator of this, $\tilde{F}_i(t)$, based on the data. The operation of calculating $\tilde{F}_i(t)$ can be repeated for each value of i. In principle, a comparison should be possible between the predictions $\tilde{F}_i(t)$ and the *later observed* t_i. A rather crude procedure, for example, might calculate the *median* of each $\tilde{F}_i(t)$, and then later note whether the observed t_i were greater than this median; for roughly one half of the time, this should be the case if the prediction system is in close accord with reality. We need other, more sensitive methods of detecting departures between $\{\tilde{F}_i(t)\}$ and the unknown $\{F_i(t)\}$.

Clearly the problem is hard. There is a sense in which it is impossibly hard: since the sequence of random variables $\{T_i\}$ is non-stationary, the number of ways $\{\tilde{F}_i(t)\}$ can depart from $\{F_i(t)\}$ will increase with i. However, we shall show that certain particularly important departures between prediction and reality can be detected.

In the previous section we showed how, for median predictions, two prediction systems could give very different results. It is clear, for example, that for later predictions either JM is too optimistic or LV is too pessimistic (or, perhaps, both). Which is the case? There is also the question of the noisiness of JM medians: does this reflect a noisiness of reality (e.g. decreases in reliability occurring because of poor fixes) which is not being detected by LV, or is it a spurious artifact of the prediction system?

The first of these questions is similar to the issue of *bias* in conventional statistics. It is the question of whether a prediction system is erring consistently in one direction (here, optimism versus pessimism). Of course, medians are only simple summary statistics for the information contained in the prediction *functions*, $\tilde{F}_i(t)$. Since these functions (of t) are functions of the *data* $(t_1, t_2, \ldots, t_{i-1})$, it will be the case that they exhibit 'sampling fluctuations'. The question we must ask of a prediction system is whether it gives $\tilde{F}_i(t)$ which are in some sense 'on average' close to the unknown $F_i(t)$. We could label such a prediction system 'unbiased' and be confident that it would not exhibit consistent departure from reality. This is a very informal argument, and it does not seem possible to construct a formal theory to detect all kinds of consistent departure. The problem, clearly, is that we only have *one observation*, $\tilde{F}_i(t)$, for each of a sequence, $F_i(t)$. of 'true states of nature'.

Nevertheless, we can go some way towards detecting biased predictors. Consider the sequence of transformations

$$u_i = \tilde{F}_i(t_i) \tag{11.3.1}$$

Each is a probability integral transform of the observed t_i using the *previously calculated* predictor $\tilde{F}_i$ based upon $t_1, t_2, \ldots, t_{i-1}$. If each $\tilde{F}_i$ were equal to the true F_i, it is easy to see that the u_i are realizations of independent, identically distributed $U(0, 1)$ random variables. Thus we have reduced the problem of examining 'closeness' of $\tilde{F}_i$ to F_i, to the question of whether $\{u_i\}$ 'looks like' a random sample from $U(0, 1)$.

There are various ways in which this question can be investigated (Abdel Ghaly *et al.* 1985); here we shall merely examine whether the u_i's are uniformly distributed by plotting their sample cdf and comparing with the cdf of $U(0, 1)$. In Fig. 11.2, these *u-plots* are shown for the LV and JM analysis of the data of Table 11.1. It is possible to conduct formal statistical tests of the closeness of these plots to the cdf of the $U(0, 1)$, which is the line of unit slope in the figure. For example, the Kolmogorov distances (maximum vertical deviation) are drawn on the figure. These are 0.190 (JM) and 0.144 (LV). In tables these are significant at 1% and 5% levels respectively.

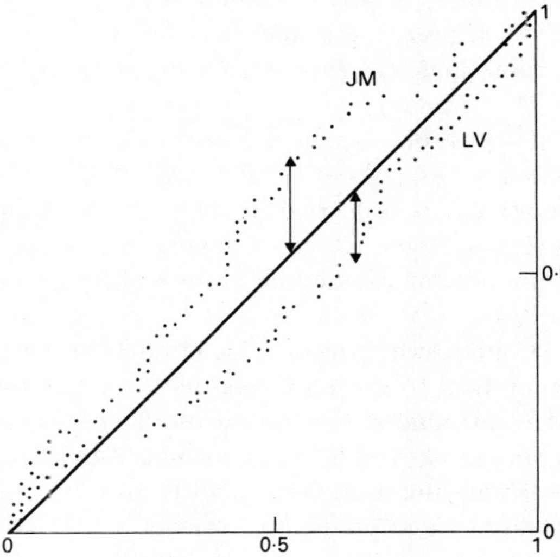

Fig. 11.2. LV, JM *u*-plots, data of Table 11.1. Steps omitted for clarity. Note that these are reproduced from line-printer plots and do not correspond exactly to true plot.

We can conclude that neither prediction system is performing very well, but that JM is notably worse. In fact, the plots tell us much more than this. The JM plot is everywhere above the line of unit slope, LV almost everywhere below. This means JM tends to give u_i's which are consistently too small. But u_i is the predicted probability that T_i will be less than t_i, so consistently too small u_i's suggest that the prediction system is consistently underestimating the chance of small t's. That is, the shape of the JM plot tells us that the JM prediction system is *too optimistic*. A similar argument suggests that LV is too pessimistic.

The plots, then, suggest that the truth might lie somewhere between the predictions made by LV and JM, but possibly closer to LV. In particular, the true median plot probably lies between the predicted median plots of Fig. 11.1.

Other methods of analysing the $\{u_i\}$ can be found in Abdel Ghaly *et al.* (1985), as can the results of comparing more prediction systems on this (and other) data sets. For the remainder of this section we shall show how we can detect problems due to what we have called 'noisiness'.

The difficulty with noisiness in this context of non-stationary prediction is that we do not know whether or not 'nature' is noisy. A predictor could be poor because $\tilde{F}_i(t)$'s fluctuated wildly when the true sequence $F_i(t)$ exhibited steady reliability growth; or it could be poor because the $\tilde{F}_i(t)$ sequence was too smooth in the presence of *real* reversals of fortune in $F_i(t)$'s (caused, for example, by occasional bad fixes).

Although it is possible to detect noisiness in predictors with relatively simple techniques (Abdel Ghaly *et al.* 1985), it is hard to tell whether the noisiness reflects reality. The next technique to be described in this section, then, is a more general one which is sensitive to various departures of the predictions from reality: among them noise and bias.

In a series of interesting papers, Dawid (1982, 1984a, 1984b, 1985) has treated theoretical issues concerned with the validity of forecasting systems. He introduced the notion of the *prequential likelihood* (PL) function, and in particular the *prequential likelihood ratio* (PLR). We shall demonstrate the usefulness of PLR as a tool for deciding the relative plausibility of two prediction systems.

The PL is defined as follows. Assume that the predictive distribution $\tilde{F}_i(t)$ for T_i based on $t_1, t_2, \ldots, t_{i-1}$ has a pdf:

$$\tilde{f}_i(t) = \frac{\mathrm{d}}{\mathrm{d}t} \tilde{F}_i(t) \qquad (11.3.2)$$

For sequential predictions of $T_{j+1}, T_{j+2}, \ldots, T_{j+n}$ (each based on all data available at that stage) the PL is:

$$\mathrm{PL}_n = \prod_{i=j+1}^{j+n} \tilde{f}_i(t_i) \qquad (11.3.3)$$

A comparison of two prediction systems can be made via their PLR:

$$\mathrm{PLR}_n = \frac{\prod_{i=j+1}^{j+n} \tilde{f}_i^A(t_i)}{\prod_{i=j+1}^{j+n} \tilde{f}_i^B(t_i)} \qquad (11.3.4)$$

Dawid (1984a) proves various results about PLR; in particular he shows that if $\mathrm{PLR}_n \to \infty$ as $n \to \infty$, prediction system B is discredited in favour of A.

For an intuitive explanation of how PL works, consider Fig. 11.3. Here the predictor $\tilde{f}_i(t)$ differs markedly from $f_i(t)$: it is too pessimistic, in our reliability context. Since the *actual observation*, t_i, will probably lie in the main body of $f_i(t)$; it will consequently probably lie in the right tail of $\tilde{f}_i(t)$ and so make a *small* contribution to the overall PL.

In the case where the true f_i's are not noisy (i.e. the sequence of $f_i(t)$'s moves slowly to the right with few reversals of order), but the $\tilde{f}_i$'s are noisy, it is easy to see that the observed t_i's will fall in the tails (left or right) of the $\tilde{f}_i(t)$'s. The same argument applies when the f_i's really are noisy and the $\tilde{f}_i$'s are too smooth. Thus unjustifiable noisiness, or unjustifiable smoothness of the predictor sequence will result in a small PL.

Clearly, PL will also detect bias. If, for example, the $\tilde{f}_i$ are consistently too pessimistic, the observed t_i will tend to lie in the right-hand tail of $\tilde{f}_i$, giving small PL.

Table 11.2 gives values of the PLR at ten-step intervals for the JM and LV analysis of the data of Table 11.1. It can be seen that until

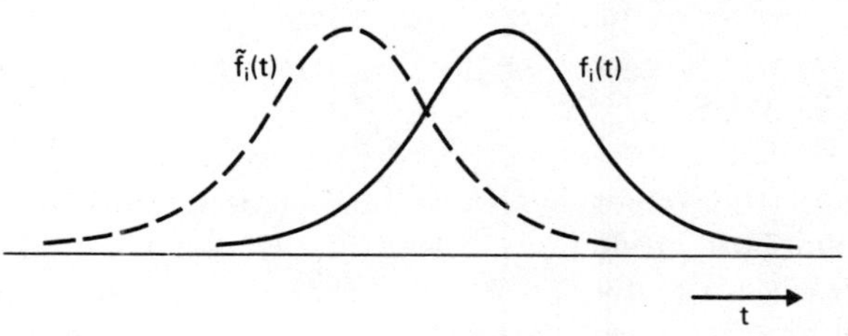

Fig. 11.3

Table 11.2. PLR of JM versus LV, data of Table 11.1. Clearly LV discredits JM overall, but less obvious for earlier predictions.

n	PLR_n
10	1.19
20	0.318
30	0.252
40	0.096
50	0.745
60	6.50
70	0.088
80	0.00177
90	0.0000813
100	0.00119

about the 60th prediction there is little to choose between the two methods, but after that LV shows a definite superiority. Of course, it is not possible to separate bias and noise from this result. We know from the u-plot that JM is more seriously biased than LV, and this, rather than the noisiness of JM, could be the reason for the PL superiority of LV.

Table 11.3 shows how PL can detect grossly too noisy predictors. D.R. Miller (personal communication, 1983) showed how the u-plot was inadequate on its own as a measure of predictive quality. He constructed, as a counter example, predictors which could be shown to be approximately unbiased, but which were totally useless because of their great noisiness. Essentially what he did was to base the prediction for T_i *only* upon the preceding t_{i-1} and t_{i-2} (ignoring t_{i-3}, t_{i-4}, ...). For the data of Table 11.1 this predictor gives a u-plot Kolmogorov distance of 0.079, which is better than either JM or LV! The uselessness of such an estimator is shown, however, in the PLR comparisons of it with LV and JM in Table 11.3. In both cases the extreme noisiness of the estimator is shown to outweigh its unbiasedness in competition with both LV and JM.

11.4 CONCLUSIONS

The theme of this paper has been direct examination of quality of software reliability predictions. Most of the existing literature comparing software reliability models (Schick & Wolverton 1978, Ramamoorthy & Bastani 1982) examines their underlying assumptions and compares their plausibility in the light of our understanding of

Table 11.3. This table shows the ability of PLR to reject an unbiased model which is *very* noisy. The Miller model predicts using only the last two observations. Here we show PLR values, at ten-step intervals, for JM versus Miller and LV versus Miller. Clearly, Miller is being discredited by each of the other prediction systems (even JM, which is known to be bad for this data).

n	JM PLR_n	LV PLR_n
10	4.00	3.26
20	30.80	82.10
30	158.00	517.00
40	8.92×10^4	7.18×10^5
50	9.32×10^5	1.01×10^6
60	4.91×10^6	5.72×10^5
70	2.48×10^6	2.53×10^7
80	6.01×10^5	2.63×10^8
90	3.67×10^6	3.37×10^{10}
100	6.34×10^8	3.96×10^{11}

software engineering practices. This can be a useful exercise, if only to weed out the more implausible candidates. However, our understanding is so limited that it is unlikely we could choose a definitive model from the survivors of such a weeding operation. In any case, since the quality of the model only forms one leg of the triad forming a prediction system, we could not be sure of good predictions even if the model were known to be good.

More importantly, it seems unlikely that there will ever exist a single model which is best in all circumstances. Analysis of several data sets by various prediction systems (Abdel Ghaly *et al.* 1985, Keiller *et al.* 1983) suggests that a model which performs well in one context may do badly in another, and vice versa. Unfortunately, it does not seem possible to decide *a priori* which model is likely to be best in a novel context.

Faced with these problems, a user might reasonably expect to try several different prediction systems on his/her data, and use the one which is best. To do this, tools need to be available to make the comparison. In the present paper, two such tools have been presented which detect particular departures of predictions from actual failure behaviour.

It would be foolish to suggest that these tools are adequate to give a user complete confidence in a prediction system. Much more work in this area is required; possibly at the expense of the proliferation of new software reliability models.

Acknowledgements

This work was partially supported by NASA Langley Research Center under grant number NAG-1-179.

References

Abdel Ghaly A.A., Chan P.Y. & Littlewood B. (1985) *Evaluation of Competing Software Reliability Predictions*. Centre for Software Reliability, City University, London, Technical Report.

Adams E.N. (1980) *Minimizing Cost Impact of Software Defects*. T.J. Watson Research Center, IBM (Research Report RC 8228).

Aitchison J. & Dunsmore I.R. (1975) *Statistical Prediction Analysis*. Cambridge University Press.

Dale C.J. (1982) *Software Reliability Evaluation Methods*. Dynamics Group, British Aerospace (Report ST-26750).

Dawid A.P. (1982) The well-calibrated Bayesian (with discussion). *Journal of the American Statistical Association* **77** (379), pp. 605–613.

Dawid A.P. (1984a) Statistical theory: the prequential approach, (with discussion). *Journal of the Royal Statistical Society, Series A* **147** (2), pp. 278–292.

Dawid A.P. (1984b) *Calibration-Based Empirical Probability*. Department of Statistical Science, University College London (Research Report 36).

Dawid A.P. (1986) Probability forecasting. In Kotz S., Johnson N.L. and Read C.B. (eds.) *Encyclopedia of Statistical Sciences* (7), pp. 210–218. Wiley.

Jelinski Z. & Moranda P. (1972) Software reliability research. In Freiberger W. (ed.) *Statistical Computer Performance Evaluation*, pp. 465–484. Academic Press.

Keiller P.A. *et al.* (1983) Comparison of software reliability predictions. *13th Annual Int. Symp. on Fault Tolerant Computing*, pp. 128–134.

Laprie J.-C. (1984) Dependability evaluation of software systems in operation. *IEEE Trans. on Software Engineering* **SE–10** (6), pp. 701–714.

Littlewood B. (1986) How to measure software reliability and how not to. *IEEE Trans. on Reliability* **R-28** (2), pp. 103–110.

Littlewood B. & Sofer A. (1987) A Bayesian modification to the Jelinski–Moranda software reliability growth model, *IEEE/BCS Software Engineering Journal*, **2** (2), pp. 30–41.

Littlewood B. & Verrall J.L. (1973) A Bayesian reliability growth model for computer software. *Applied Statistics* **22** (3), pp. 332–346.

Musa J.D. (1975) A theory of software reliability and its application. *IEEE Trans. on Software Engineering* **SE–1** (3), pp. 312–327.

Nagel P.M. & Skrivan J.A. (1981) *Software Reliability: Repetitive Run Experimentation and Modelling*. Boeing Computer Services Company (BCS-40399).

Ramamoorthy C.V. & Bastani F.B. (1982) Software reliability — status and perspectives. *IEEE Trans. on Software Engineering* **SE–8** (4), pp. 354–371.

Schick G.J. & Wolverton R.W. (1978) An analysis of competing software reliability models. *IEEE Trans. on Software Engineering* **SE–4** (2), pp. 104–120.

Shooman M.L. (1973) Operational testing and software reliability estimation during program development. *Record IEEE Symp. on Computer Software Reliability*, pp. 51–57.

Chapter 12

Entropy/Information Theory and (Software) Reliability

B. DE NEUMANN
GEC Research, Great Baddow, Chelmsford, Essex CM2 8HN

12.1 INTRODUCTION

The purpose of the workshop talk upon which this résumé is based, was to speculate upon some ways in which entropy/information theory might be useful to software reliability modellers. Three specific topics were chosen in order to complement the work covered in the companion paper (Anderson 1986). These were environment, the software process, and structure.

12.2 ENVIRONMENT

It is widely accepted that hardware reliability is environment dependent, and particular reliability models recognize this. The operating environment is characterized in some way; for example the environment of mechanical systems is characterized by 'loading roughness' (Carter 1979), whereas the electronic environment is characterized in other ways (MIL-HDBK-217B 1974). Hardware reliability is also influenced by the quality of the constituents and other factors, but essentially we determine the reliability by the failure characteristics, on the assumption that the design is correct. In the case of software we have perfect components, and failures occur when errors (and oversights) in the design are exercised by its environment. These errors are randomly (in some sense) distributed throughout the software, and hence we should expect that the reliability is a function of the development process and the environment.

We will consider the problem of characterizing the environment. It seems reasonable to suppose that the software environment is indeed random, since if it were not the software would be largely superfluous. Thus, in principle at least, it would be possible to completely characterize the environment by specifying the probability $\rho(S_i)$ of each element of the entire input space $\{S_i\}$. Such an approach is extremely clumsy, and perhaps instead we should consider an entropy related measure of the environment:

$$\text{Entropy } H \triangleq -\sum_i \rho(S_i) \log (\rho(S_i)).$$

Entropy alone will not be sufficient to capture the nuances of a software environment but it does at least capture the uncertainty aspects, since it is zero for a deterministic source and maximum for the most unpredictable source.

It is perhaps worth emphasizing the value of being able to characterize environment suitably. We have already discussed the dependence of reliability upon environment, thus mathematically we would say $R = f(\mathbf{E})$. This as it stands is no use at all, but if, as mathematical modellers, we are able to determine some properties of f as a function of $\mathbf{E}$ (which implies we can characterize $\mathbf{E}$) then we are in a better position to predict the reliability of software in $\mathbf{E}^*$ say, when we have tested and analysed the software in $\mathbf{E}_0$. This opens the door to accelerated testing and optimal testing.

12.3 THE SOFTWARE PROCESS

Schematically this may be depicted as in Fig. 12.1.

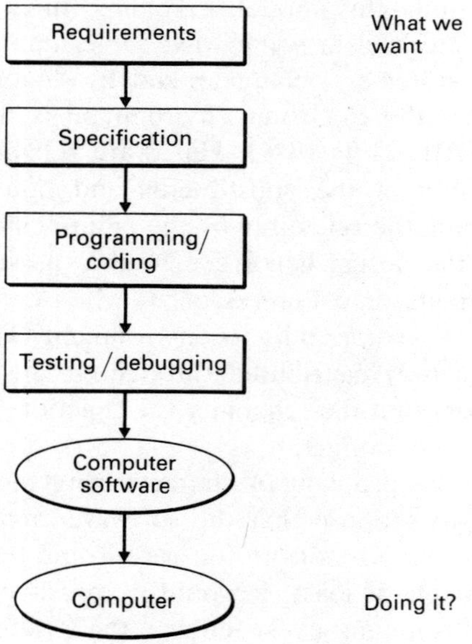

Fig. 12.1

Clearly there is a need for communication between the various phases of the process. In fact, there is a strong analogy with an idealized source/channel/receiver model of information theory (Fig. 12.2).

From information theory (see, for example, McEliece 1977), it is well known that, if noise affects the channel, then we need coding/decoding (e.g. Hamming, BCH, Goppa codes) to improve the quality of the received message (Fig. 12.3).

We want the 'noisy' programmers to convey our desires to the computer. This is a process which is still fraught with difficulty and which has led to research into formal methods, etc. It is possible here that information/coding theory would give us lower bounds on the redundancy which should form a part of the specification language. For an information theoretic analysis of the balanced redundancy/richness of the DNA language, see Gatlin (1972).

12.4 STRUCTURE

Structure exists in software and hardware, has different aspects and exists for various reasons (e.g. logical structure, data flow structure, control flow structure, fault tolerant structure, etc). Indeed, 'structured programming' has become a vogue in order to exhibit certain software structures. In particular, the 'reliability structure' (fault tolerant structure) exists to reduce the vulnerability of the system to coding

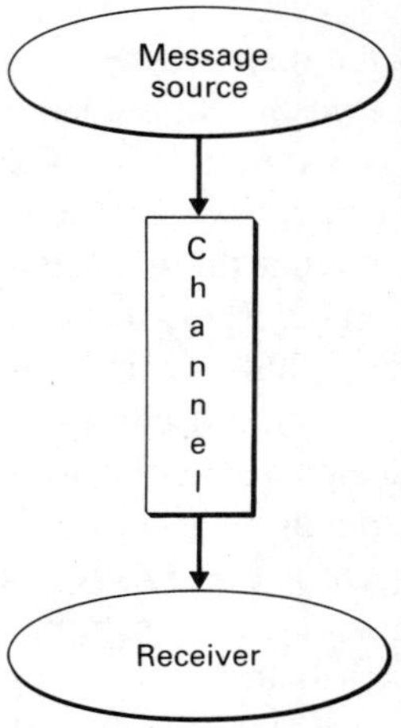

Fig. 12.2

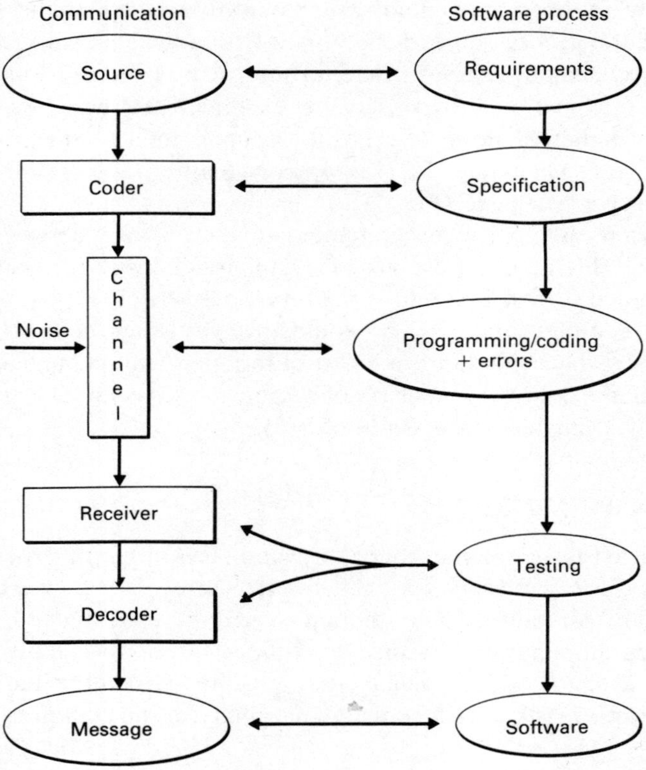

Fig. 12.3

errors and faults. Thus reliability structure reflects the reliability of its constituents and the required operational reliability.

Reliability theory tells us that, for maximum reliability from a component set assembled into a system, redundancy should occur at the lowest level. This means that there exists a large number (exponentially many) of different realizations of the same system. Why should we assume, naïvely perhaps, that our first guess at the reliability structure is the best? Maybe we should consider the other feasible structures — and even introduce an element of randomness in the structural design! Clearly existing, functioning large systems could possibly shed some light here if investigated (e.g. DNA, biosystems, telephone networks, etc.). The human brain, for example, which broadly performs the same functions for each bearer, has a high level organization and structure, which is similar for each, in which it is possible to discern the function of various regional parts. However, at the neuronal axon/

synapse level the linkages appear to be almost random and no similarities in the interconnection can be discerned when comparing brains.

Perhaps we should take the pragmatic view that we should not concern ourselves with how a system achieves its functions, so long as it does. Maybe we should be investigating 'maximum entropy' structures. This would ensure that our uncertainty about how a system is functioning in detail is maximized, and maximize its changes of not failing.

12.5 CONCLUSIONS

An attempt has been made in this paper and also in Anderson (1986) to introduce the concepts of entropy/information theory to the software engineering community. This paper was particularly concerned with speculating upon some areas in which these techniques maybe useful, and in which some advance is required. The three topics remain an active and important area of research.

Some early work on 'reliable computation structure', supporting the structural speculations of this chapter, is reported in Winograd & Cown (1963). They show that reliable machines can be constructed even when there are interconnection errors between modules.

References

Anderson B.G. (1987) The rôle for entropy and information in software reliability. Chapter 13, this volume.

Carter A.D.S. (1979) Reliability reviewed. *Proc. Inst. Mech. Eng* **193**.

Gatlin L.L. (1972) *Information Theory and the Living System*. Columbia University Press.

MIL-HDBK-217B(1974) *Military Standardization Handbook, Reliability Prediction of Electronic Equipment, US Dept of Defence.* Publisher McEliece R.J. (1977) *The Theory of Information and Coding*.

Winograd S. & Cown J.D. (1963) *Reliable Computation in the Presence of Noise*. MIT Press.

Chapter 13

The Rôle for Entropy and Information in Software Reliability

B.G. Anderson
British Aerospace, Army Division, Stevenage, Hertfordshire SG1 2DA

13.1 INTRODUCTION

Past attempts to model software reliability have been defeated by the inability to identify the failure-probability distributions which exist if only because of the probabilistic nature of the program's input. Researchers have assumed base distributions, hoping to repeat the success of the exponential distribution for hardware reliability or the success of the normal distribution in science and engineering. When this approach failed they modified these distributions by allotting time-varying or distributed parameters. The net result is a vast number of different software reliability models, and it is suggested that users try a number of these and choose the best. This is the 'eclectic' approach, and although the word best implies some form of criterion, no attempt has been made to derive the required distributions by optimizing such a criterion.

Now this is exactly the position that occurred in time-series analysis and image-processing about a decade ago. There the problem was to find a data-processing window which yielded accurate spectral density estimates. However, each window, no matter how successful, produced sidelobe artifacts, and spectral density analysis became an art form in balancing the opposing effects of estimate accuracy versus sidelobe generation. This is just the eclectic path suggested by present day reliability researchers, except that the number of software models far exceeds the number of spectral windows then available. The advent of the maximum entropy technique ended this by producing a universal spectral density estimation procedure along with the Burg-Levinson algorithm for autoregressive processes, which not only reduced the production of artifacts but also enabled interpolation and extrapolation into areas not explicitly covered by the data.

It is the author's contention that this success story can be repeated in the software and hardware reliability fields. The following report is intended to convey the power, beauty and potential of the entropic or information formalism when it is applied to reliability problems.

13.2 ENTROPY AND INFORMATION

If f_i is the probability of an outcome of an event i, then the amount of uncertainty I_i existing before the event is also the information gained by observing the outcome. Define:

$$I_i \equiv -\log f_i \qquad (13.2.1)$$

then it is seen that if $f_i \rightarrow 1$, $I_i \rightarrow 0$, so the outcome is certain and no information is gained from the observation, whilst if $f_i \rightarrow 0$, $I_i \rightarrow \infty$ in which case the outcome is very uncertain, and so observing the outcome conveys a large amount of information. The logarithmic function was not chosen just to get the scaling right, it also provides the property of additivity. Thus if there are two independent events then the total uncertainty becomes:

$$I_{ij} = -\log f_i f_j = I_i + I_j \qquad (13.2.2)$$

which ties in with our intuition.

For n independent events the total uncertainty is thus:

$$I = -\sum_{i=1}^{n} \log f_i \qquad (13.2.3)$$

and entropy, H, is defined as the average uncertainty or average information gained, i.e:

$$H \equiv -\sum_{i=1}^{n} f_i \log f_i \qquad (13.2.4)$$

13.3 MAXIMUM-ENTROPY

13.3.1 The maximum-entropy principle

If f_i are the unknown relative frequencies existing before the events, and some data (a function of the outcome of the events) are observed, then the least prejudiced or biased assignment of frequencies is that which maximizes the entropy H subject to the data, i.e. the data conveys the maximum information. This avoids accidental inclusion of information that is not present, i.e. artifacts.

Consider N values of a continuously distributed variate, $y_1, \ldots, Y_N$, e.g. values of a waveform $y(t)$ at times $t_1, t_2, \ldots, t_N$. The entropy of these values, obtained by generalizing equation (13.2.4), is thus:

$$\mathbf{H(p)} = - \int_{\mathbf{y}} p(\mathbf{y}) \log p(\mathbf{y})\, d\mathbf{y} \qquad (13.3.1)$$

where the vector format has been used to simplify the presentation. The maximum-entropy principle requires the maximization of $H(p)$ with respect to the joint probability-density function $p(\mathbf{y}) = p(y_1, \ldots, y_N)$ subject to the probability-defining constraint:

$$\int_{\mathbf{y}} p(\mathbf{y})\, d\mathbf{y} = 1 \qquad (13.3.2)$$

plus expected-value constraints:

$$\mathbf{A}^d = \int_{y} p(\mathbf{y})\mathbf{A}(\mathbf{y}) d\mathbf{y} \qquad (13.3.3)$$

where

$$\mathbf{y} \equiv \{y_1, \ldots, y_N\} \qquad (13.3.4)$$

$$\mathbf{A(y)} \equiv \{A_1(\mathbf{y}), \ldots, A_M(\mathbf{y})\} \qquad (13.3.5)$$

and $\mathbf{A}^d$ is the data or observed value of $\mathbf{A}$. $\mathbf{A}^d$ can also be considered as the estimate for the vector $\mathbf{A}$ containing M elements.

13.3.2 The maximum-entropy algorithm

The solution of constrained maximization is obtained by maximizing the Lagrangian function defined by:

$$H_L(p) \equiv H(p) + \Lambda\left\{1 - \int_{\mathbf{y}} p(\mathbf{y})\, d\mathbf{y}\right\} \qquad (13.3.6)$$

$$+ \boldsymbol{\lambda}\cdot\left\{\mathbf{A}^d - \int_{\mathbf{y}} p(\mathbf{y})A(\mathbf{y})\, d\mathbf{y}\right\}$$

where Λ and the elements of the vector $\boldsymbol{\lambda}$ $\equiv \{\lambda_1, \ldots, \lambda_M\}$ are the Lagrangian multipliers. The dot notation is used for the inner-product of two vectors, thus:

$$\boldsymbol{\lambda}\cdot\mathbf{A}^d \equiv \sum_{m=1}^{M} \lambda_m A_m^d \qquad (13.3.7)$$

This is a classic calculus of variations problem, since $p(\mathbf{y})$ is a function of N continuous variables, for which the solution is:

$$p(\mathbf{y}) = Z^{-1} \exp\{-\boldsymbol{\lambda}\cdot\mathbf{A}(\mathbf{y})\} \qquad (13.3.8)$$

where

$$Z(\boldsymbol{\lambda}) = \int_{\mathbf{y}} \exp\{-\boldsymbol{\lambda}\cdot\mathbf{A}(\mathbf{y})\}\, d\mathbf{y} \qquad (13.3.9)$$

is a consequence of the first condition on $p(\mathbf{y})$, equation (13.3.2), and effectively determines Λ as a function of $\lambda_1, \ldots, \lambda_M$. The remaining Lagrangian multipliers are determined from:

$$\frac{\partial}{\partial\lambda_m}\{\log Z(\boldsymbol{\lambda})\} = \frac{1}{Z}\frac{\partial \log Z}{\partial\lambda_m} = -A_m^d \qquad (13.3.10)$$

for $m = 1, \ldots, M$

whilst the maximum value attained by the entropy is found to be:

$$H_{\max} = -\log Z - \boldsymbol{\lambda}\cdot\mathbf{A}^d \qquad (13.3.11)$$

13.3.3 Properties of the maximum-entropy solution

The maximum-entropy principle is supported by a concentration theorem: a fraction F of all possible outcomes of a random experiment will yield an entropy H within the range:

$$H_{\max} - \equiv H \leq H(p) \leq H_{\max} \qquad (13.3.12)$$

where $H_{\max}$ is determined by the algorithm and:

$$2N \equiv H = \chi_k^2\,(1 - F) \qquad (13.3.13)$$

with N the number of trials and k the degrees of freedom. These limits are remarkably tight and contain a high proportion of all likely outcomes, i.e. of possible probability distributions $p(\mathbf{y})$.

Embodied in the principle is the statement that when making inferences based on incomplete information draw them from the probability distribution that possesses the maximum-entropy. An important and practical use of such inference is provided by considering the joint characteristic-function for all the constraints of $\mathbf{A}(\mathbf{y})$. Thus:

$$\Phi_{\mathrm{A}}(\mathbf{u}) \equiv E_p\,[\exp\{i\mathbf{u}\cdot\mathbf{A}(\mathbf{y})\}] \qquad (13.3.14)$$

$$= Z^{-1}(\boldsymbol{\lambda}) \int_{\mathbf{y}} \exp\{-(\boldsymbol{\lambda} - i\mathbf{u})\cdot\mathbf{A}(\mathbf{y})\}d\mathbf{y}$$

$$= Z(\boldsymbol{\lambda} - i\mathbf{u})/Z(\boldsymbol{\lambda}) \qquad (13.3.15)$$

The joint cumulant-generating function $\boldsymbol{\chi}_A(\mathbf{u})$ follows by definition:

$$\boldsymbol{\chi}_A(\mathbf{u}) \equiv \log \Phi_A(\mathbf{u}) = \log Z(\boldsymbol{\lambda} - i\mathbf{u}) - \log Z(\boldsymbol{\lambda}) \qquad (13.3.16)$$

The kth cumulant of the elemental constraint $A_m(\mathbf{y})$ is thus:

$$\chi_k(A_m) = \lim_{i\mathbf{u}\to 0} \frac{\partial^k \chi_A(\mathbf{u})}{\partial(iu_m)^k} = (-1)^k \lim_{\lambda_m \to 0} \frac{\partial^k \log Z(\boldsymbol{\lambda})}{\partial \lambda_m^k} \tag{13.3.17}$$

The first two cumulants are seen to be given by:

$$E_p[A_m] = -\frac{\partial \log Z(\lambda)}{\partial \lambda_m} = A_m^d \tag{13.3.18}$$

as required by condition (13.3.3), and:

$$\text{VAR}_p\,[A_m] = \frac{\partial^2 \log Z(\boldsymbol{\lambda})}{\partial \lambda_m^2} \tag{13.3.19}$$

which is now a function of the data A_m^d for $m = 1, \ldots, M$.

Following the maximum-entropy principle it is now possible to infer the cumulative-probability distribution for the A_m. Thus define:

$$\zeta \equiv (A_m - A_m^d)/\sqrt{(\text{VAR}[A_m])} \tag{13.3.20}$$

then the Edgeworth expansion for ζ becomes:

$$\text{Prob}\,\{\zeta \leq \zeta_o\} = \Phi\,(\zeta_o) - \frac{\chi_{3\zeta}}{3!}\,\phi^{(2)}\,(\zeta_o) + \frac{\chi_{4\zeta}}{4!}\,\phi^{(3)}\,(\zeta_o) - \ldots \tag{13.3.21}$$

where Φ and $\phi^{(k)}$ are the normal integral and its derivatives, respectively. This example shows that probabilistic statements can be made concerning the spread of the function A_m. The process can be repeated for arbitrary functions of $\mathbf{y}$, but the calculation is not so straightforward as in this example.

13.4 APPLICATIONS OF MAXIMUM-ENTROPY

13.4.1 Moment-based data

First-order moments

Consider the reliability engineer who puts a single repairable item on test and measures the time of successful operation T for a *fixed* number of failures, N say. Thus:

$$T = \sum_{n=1}^{N} y_n$$

where y_n are the operational times between failure and $0 \leqslant y_n < \infty$. The only constraint in this case is:

$$A = \sum_{n=1}^{N} y_n \tag{13.4.1}$$

where the observed value of $A^d \equiv T$. Note that the individual sample values of y_n are used as such, i.e. T is the only observation required and corresponds to the case where the samples of y_n, y_n^d, are not recorded. If the samples y_n^d are recorded then it is always possible to generate more data functions, and this topic will be discussed later under the heading of cross-entropy.

The maximum-entropy solution for this case is:

$$p(y_1, \ldots, y_N) = Z^{-1} \exp \left\{-\lambda \sum_{n=1}^{N} y_n\right\} \tag{13.4.2}$$

where

$$Z = \prod_{n=1}^{N} \left[\int_0^\infty \exp \{-\lambda y_n\} dy_n\right] = \lambda^{-N} \tag{13.4.3}$$

The value of the Lagrangian multiplier λ is determined from:

$$\left.\begin{aligned} &d/d\lambda \log Z = -N/\lambda = A^d = T \\ &\text{so that } 1/\lambda = T/N \end{aligned}\right\} \tag{13.4.4}$$

which is the mean-time between failures. The maximum-entropy probability-density function for the variate y is thus the exponential distribution

$$p(y) = \lambda \exp \{-\lambda y\} \tag{13.4.5}$$

which, from equations (13.3.12) and (13.3.13), accounts for the robustness of this distribution for hardware applications. Note that the distribution $p(\mathbf{y})$ is the product of N distributions (13.4.5) because the data contains no information on cross-coupling.

An alternative reliability measurement scheme is to measure the number of failures in a *fixed* time T so that the observable data would be $\bar{y} = 1/N^d \sum_{n=1}^{N^d} y_n^d$ and N^d.

The constraints are thus:

$$A_1 = \sum_{n=1}^{N} y_n$$

and

$$A_2 = \sum_{n=1}^{\infty} \int_0^T \delta \left\{ y - \sum_{s=1}^{n} y_s \right\} dy \tag{13.4.6}$$

where $\delta(\ )$ is a counting function and $A_1^d = N^d \bar{y}$, $A_2^d = N^d$. The maximum-entropy formulation highlights the difference between the two approaches and guards against the use of incorrect assumptions.

If the applications above involved a variate defined for all real numbers, $-\infty < y < \infty$, then the integral for Z would not converge for the constraint $\sum_{n=1}^{N} yn$. One solution is to modify the data and take:

$$A_1 = \sum_{n=1}^{N} |y_n| \tag{13.4.7}$$

i.e. the absolute deviation.

Second-order moments

Suppose that the mean and mean-square values of the samples y_n^d are the observables, then the constraints become:

$$A_1 = \sum_{n=1}^{N} y_n$$

and

$$A_2 = \sum_{n=1}^{N} y_n^2 \tag{13.4.8}$$

The maximum-entropy solution in this case is found to be:

$$p(y_1, \ldots, y_N) = Z^{-1} \exp \left\{ -\lambda_1 \sum_{n=1}^{N} y_n \ - \lambda_2 \sum_{n=1}^{N} y_n^2 \right\} \tag{13.4.9}$$

and since no cross-product terms are involved in the constraints then:

$$p(y) = \frac{1}{\surd(2\pi\sigma_s^2)} \exp \left\{ -\frac{1}{2} \left(\frac{y - m_s}{\sigma_s} \right)^2 \right\} \tag{13.4.10}$$

where m_s and σ_s^2 are the sample mean and variance, respectively. Define:

$$\left.\begin{aligned} &m \equiv A_1/N \\ &\text{and} \\ &\sigma^2 \equiv 1/N \sum_{n=1}^{N} (y_n - m)^2 = \{A_2/N - (A_1/N)^2\} \end{aligned}\right\} \quad (13.4.11)$$

then the variance of the mean, m, and variance of y, σ^2, are obtained by implementing equation (13.3.19), resulting in:

$$\left.\begin{aligned} &\text{VAR}_p[m] = 1/N^2 \, \text{VAR}_p[A_1] = \sigma_s^2/N \\ &\text{and} \\ &\text{VAR}_p[\sigma^2] = 1/N^2 \, \text{VAR}_p[A_2] = 2\sigma_s^2(\sigma_s^2 + 2m_s^2)/N \end{aligned}\right\} \quad (13.4.12)$$

as expected.

For a one-sided variate, $0 \leqslant y < \infty$, the cumulative-probability solution is found to be:

$$P(y) = \frac{\Phi\left(\dfrac{y - m'}{\sigma'}\right) - \Phi\,(-m'/\sigma')}{1 - \Phi\,(-m'/\sigma')} \quad (13.4.13)$$

The parameters m' and σ' are different from the sample values m_s and σ_s so the solution is not the trivial truncation result.

Higher-order moments

Generalizing the previous applications results in the constraints:

$$A_k\,(y_1, \ldots, y_N) = \sum_{n=1}^{N} y_n^k \text{ for } k = 1, \ldots, K \quad (13.4.14)$$

which are proportional to the first K sample moments about the origin. It is possible to omit intermediate values of k whilst a possible alternative scheme is to use orthogonal polynomials in y_n instead of simple powers. The maximum-entropy solution for the constraints (13.4.14) is again independent for each $y_1, \ldots, y_N$ and so the probability-density function for y is:

$$p(y) = Z^{-1/N} \exp\left\{-\sum_{k=1}^{K} \lambda_k y^k\right\} \tag{13.4.15}$$

with

$$Z^{1/N} = \int_{0,-\infty}^{\infty} \exp\left\{-\sum_{k=1}^{K} \lambda_k y^k\right\} dy \tag{13.4.16}$$

The solution for the Lagrangian multipliers requires the solution of

$$\int_{0,-\infty}^{\infty} \exp\left\{-\sum_{k=1}^{K} \lambda_k y^k\right\} dy = A_k^d/N \text{ for } k = 1, \ldots, K \tag{13.4.17}$$

which is theoretically intractable but numerical techniques are possible for the strictly distribution-fitting purposes. However, expanding the exponential into the equivalent form:

$$\exp\{-\lambda_1 y - \lambda_2 y^2\} \exp\left\{-\sum_{k=3}^{K} \lambda^k y^k\right\}$$

$$\equiv \exp\{-\lambda'_0\} \exp\{-\lambda'_2(y-m)^2\}\left[1 + \sum_{k=3}^{\infty} \frac{G_k}{k!}(y-m)^k\right] \tag{13.4.18}$$

results in the distribution $p(y)$ possessing the form:

$$p(y) = 1/\sigma\ \phi\left(\frac{y-m}{\sigma}\right)\left\{\frac{1 + \sum_{k=3}^{2K\mu} (y-m)^k\ G_k/k!}{1 + \sum_{k=2}^{K\mu} \mu(N, 2k)\ G_{2k}/k!}\right\} \tag{13.4.19}$$

This result is recognized as a form of Gram-Charlier expansion whereby the Hermite polynomial terms are collected together into the coefficients of $(y-m)^k$ and the parameters m, σ and G_k are obtained from $\lambda_1, \lambda_2, \ldots \lambda_K$. The terms $\mu(N, 2k)$ are normal moments about the mean for variates distributed over $-\infty < y < \infty$.

The maximum-entropy principle permits the estimation of higher moments than the K'th, thus:

$$E_p\ (y-m)^r = \int_{-\infty}^{\infty} (y-m)^r\ p(y)\ dy$$

$$= \left\{ \frac{\mu_r + \sum_{k=3}^{2K\mu} \mu_{k+r}\, G_k/k!}{1 + \sum_{k=2}^{K\mu} \mu_{2k}\, G_k/k!} \right\} \tag{13.4.20}$$

for $r > K$. Intermediate moments, $r < K$, may be omitted from the computation of the distribution and then estimated as above. It is also possible to infer the accuracy of the constraints A_k/N in the usual manner.

Having obtained this general, albeit cumbersome, result, the question is then posed: if the origin data samples y_n^d are readily available, where does one stop in the representation? There is, in fact, a method of determining the optimum value of K which will be discussed later under the cross-entropy heading.

13.4.2 Correlation-based data

Readers conversant with spectral and regression analysis will appreciate the importance of the sample autocorrelation function defined by:

$$R_k \equiv \frac{1}{N-k} \sum_{n=1}^{N-k} y_n y_{n+k} \text{ for } k \geqslant 0 \tag{13.4.21}$$

This function suggests the use of constraints:

$$\xi_k \equiv 1/2 \sum_{nCN(k)} y_n y_{n+k} \tag{13.4.22}$$

for spectral-analysis studies using maximum-entropy, and illustrates the techniques when cross-product terms are present, as distinct from the previous applications. In the definition for ξ_k, $N(k) \equiv 1, \ldots, N-k$ for $k \geqslant 0$ whilst $N(k) \equiv |k| + 1, \ldots, N$ for $k < 0$. Also note that:

$$\xi_0 = 1/2 \sum_{n=1}^{N} y_n^2 \tag{13.4.23}$$

so there should be no convergence problems.

The maximum-entropy solution with the constraints ξ_p is found to be:

$$\begin{aligned} p(\mathbf{y}) &= p(y_1, \ldots, y_N) \\ &= Z^{-1} \exp\left\{-1/2 \sum_{k=-K}^{K} \sum_{nCN(k)} \lambda_k y_n y_{n+k}\right\} \\ &= Z^{-1} \exp\{-1/2\, \mathbf{y}^+ \Lambda\, \mathbf{y}\} \end{aligned} \tag{13.4.24}$$

where the matrix Λ is Toeplitz with determinant $|\Lambda|$ so that $\lambda_{ji} = \lambda_{j-i}$ for $|j-i| \leqslant K$ and is zero for $|j-i| > K$. The distribution is obviously multi-normal, hence:

$$Z = (2\pi)^{N/2}\ |\Lambda|^{1/2} \tag{13.4.25}$$

However, the evaluation of the Lagrangian multipliers λ_k requires a special property of the Toeplitz matrix. Thus define the polynomial $V(e^{i\theta})$ by:

$$V(e^{i\theta}) \equiv \sum_{k=-K}^{K} \lambda_k e^{ik\theta} \tag{13.4.26}$$

then it can be shown that:

$$2/N \log Z \rightarrow -\frac{1}{2\pi}\int_0^{2\pi} \log V(e^{i\theta})\, d\theta \text{ for } N \gg 1 \tag{13.4.27}$$

Using this result on equation (13.3.10) yields:

$$R_k^d = \frac{1}{2\pi}\int_0^{2\pi} \frac{\exp\,(ik\theta)}{\left[\sum\limits_{k=-K}^{K} \lambda_k \exp\,(ik\theta)\right]}\, d\theta \tag{13.4.28}$$

which can be solved by applying the Burg-Levinson algorithm to the denominator, expressed as:

$$C\left\|\left[1 + \sum_{k=1}^{K+1} f_k \exp\,(ik\theta)\right]\right\|^2 \tag{13.4.29}$$

and then defining f_k and hence λ_k.

Suppose now that data is missing, i.e. for $k' < K$, or it is required to extrapolate into $k > K < N$, then it can be shown using the characteristic function technique that the autocorrelation function estimate to use is:

$$R_{k'} = \frac{1}{2\pi}\int_0^{2\pi} \frac{\exp\,(ik'\theta)}{\left[\sum\limits_{kCK} \lambda_k \exp\,(ik\theta)\right]}\, d\theta \tag{13.4.30}$$

which is optimum in a mean-square error sense.

The spectral-density $W(f)$ is now obtained from the Wiener-Khinchtine relationship:

$$W(f) = \sum_{k'=-\infty}^{\infty} R_{k'} \exp\,\{2\pi\, ifk'\} \tag{13.4.31}$$

which uses the extrapolated values of $R_{k'}$ where necessary. The result of substituting the expression for $R_{k'}$ into the above gives:

$$W(f) = \left[\sum_{kCK} \lambda_k \exp\{2\pi\, ifk\} \right]^{-1} \tag{13.4.32}$$

for all $|f| \leqslant 1/2$, which only depends on the λ_k for the observed data.

This form of spectral-analysis does not require the selection of data windows and reduces sidelobes, i.e. it does not introduce artifacts not supported by the data.

The accuracy of all estimates $R_{k'}$ is given by:

$$\text{VAR}_p[R_{k'}] = 2/\text{N}\ 1/2\pi \int_0^{2\pi} \frac{\exp(2ik'\theta)}{\left[\sum_{kCK} \lambda_k \exp(ik\theta)\right]^2}\, d\theta \tag{13.4.33}$$

for all k' whilst the higher-cumulants required for distribution studies of the estimates, $R_{k'}$, are given by:

$$\chi_r(R_{k'}) = (2/\text{N})^{r-1}(r-1)!\ 1/2\pi \int_0^{2\pi} \frac{\exp(irk'\theta)}{\left[\sum_{kCK} \lambda_k \exp(ik\theta)\right]^r}\, d\theta \tag{13.4.34}$$

This result does not arise in the conventional spectral-analysis techniques.

Now in practice, e.g. in pattern-recognition and image processing schemes, fast algorithms are required and this opens up an area of research in maximum-entropy spectral analysis by considering, as a first priority, the simplification of the data collected. Some possible modifications are to use constraints of the form:

$$\xi_k = \sum_{nCN(k)} \text{sign}\,[y_n]\, y_{n+k} \text{ for } |k| = 0, 1, \ldots, K \tag{13.4.35}$$

or

$$\xi_k = \sum_{nCN(k)} \text{sign}\,[y_n]\, \text{sign}\,[y_{n+k}] \text{ for } |k| = 1, \ldots K \tag{13.4.36}$$

with

$$\xi_0 = \sum_{n=1}^{N} y_n$$

where

$$\begin{aligned} \text{sign}\,[y] &\equiv 1 \text{ for } y \geqslant 0 \\ &= -1 \text{ for } y < 0 \end{aligned} \tag{13.4.37}$$

13.4.3 Distributional data

The moment-based data section has produced some interesting results, e.g. the reasons for the success of the exponential and normal distributions, the ability to assess the accuracy of estimates and to discuss their distribution, the prediction of higher-moments and so on. However, the use of moments is not the only way to represent a distribution, especially if the areas of interest are the distributional tails for the detection of outliers, say. An alternative description is to specify the proportion of samples falling above or below stated variate-levels. Thus complication in the exponent as required for the study of time-varying failure rates is exchanged for a piece-wise representation for the distribution. This process will result in a computationally more efficient algorithm.

Given the variate-levels L_m for $m=1, \ldots, M$ define

$$\xi_m \equiv \sum_{n=1}^{N} U(y - L_m) \tag{13.4.38}$$

where $U(y)$ is the Heaviside step-function, then ξ_m^d will be the observed number of samples, y_n^d, out of N falling above or equal to L_m or:

$$P_m^d \equiv 1 - \xi_m^d/N \tag{13.4.39}$$

will be the proportion of samples falling below L_m. In this case it is necessary to take a measure of deviation or dispersion so, for illustration of the technique, assume the simplest constraint:

$$\xi_1 = \sum_{n=1}^{N} |y_n| \tag{13.4.40}$$

for variates ranging over $-\infty < y < \infty$

The maximum-entropy solution for this case is the interpolative scheme for the cumulative-distribution given by:

$$P(y) = P_{m+1}^d - (P_{m+1}^d - P_m^d)\left\{\frac{\exp(-\lambda_1|y|) - \exp(-\lambda_1|L_{m+1}|)}{\exp(-\lambda_1|L_m|) - \exp(-\lambda_1|L_{m+1}|)}\right\} \tag{13.4.41}$$

for all $L_m \leqslant y < L_{m+1}$ and $m = 0, \ldots, M$. By definition, $L_o = -\infty$, $L_{M+1} = +\infty$, $P_o^d \equiv 0$ and $P_{M+1}^d \equiv 1$. The solution for variates distributed over $0 \leqslant y < \sigma$ is derived by simply removing the modulus signs, which are superfluous, and putting $L_o \equiv 0$. The solution for the parameter λ_1 is non-linear but tractable using successive iteration or

Newton-Ralphson techniques. It is seen that the solution allows extrapolation into the tails without making assumptions about the distribution there, whilst it is possible to determine the accuracy of the parameters P_m and the prediction accuracy in the tails.

It is also possible to invert the distribution which is an advantage in simulation applications. Thus, that y_o which produces $P(y_o) = P_o$ is given by:

$$y_o = 1/\lambda_1 \log \left\{ \frac{(P^d_{m+1} - P^d_m)}{(P^d_{m+1} - P_o)\exp(-\lambda_1|L_m|) + (P_o - P^d_m)\exp(-\lambda_1|L_{m+1}|)} \right\} \tag{13.4.42}$$

The use of second-order moment data produces a similar maximum-entropy cumulative-probability scheme, namely:

$$P(y) = P^d_{m-1} - (P^d_{m+1} - P^d_m) \left\{ \frac{\Phi\left(\frac{y-\mu}{\sigma}\right) - \Phi\left(\frac{L_{m+1}-\mu}{\sigma}\right)}{\Phi\left(\frac{L_m-\mu}{\sigma}\right) - \Phi\left(\frac{L_{m+1}-\mu}{\sigma}\right)} \right\} \tag{13.4.43}$$

for all y in $L_m \leqslant y < L_{m+1}$ and $m = 0, \ldots, M+1$ with L_o, L_{M+1}, P^d_o, and P^d_{M+1} defined as before. The case $0 \leqslant y < \infty$ simply requires putting $L_o \equiv 0$. There is no point in going to higher-order moment constraints since accuracy is increased more efficiently by increasing the number of levels, M. Now this is obvious for a number of levels which retain a fair number of samples within the defined intervals, but is it so if the number of intervals increases without bound? Thus the question is again posed, how many levels are optimum to represent the distribution? Once again the reader is referred to the discussion of cross-entropy.

Summarizing the distributional-data case:

1 The maximum-entropy distribution can be stored using $2M+1$ stores.

2 It can extrapolate and interpolate between levels and its cumulative form passes through the points (L_m, P^d_m).

3 The distribution can be readily inverted, i.e. given P_o find y_o such that $P(y_o) = P_o$. For the second-order case it is seen that:

$$\Phi\left(\frac{y_o-\mu}{\sigma}\right) = \Phi\left(\frac{L_{m+1}-\mu}{\sigma}\right) - \left(\frac{P^d_m - P_o}{P^d_m - P^d_{m+1}}\right)\left\{\Phi\left(\frac{L_{m+1}-\mu}{\sigma}\right) - \Phi\left(\frac{L_m - \mu}{\sigma}\right)\right\} \tag{13.4.44}$$

and so inversion is effected at the same cost as inverting the normal integral using rational polynomials.

4 The mean and variance of $P(y)$ is given by:

$$\left.\begin{aligned} &E[P(y)] = P(y) \\ &\text{and} \\ &\text{VAR}[P(y)] = 1/N\ P(y)\ \{1 - P(y)\} \end{aligned}\right\} \qquad (13.4.45)$$

whilst higher-moments can be found.

5 The piece-wise solution means that time-varying failure-rates are accommodated according to the data requirement.

13.4.4 Further applications

The extension of the technique to multi-variate distributions is straightforward, using either the strictly functional exponent form over the whole domain of the variate, or a cellular approach where the data consists of samples falling in particular cells. The proportional hazard technique is a special case of this extension. Also, extreme value statistics can be studied by observing as data the m'th largest sample within sets of sample, size N say. Finally, the exponent form in both representations allows for the construction of simplified classification and detection algorithms since:

$$\log p(y) = -\log Z - \boldsymbol{\lambda} \cdot \mathbf{A}(\mathbf{y}) \qquad (13.4.46)$$

13.5 CROSS-ENTROPY

13.5.1 The principle of minimum cross-entropy

The maximum-entropy technique is most suitable when working with raw data but, as presented, there is no way of feeding previously acquired information into the problem. Thus a generalization of the method is required to allow the introduction of prior information and this is accomplished by the concept of cross-entropy, which is also known as weight of evidence, directed divergence, relative entropy, etc. Cross-entropy is defined as:

$$H(q,p) \equiv \int_{\mathbf{y}} q(\mathbf{y}) \log \{q(\mathbf{y})/p(\mathbf{y})\}\ dy \qquad (13.5.1)$$

where $p(\mathbf{y})$ is here the requisite prior distribution. The constraints on the probability-density function $q(\mathbf{y})$ are the same as before, namely:

$$\int_{\mathbf{y}} q(\mathbf{y})\, d\mathbf{y} = 1 \tag{13.5.2}$$

and

$$\mathbf{A}^{\mathrm{d}} = \int_{\mathbf{y}} q(\mathbf{y})\, \mathbf{A}(\mathbf{y})\, d\mathbf{y} \tag{13.5.3}$$

It is seen that if there is little or no prior information, then $p(\mathbf{y})$ will be constant, i.e. $\mathbf{y}$ initially uniformly distributed, and cross-entropy reduces to entropy by simply reversing the sign of $H(q,p)$. The principle of minimum cross-entropy entails the minimization of $H(q,p)$ subject to the constraints of equation (13.5.2) and (13.5.3).

13.5.2 The minimum cross-entropy algorithm

The Lagrangian function in this case is:

$$H_L(q,p) = H(q,p) + \Lambda \{1 - \int_{\mathbf{y}} q(\mathbf{y})\, d\mathbf{y}\} + \boldsymbol{\lambda} \cdot \{\mathbf{A}^d - \int_{\mathbf{y}} q(\mathbf{y})\mathbf{A}(\mathbf{y})\, d\mathbf{y}\} \tag{13.5.4}$$

and the calculus of variations solution to minimizing $H_L(q,p)$ is the probability-density function:

$$q(\mathbf{y}) = Z^{-1}\, p(\mathbf{y}) \exp\{-\boldsymbol{\lambda} \cdot \mathbf{A}(\mathbf{y})\} \tag{13.5.5}$$

where

$$Z \equiv \int_{\mathbf{y}} p(\mathbf{y}) \exp\{-\boldsymbol{\lambda} \cdot \mathbf{A}(\mathbf{y})\}\, d\mathbf{y} \tag{13.5.6}$$

The Lagrangian multipliers are again obtained from:

$$\frac{\partial \log Z(\boldsymbol{\lambda})}{\partial \lambda_m} = 1/Z\, \frac{\partial Z(\boldsymbol{\lambda})}{\partial \lambda_m} = -A_m^d \tag{13.5.7}$$

whilst the minimum value obtained by the cross-entropy is:

$$H_{\min}(q,p) = \log Z + \boldsymbol{\lambda} \cdot A^d \tag{13.5.8}$$

The properties and usage of the minimum cross-entropy distribution follow exactly as in the maxium-entropy case, e.g. it is possible to evaluate the cumulants of the constraint functions $A_m(\mathbf{y})$, etc.

13.5.3 A software reliability application

The application most relevant to software reliability problems of estimation and growth models utilizes the distributional constraints:

$$\xi_m = \sum_{n=1}^{N} U(y_n - L_m) \text{ for } m = 1, \ldots, M \tag{13.5.9}$$

where y_n are the intervals between software failures or, alternatively, the times to software failure.

The solution with additional first-order moment data is:

$$P_q(y) = P^d_{m+1} - (P^d_{m+1} - P^d_m) \left\{ \frac{F(y) - F(L_{m+1})}{F(L_m) - F(L_{m+1})} \right\} \tag{13.5.10}$$

for $m = 0, \ldots, M$ as before, $L_m \leqslant y < L_{m+1}$ and where:

$$F(y) \equiv \int_y^{\infty} p(y') \exp\{-\lambda y'\}\, dy' \tag{13.5.11}$$

and λ is derived by solving equation (13.5.7) for this case.

When second-order moment data is collected the solution is:

$$P_q(y) = P^d_{m+1} - (P^d_{m+1} - P^d_m) \tag{13.5.12}$$

$$\left\{ \frac{\Phi_q\left(\frac{y-\mu}{\sigma}\right) - \Phi_q\left(\frac{L_{m+1}-\mu}{\sigma}\right)}{\Phi_q\left(\frac{L_m-\mu}{\sigma}\right) - \Phi_q\left(\frac{L_{m+1}-\mu}{\sigma}\right)} \right\}$$

where now:

$$\Phi_q(y) \equiv 1/\sqrt{(2\pi\sigma^2)} \int_{-\infty}^{y} p(y') \tag{13.5.13}$$

$$\exp\left\{-1/2 \left(\frac{y' - \mu}{\sigma}\right)^2\right\} dy'$$

It is seen that the introduction of prior information into the problem is much simpler than the usual Bayesian approach and does not require simplifying assumptions about the prior distribution in order to make the problem tractable. The cumulative-probability distribution $P_q(y)$ is continuous through the data points (P^d_m, L_m) and can be used either to interpolate between levels L_m or to extrapolate into failure regions not yet examined. Also probability statements can be made on these estimates which is a property not available with present-day software models.

13.5.4 Cross-entropy as a resemblance measure

Although cross-entropy is a very useful generalization of the maximum-entropy technique, it possesses further properties as a measure of resemblance between two distributions. In fact, cross-entropy satisfies all the axioms of a distance measure except the triangularity property, hence the use of the term resemblance.

The first application of this property concerns the question raised in the preceding sections; namely how many constraints, either functional or distributional, provide the best representation of the data? Suppose that $q_0(y)$ is the distribution obtained by a given set of data constraints and that $q_1(y)$ is the distribution derived by including additional data constraints. Then if $H(q_1, p)$ is less than $H(q_0, p)$ then q_1 is the better representation when the criterion is cross-entropy. The process is repeated until $H(q_{n+1}, p)$ first becomes greater than $H(q_n, p)$ then $q_n(y)$ is the preferred distribution.

Another use of cross-entropy is in the field of hypothesis testing and classification. Thus, if $q_1(y)$ is the maximum-entropy or minimum cross-entropy distribution obtained for data belonging to the class H_1 and $q_0(y)$ is the similar distribution for the class H_0, then if a further set of samples $y_{N+1}, \ldots, y_{N+N'}$ are obtained then they are deemed to have derived from hypothesis H_1 or H_0 according to the decision rule:

$$\sum_{n=N+1}^{N+N'} \log \left\{ \frac{q_1(y_n)}{q_0(y_n)} \right\} = \tag{13.5.14}$$

$$\sum_{n=N+1}^{N+N'} \log q_1(y_n) - \log q_0(y_n) \quad \underset{\text{DECIDE } H_0}{\overset{\text{DECIDE } H_1}{\gtrless}} \quad \eta$$

In this decision process η is the threshold level designed to provide a given level of protection against false decisions. This process is seen to be the presequential likelihood-ratio test that is the current vogue, and using entropic distributions it is seen to reduce to the simplified form:

$$\sum_{n=N+1}^{N+N'} (\boldsymbol{\lambda}_1 - \boldsymbol{\lambda}_0) \cdot \mathbf{A}(y_n) \quad \underset{\text{DECIDE } H_0}{\overset{\text{DECIDE } H_1}{\gtrless}} \quad \eta - N' \log \{Z_1/Z_0\} \tag{13.5.15}$$

Similarly, in the classification problem the sample is allocated to the population for which:

$$\sum_{n=N+1}^{N+N'} \log \{q_r(y_n)\} = N' \log Z_r + \boldsymbol{\lambda}_r \cdot \sum_{n=N+1}^{N+N'} \mathbf{A}(y_n) \qquad (13.5.16)$$

is a maximum, where $r = 1, 2, \ldots, R$ represents the R mutually exclusive contending populations.

Thus the entropic or information technique provides a systematic method of representing a set of data and of allocating further sample data to its true population.

13.6 SUMMARY

- The entropic technique is distribution-free in the sense that it makes no assumption about the distribution of variate y. This makes the method ideal for the study of software reliability and growth models.
- The method makes no assumptions outside the available data, which reduces the production of artifacts.
- The introduction of prior information is much simpler than the usual Bayesian approach.
- The probability distributions and their inverses are simple to evaluate, which is particularly useful when Monte-Carlo generation of random numbers is being performed to an empirical distribution.
- Estimation of parameter accuracy is a viable proposition and probability statements can be made regarding the range of an estimate.
- Time-varying data can be incorporated resulting in time-varying Lagrangian multipliers and non-homogenous processes.
- If the results are not satisfactory then the form of the data constraints chosen should be re-examined and the procedure is not altered.
- The eclectic approach is not necessary.
- The minimum cross-entropy concept provides the ability to choose between distributions representing data sets.
- It is possible to compare data constraint forms in order to obtain the best representation consistent with easily derived data functions.
- The generality of the technique raises the possibility of producing a universal suite of programmes to implement the procedures.
- The emphasis of the report is on presenting a methodology for dealing with statistical distribution problems and is not to be regarded as just another software model, since the class of distributions produced subsumes all previous models.

Further reading

Anderson B.G. (1983) *Adaptive Target Detection*. Dynamics Group, British Aerospace (Report ST-27541).

Anderson B.G. (1985a) *Clutter and Target Simulation*. Dynamics Group, British Aerospace (Report ST-29206).

Anderson B.G. (1985b) *Storage, Reconstruction and Generation of Statistical Distributions for Simulation Purposes*. Dynamics Group, British Aerospace (Report ST-29205).

Anderson B.G. (1986) *Classification and Detection in Parameter Space*. Dynamics Group, British Aerospace (Report ST-30172).

Anderson B.G. (1986) *Adaptive Detection in Parameter Space*. To be published.

Anderson B.G. (1986) *Registration and Tracking: an Information Theoretic Approach*. Dynamics Group, British Aerospace (Report ST-31571).

Anderson B.G. (1986) *Information Theory in Software and Hardware Reliability: the Generalized Approach*. Dynamics Group, British Aerospace (Report ST-30582).

Anderson B.G. (1986) *A Simple Maximum-Entropy Detection Process using Absolute Deviation*. Unpublished MS (available from Author).

Good I.J. (1950) *Probability and the Weighing of Evidence*. Griffin.

Jaynes E.T. (1982) On the rationale of maximum-entropy methods. *Proc. IEEE* **70** (9), pp. 939–952.

Kullback S. (1959) *Information Theory and Statistics*. Wiley.

Shore J.E. & Johnson R.W. (1980) Axiomatic derivation of the principle of maximum entropy and the principle of minimum cross-entropy. *IEEE Trans. on Information Theory* **IT-26** (1), pp. 26–37.

Tribus M. (1961) *Thermostatics and Thermodynamics*. Van Nostrand.

Chapter 14

The Use of Models in Reliability*

L.N. HARRIS
Dynamics Group, British Aerospace, Stevenage, Hertfordshire SG1 2DA

14.1 INTRODUCTION

Much of the published work on the quantification of reliability presumes that this can be achieved through the use of a model. This is understandable on two counts; first, the introduction of the computer has given engineers a fast and accurate means of doing calculations; hence, given a simple mathematical description, deductions can be made almost at will. Second, the statistician has played the dominant role in developing mathematical theories of reliability. There can be little doubt that a faction of this community has moved from the approach of analysis to the approach of modelling. The difference between these approaches is what they emphasize as being important. Analysis is the process of interrogating data to detect patterns. If we recognize these patterns, and experience has taught us their significance, this gives us reasons for claiming that we know something about the source of the data. On the other hand, modelling presumes that we already know something about the source of the data. Hence the object of an exercise is to show that a data set is adequately represented by a model.

Although these developments are understandable, they make modelling neither right nor useful in all circumstances.

This article addresses the question 'what is a model, and what is its role in reliability?' The discussion is philosophical; a fact for which I give no apology since in my view, philosophy is of fundamental importance in the development of science. The objective of the philosophy of science is to give us the assurance that our scientific reasoning is correct. This can be seen by considering its relationship to science itself (Fig. 14.1).

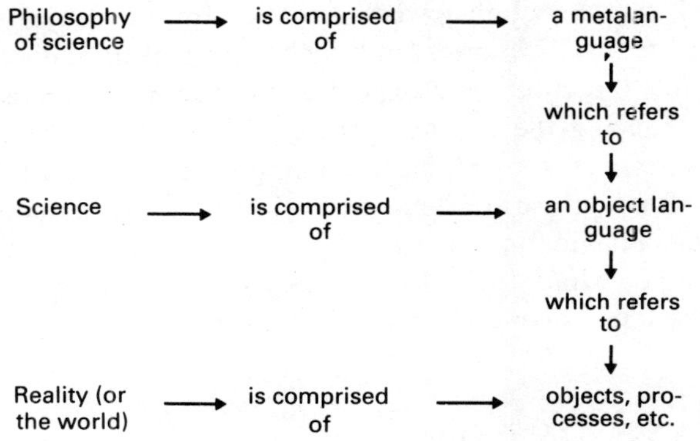

Fig. 14.1

From this we can see that whereas science uses a specialized language to talk about the objects of the world, and to explain why facts are facts (known as theory), the philsophy of science uses a metalanguage to talk about science itself, and is the means by which we gain assurance that the language of science is itself correct.

14.2 LAWS, THEORIES AND MODELS

The word 'model' has come to be used in scientific discourse to mean almost any structure of knowledge that has the potential for deriving inferences. At one extreme it may be an affectation for saying 'theory', whereas at the other extreme, it may be an implausible conjecture dressed in mathematical clothes in the hope that it will appear respectable. We can note that the words 'law', 'theory' and 'model' are often used synonymously. However, proper use requires us to recognize that the concept of a law in science invokes 'necessity' or its weaker companion 'propensity', and so when laws of science are discovered it is presumed that they have always existed. On the other hand, theories are inventions. Their development relies on mankind's ability to see abstract structures between the observable facts of the world. The credibility of a theory rests on its ability to be confirmed experimentally, and its logical structure gives it deductive links with other theories. Models, unlike laws or theories, are solely prescriptive. They are not regarded as having the property of being a true account of science, nor are they required to have a deductive link with other models. The relation between a model and reality is that we regard a model's behaviour as if it were true, knowing full well that it cannot fulfil the function of laws and theories.

A model can also be viewed as a descriptive device that links theories with reality. Theories, although powerful in explanation, are often poor in prediction. For example, the theory of metals is inadequate for deducing the characteristics of a metal. The purpose of a model in this respect is to emphasize an important feature of a phenomenon, either for purposes of detailed explanation or prediction, or as a spur to one's imagination in developing a theory. We can gain an understanding of what a model is and its role in engineering by simply reviewing the types of models used in engineering.

14.3 A TAXONOMY OF MODELS

14.3.1 Models as analogies

In describing the behaviour of an unfamiliar phenomenon, an educator may base his description on a better understood phenomenon. For example, in trying to describe the structure of the nuclear atom, the educator may liken it to a solar system in miniature. In this the atom is considered as being analogous to the solar system. The educator's reason for making this analogy is that it causes the student to think about the structure within a conceptual framework that will make what is to follow more readily understood. In like manner scientists and engineers, in trying to understand a phenomenon, use the same approach.

In this conception of a model, one is only pointing out that a certain similarity exists between one system X and another system Y. The similarity can be any similarity. However, for scientific discourse in general, restrictions are made so that only specific classes of similarity are included. Examples are:

1 X and Y may be regarded as similar by virtue of satisfying a common physical principle.

2 X and Y may be regarded as similar by virtue of a near common geometrical configuration.

3 X and Y may be regarded as similar by virtue that they appear to serve similar functions.

These examples are adequate to illustrate that the properties of similarity in X and Y are normally of an abstract kind. It is not usual to make an analogy between a system X and a system Y because they have categorical properties in common, e.g. they are both red, large, heavy or hot.

The major faculty of this type is that it provides a vivid way of illustrating and thinking about a complex phenomenon.

Although not immediately apparent, the utility of such models rests on the fact that X and Y in most respects are dissimilar. For instance, we do not regard the tearing of an aluminium sheet as being analogous to the tearing of a copper sheet. The two materials have too many similarities for this purpose. However, what is useful is to regard the macroscopic formation of a tear in a plastic film as analogous to the microscopic formation of a tear in an aluminium film. Although this point is trivial, it is nonetheless important. It demonstrates that analogies are primarily descriptive and, as such, although useful for qualitative inferences, they are unreliable for quantitative inferences.

14.3.2 Representational models

In engineering, it is common practice to make simplified models for purposes of investigations. These models incorporate many of the known features of the prototype (the equipment being represented).

There are various classes of these models; typically

1 *The true model*, where X, the model, incorporates all the features of Y, the prototype, as faithfully as is realistically possible.

2 *The adequate model*, which is a simplified version of the true model where only one or two features of Y are faithfully reproduced in X.

3 *The distorted model*, which is a further simplification and is used where accurate scaling of all of the properties in Y would be misleading. E.g. A true 50:1 scaling of a pressure vessel would be undesirable since this model would not accurately reflect the behaviour of the prototype. Although size may be scaled by 50:1, wall thickness may be scaled by only 15:1. The transformations are usually handled by empirically determined conversion factors.

4 *The analogue model*. In this type of model the characteristics of the prototype are not reproduced in the model. They are represented by an analogy between Y and an essentially dissimilar, but easier to handle, system X. The presumption is made that the laws that govern the behaviour of the characteristics of interest in Y are similar in form to the laws that govern the equivalent characteristics in X.

It is normal to consider representational models as actually being built. In doing so, true properties can be ascertained by reference to experiments, measurements, investigations and calculations actually made upon the model.

The advent of the computer has introduced a revolution in this form of model. It can be represented or coded by mathematical equations and algorithms and manipulated by computer. However, one should be wary, as the presumption of physical modelling is that our knowledge is incomplete. The presumption of mathematical equations is that our knowledge is adequate and that the details of our design inferences are latently embedded within the equations.

14.3.3 Theoretical models

Analogy and representation invoke the concept of similarity between X and Y. The theoretical model does no such thing. It is a set of assumptions, either explicitly stated, or, as is often the case in reliability, not stated. It postulates that the model has the potential for characterizing behavioural aspects of the prototype. The truth of this cannot be ascertained by merely considering the model. This has to be achieved either by rational justification or empirical confirmation.

More than any other class of model, this model invites speculative inferences. It is therefore of the utmost importance that one has a full understanding of the structure of a model, what a model claims to do, its relationship to normal science and finally its scope and limitations. An important aid to achieving this insight is to recognize the constructional properties of such models, typically:

1 A theoretical model, to make any claim to be plausible, must be essentially an explanatory model. A model incapable of explaining a phenomenon is also incapable of predicting the behaviour of that phenomenon.

2 For a theoretical model to be powerful in explanation, it also has to be powerful in description. This is because in describing a system, a model attributes to itself an internal structure, reference to which is intended to explain various properties exhibited by the system.

3 The description is required to be more than just a list of features. It needs to be dynamic and is likely to invoke some theoretical generalities. It is only by appealing to theoretical generalities that a description can become an explanation.

4 The structure depicted by the theoretical model must always be considered with reference to those properties it serves to explain, and not to something incapable of further detailed or more substantial explanation.

5 In most senses of the word 'simplification', a theoretical model, is a simplification of, or approximation to, the properties or behaviour of the object it models. However, this does not mean that the model is necessarily less accurate in prediction than more sophisticated or complete theories, since, as already pointed out, one of the purposes of a theoretical model is to increase the accuracy of prediction.

6 To term a model as either good or bad is inappropriate. It either serves its task or does not. In this it is similar to the pocket calculator, where one is required to find the product of two numbers to 5 decimal places. A calculator that displays 7 significant digits is not a worse calculator for this task than a calculator that displays 9 significant digits.

Many representational and theoretical models, especially when coded by mathematical formulae, are regarded as somehow approximately representing reality. It is important to distinguish precisely what is meant by an approximate representation of reality. An approximation can be thought of in two ways: the first is the way we think of approximations within mathematics. That is, we allow one function, say a polynomial, to approximate a more complicated function, in which case that polynomial is thought of as representing the more complex function in terms of accuracy, which we express as limits. On the other hand, we can think of an approximation in terms of it being an analogy. For example, we can think of some empirical phenomenon, such as the distribution of the times between failures of an equipment, as being approximately represented by a statistical distribution, in which case the accuracy must be determined empirically, and thus cannot be thought of in terms of limits. The consequence of this is not that it produces a limitation in accuracy, but that it restricts its domain of applicability. The difference is subtle but important.

14.4 THE SPECTRUM OF MODELS

Merely classifying models gives us no real idea as to an individual model's potential. Besides, there are many ways of classifying models. The one outlined in no way claims to be superior in providing a clearer insight as to the potential of a model than any other (the one described owes much to Achinstein's 'semantic theory of models'). The potential, the scientific content or the plausibility of an individual model is best determined by considering the variety of models as being ordered on a spectral line. By identifying the extreme points of this line, and the relative position of a model on the line, one can intuitively grasp its scope and its limitations. It may also serve to show how a model can be improved.

To explain what one means by a spectral line, consider a simple example of arithmetic. Consider a child of two or three years of age who we know has learned to count to 10 and whom we have told that 2 + 1 = 3, and 2 + 3 = 5. If we now ask this child what 2 + 2 is equal to, we would not be surprised to receive the answer 4, but if we ask the child how it knows this, it will not be able to answer. If we ask the same questions at the age of ten we may receive an answer 'this is what I have been taught at school'. At the age of 13, the response could be, 'this is a problem of arithmetic; I understand arithmetic is a matter of knowing the rules of calculation that are permissible. These I have been taught and am well practised in using them. In calculating what 2 + 2 is, I have used these rules correctly, therefore I am justified in believing that the answer is 4'. We can pursue this line a little further: an older person, say aged 15, who has studied mathematics, may respond by referencing the axioms of arithmetic. In doing this, reference will be made to a rigorous mathematical model, the 'axiomatic system'. Here, we take the statement 2 + 2 = 4 as a proposition which has to be proved from other theorems which we call axioms. Axioms can be regarded as theorems in themselves which are admitted without proof, since they are held to be self evidently true. Proof is then a matter of obtaining further theorems by certain admitted procedures of deduction.

To a person who has majored in mathematical logic, the answer previously given would not be satisfactory. He or she would point out that the axiomatic system had been commonplace for a long time in many branches of mathematics, but mathematicians have gained further insight. Even the same branch of mathematics might have alternative axioms. For instance, in geometry, alternatives to Euclidian geometry are being proposed, the best known of which is that of Riemann. It was also recognized that a set of axioms becomes mathematically 'possible' if they are logically 'consistent'. That is, one cannot deduce from the set of axioms two theorems, one of which is a proposition, the other a negation of that proposition.

It was soon realized that not only the axioms but also the rules of inference themselves might be, and even ought to be, subject to variations. Now, if axioms and the rules of inference are both viewed as being subject to change, to understand mathematics we have to think in terms of 'mathematical systems' or, as they are also referred to, 'formal systems' of inference. The first and most important requirement of a formal system is that it should be consistent, e.g. it does not lead to contradictions. Consistency, although important, is not the only property of concern. One has to show that the system is also complete.

A system is complete if and only if, for any proposition which can be formulated, it can be proved that it holds or that its negation holds. Now, if we return to the question 'what is 2 + 2?' the answer may be, 'I know that 2 + 2 = 4 by virtue of the formal system known as arithmetic which has been shown to be, in this respect, consistent and complete'. We should note that Godel's incompleteness theorem is a proof that arithmetic, as a system, is incomplete. Thus there are truths in arithmetic that can neither be demonstrated nor proved to be true, but this consideration does not affect the property of addition.

Our example shows that initially, that is at the age of three, answers to questions are based on intelligent guesswork. They are to be admired, since they introduce the faculty of reasoning. The answer given at the age of ten is also worthy of admiration since it shows that in all matters one has to be taught. The answer given at the age of 15 is to be applauded. It now shows concern for rigour, but it is the final answer that is the most worthy, since not only does it show recourse to reason, learning and rigour, but it also refers to formalism.

We can see from this that the line of development involves a gradual shift from guesswork to fully using the faculties of logical and deductive reasoning. It is this line that I refer to as the spectral line. It is the line that all science and mathematics in the 20th century attempts to pursue and it is this line that we as modellers should also pursue.

14.5 THE NOMOLOGICAL MODELS

The essence of the spectral line is to show that, although the development of models is a worthy pursuit, at the same time we need to develop a logic by which we can know that our models have the properties we desire them to have. This line of enquiry is a pursuit of what is known as the logic of confirmation, on which much work has been done in the last few decades. One of the most respected treatments of this topic is that of Carl Hempel, which is outlined in his book *Aspects of Scientific Explanation* (Hempel 1970) and further treated in his paper 'Deductive nomological versus statistical explanation' (Hempel 1962).

We can regard the nomological model as one of the end points of the spectral line. It is the end point that we should aim to achieve. This model is based on the concept of explanation as an attempt to state the causes of something. We can use Klemke's schema (Klemke 1980) to outline it. In this account, explanation is taken to be a set of statements. The statements describing the event or phenomenon to be explained are called the 'explanandum'. The statements put forward to account for the event or phenomenon expressed in the explanandum are called the 'explanans'. Klemke's schema is as follows:

E, some purported explanation, is an explanation if and only if:

1 The explanandum of E is a deductive consequence of the explanans.
2 The explanans of E contain at least one law of nature.
3 The law of nature is necessary for the derivation of the explanandum.
4 The sentences of the explanans are testable by observation.
5 The explanans are true (highly probable or highly confirmed).

From this we can see the essential components of an explanation. First, it has a logical structure. The explanans serve as the propositions of which the major proposition is a law of nature, and the explanandum is then the conclusion. Second, it is not only the explanandum that is required to be empirically confirmed, but also the explanans must have at least the same potential, as they are required to have some basis in fact.

The importance of this structure to reliability is that in this form an explanation can also serve as a prediction. Again we refer to Klemke for our example.

Given the law of conservation of momentum, that for an isolated system of bodies momentum is constant, we wish to explain why the velocity of a car–truck crash is 6 m/s. We do this by appealing to the law of conservation of momentum and the initial conditions of the car and truck. In Hempelian (nomological) form the explanation would look like this:

1 $(Mv)_t + (Mv)_c = (Mv)_{t+c}$.
2 Mass of truck $M_t = 1400$ kg.
3 Mass of car $M_c = 600$ kg.
4 Velocity of truck $\acute{v}_t = 0$.
5 Velocity of car $V_t = 20$ m/s.
6 Therefore $v_{t+c} = 6$ m/s.

Now, **1** to **6** constitute the explanation, but we note we can use **1** to **5** to predict **6**. We can now see that in the nomological schema the difference between an explanation and a prediction is a matter of when the event being explained occurs relative to when the argument explaining it is constructed.

An important property of the nomological explanation is that when complete it has deductive closure. This means that any deductive inference made on the basis of a subset of the model's propositions is itself one of the propositions of that model. Referring back to our example of the car–truck crash, any one of the six stated propositions is itself deducible from the remaining five.

Our example uses non-statistical measures. When using statistical measures, it is not always possible or even likely that the property of deductive closure is attainable. However, statistical closure may be attainable. The concept of statistical closure is due to Henry Kyburg Jnr (Kyburg 1974). Kyburg defines statistical closure thus: 'A rational corpora which is statistically closed, is one that contains all the logical consequences of any set of statistical statements about a given subject matter. We can note that whilst deductive closure implies statistical closure, statistical closure does not imply deductive closure'.

The property of statistical closure is of the utmost importance in the development of practical reliability models.

Finally, the nomological explanation can be viewed as a 'formal system' of explanation and prediction, in which the explanandum is viewed as being the equivalent to the theorem in mathematics, which is derivable by the use of a calculus from the explanans. The explanans now takes on the role of axioms in mathematics. Thus we have introduced the three most important requirements of logic, consistency and completeness.

14.6 ABDUCTIVE ENTHYMEMES

Many well substantiated areas of science easily succumb to the nomological explanation, but others require development in understanding of fundamental notions for progress to be made. In fact, these areas constitute the majority of science. It is usual for some philosophers to consider these areas as being statistical. I regard non-nomological models as 'abductive enthymemes', because this more clearly describes their structure. In Aristotelian logic, an abduction is an argument of syllogistic form in which the minor premise is not asserted as being true, but as either a probability or as being probably true. In a standard syllogism we may for example, argue:

All metals are good conductors of electricity	(Major)
Copper is a metal	(Minor)
Therefore copper conducts electricity	(Middle)

In this argument, the truth value of the conclusion (the middle premise) is a logical consequence of the major and minor premises.

In the abduction we argue:

All metals are good conductors of electricity
Substance X is probably copper

Therefore substance X probably conducts electricity

If we inspect the above example, we may question how we arrived at the premise that substance X was probably copper. Clearly this must have been through some process of reasoning. Perhaps we considered copper because as substance X has a coppery appearance, or because we determined that it is a good conductor of heat, or that it is easily soldered. In not stating our reasons we are truncating our syllogism. The name given to a truncated syllogism is an 'enthymeme'. An enthymeme is an argument of syllogistic form in which one (or more) of its premises are taken as being understood, but not stated. They have the quality of being rhetorical, are very persuasive, but all the same may lead to invalid conclusions.

We can now reconstruct our abduction, this time stating more of our presumed premises, from which we can see how the nature of the argument changes in the light of the previously unstated premises, e.g.

All metals are good conductors of electricity. Substance X is probably copper, because it looks like copper, is easily soldered and conducts heat

---

Therefore substance X is probably a good conductor of electricity

Alternatively, the argument may be:

All metals are good conductors of electricity. Substance X is probably copper, because it came out of a box marked 'Copper'

Therefore substance X is probably a good conductor of electricity

Our first example gives greater reason for believing that substance X will conduct electricity, since it conducts heat. Careful consideration shows that the conclusion is more likely based on this consideration than any possible reason for believing that our substance is copper. It results from our knowing that materials that conduct heat also conduct electricity because the same atomic principles are involved in both phenomena. However, in the second example the probability of the conclusion is a direct consequence of the minor premise, and there we have developed no arguments that state why a substance in a box marked 'Copper' should in fact be copper.

To my knowledge, all reliability models used in prediction are both abductive and enthymeme in structure. In not fully stating the premises that support a particular model, the practitioner faces difficulties in both corroborating them and interpreting them, as he has not the vaguest idea of the ultimate principles upon which they are based. Much of the discussion given in the literature on reliability prediction is a seeking of clarification of these principles. They could for example be:

- James Bernoulli's assumption that things in the future will exhibit the same pattern as things in the past. This is in fact advocating the use of simple enumeration in statistical reasoning, a principle long rejected by scientists as the sole justification for a scientific inference.
- Daniel Bernoulli's claim that statistical evidence reveals the underlying probability of occurrence for certain types of events, since we know that the actual outcomes are proportional to the probabilities.
- Laplace and Bayes' notion that observed results give us evidence which can be used to compute the probability that the underlying probability has a given value within a given range.

These examples are rules developed from 'classical probability', and although they have been abandoned or modified by 20th century statisticians, probability theorists and scientists as being an insufficient basis for prediction, in the main they are the only basis for accepting as valid many of our current reliability models. An acquaintance with the reliability literature leads me to believe that the advocates of some models do not know what philosophical principles are being invoked in asserting that a model can be used in prediction. If this is the case, how much more difficult must it be for the practitioner, since he can inspect the mathematical formulation of the model and detect no apparent errors in mathematical reasoning. However, current statistical theory is not a coherent body of knowledge. It consists of many incommensurate viewpoints, and statisticians disagree even on the nature of statistical inference, let alone their procedures. Also, there is currently no single accepted view of probability theory, there being a number of apparently incommensurate theories, e.g. classical, frequentist, logical, propensity, subjective etc. All statistical inferences in one form or another invoke a probability theory — but not necessarily of common philosophical origins.

One should not be deceived into believing that, since probability has been successfully axiomatized and thus can be treated mathematically, we know how to interpret it. For example, an acquaintance with the development of mathematical logic tells us that, although the Peano axioms of arithmetic are capable of developing the rules of arithmetical calculation, there are many numbering systems other than the one we use that have no useful interpretation and yet do not violate any of Peano's axioms.

So far we have talked only of logical truth, which in general rests on the principles of consistency and completeness, but in science this is not the truth we ultimately seek. We seek factual truth, which rests on the principle of correspondence, in that 'truth' corresponds to the facts. One needs to point out that it is impossible for a truth to be factually true and at the same time be logically untrue. However, it is possible for a truth to be logically true but factually untrue. Consequently, in science an abduction is interpreted as being a set of statements that have the potential for explaining facts. They are hypotheses or possibilities. In recognizing this we can no longer regard the premises, nor for that matter the structure of the argument, as grounds for asserting factual truth or factual probability. We do this by the procedure known as the 'hypothetico-deductive method'. In this method we are required to regard the hypothesis as potentially true and to deduce or predict further consequences from it. We now have to demonstrate empirically that these deductions correspond with fact. If they do, we have a propensity to accept the hypothesis: if they do not, we are required to abandon or at least modify the hypothesis.

Much talk of the 'hypothetico-deductive method' can be found in the literature on scientific inference. Unquestionably its development and use accounts for much of the growth of scientific knowledge at about the turn of the century. Occasionally, reference to it can be found in the more advanced (philosophical) literature on statistics. The most immediate reference is that of Bartlett (Bartlett 1980), who develops and explains its use and function by what I shall refer to as 'the Bartlett ladder' shown in Fig. 14.2.

In general, the procedure of the hypothetico-deductive method has led to the discovery of much that we know in science, and in consequence underpins much of our knowledge of the more substantial areas of physics. Hanson's account of scientific discovery (Hanson 1958) accounts for this method as partially a search for the explanans from knowledge of the explanandum.

As the abductive enthymeme does not specify fully all of the explanans from which the explanandum is inferred, and as the explanandum is often an assertion of probability rather than truth,

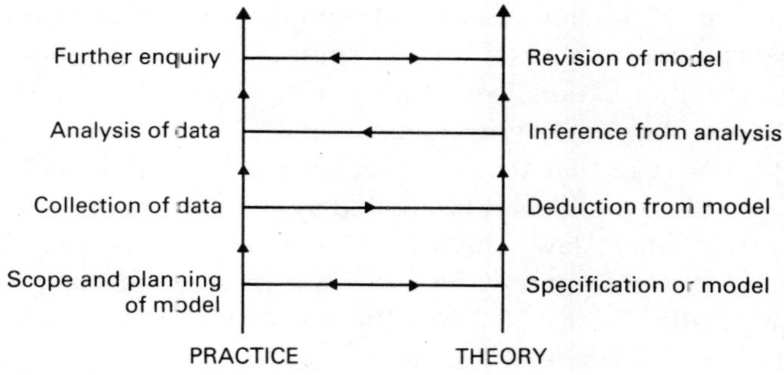

Fig. 14.2

confirmation can only be determined by directly operating on the explanandum. We argue that if every factual eventuality depicted by the explanandum can be confirmed, so can the model. This has led to the development of a number of quantifiable theories of confirmation. Broadly speaking, they fall into three classes:

1 Those based on the logical interpretation of probability. It is Rudolph Carnap's theory (Carnap 1950) that is the most highly developed. In this theory the logical interpretation of probability is used within the formal apparatus of a constructed language. A constructed language consists of giving a proper name to each individual or particular of the model, a predicate for each basic property, truth functional connectives and parentheses (rules of punctuation). In this theory a logical probability is seen as a logical relation somewhat similar to logical implication, but which can be regarded as partial implication. If the evidence overwhelmingly favours our hypothesis (model), i.e. is logically implied by it, the logical probability value is equal to 1. On the other hand, if the evidence is such that the negation of the hypothesis is implied, the logical probability value is 0. Between these extremes there is a continuum of cases in which deductive logic tells us nothing beyond the negative assertion that neither the hypothesis nor its negation can be deduced from the evidence. On this continuum, inductive logic takes over. By a logical analysis of the stated hypothesis h and stated evidence e we conclude that h is not logically implied but is, so to speak, partially implied by e to the degree of so-and-so much. In this formulation, probability is more often talked of as degrees of confirmation and is represented by $c(h,e)$.

2 Entropy and Bayesian concepts, surprisingly (considering their different philosophical roots) amount to what is a common approach.

Within the information sciences, entropy is taken to be a measure of information. Now, any model that completely explains a phenomenon makes data redundant. Thus confirmation is a question of evaluating the information content given by a model, and the information content within data. For example, if we know Ohm's law, the empirical knowledge that the voltage across a resistor of 1 ohm conducting 1 amp is 1 volt cannot be treated as new information since it is deducible from Ohm's law. This type of reasoning has led to a number of proposals that entropy can be used as a measure of confirmation. One of the earliest is that of Hans Reichenbach (Reichenbach 1956). In his structure, Reichenbach advocates that within any confirmation framework we have two sources of information, those he refers to as 'intensional' information, whose measure increases with a percentage of true predictions, and 'extensional' information, whose measure increases with the percentage of false predictions. Given that these two measures are equal, the degree of predictability of a model is zero. Confirmation is thus taken as the measure of the relationship between intensional and extensional information.

The Bayesian concept is based on the measure of the 'weight of evidence' which was formulated by Alan Turing. Its mathematical development is due to I.J. Good (Good 1983). In standard statistical reasoning, we often imply a probable effect of a cause. If this is a legitimate preoccupation, so is determining the probable cause of an effect. Thomas Bayes formalized how this may be logically achieved in the well-known Bayes theorem.

We can describe how it works by reference to a simple experiment. Say we have two boxes, each of which contain three balls. We know that in one of the boxes there are two white balls and one black, whereas in the other there are two black balls and one white. We now have to guess which box contains which set of balls. The only information that we have is that we can select at random one ball from one box. Now, say we select a white ball from box (A). Common sense tells us that it is twice as likely that this is the box that contains the two white balls. Instead of talking about what is likely, we can talk in terms of betting odds. We could say that the odds are 2:1 that box (A) contains the white box.

Alan Turing saw that within this concept there was a means of deciding between alternative hypotheses. Turing's insight was to consider what would happen within a series of such experiments. He reasoned that if the hypothesis 'box (A) contains the white balls' is true, the odds in favour of this would accumulate to a very large number as the experiments continued. For purposes of mathematical ease, Turing preferred the idea of summing the logarithms of the odds rather than multiplying them. In our example, the discovery of a white ball from box (A) then added a weight of evidence of log 2 that it was box (A) that contained the two white balls. A consequence of this reasoning is that we can explicitly state a mathematical theory that gives us a measure in favour of a hypothesis as the evidence accumulates. This theory has been fully developed by I.J. Good (Good 1983). The relationship between this concept using the 'weight of evidence' and entropy, is that within information science it is called relative entropy or cross entropy. Thus the mathematical formulation of confirmation within entropy theory, and Bayesian confirmation theory, are very much the same thing.

3 Boot-strapping. This conception is almost entirely due to Clark Glymour and is outlined in his treatise *Theory and Evidence* (Glymour 1980). He claims it to be a rejection of Bayesianism.

Glymour has noted that in practice, confirmation based upon confirming all the explanans is not possible since some involve measurable characteristics whereas others involve theoretical entities, e.g. failures, which are factual, as against MTBFs which are theoretical. Glymour's theory shows how 'boot-strapping' can be used to confirm such models. What he does is to confirm a model relative to a particular theory.

14.7 NOMOLOGICAL MODELS VERSUS ABDUCTIVE ENTHYMEMES

No one would claim that we are in the position to, or need to, abandon the abductive enthymeme class of models. However, we have to recognize that it is not a secure basis for giving answers to all problems. In this respect it is somewhat like geometry, in that geometry was incapable of doing many things that mathematicians sincerely thought it should be capable of, e.g. squaring the circle, trisecting the angle. What is clear is that it is the nomological form of modelling that is in the ascendant, at the cost of the abductive enthymeme. This trend is a consequence of what is currently demanded from science.

The shift over the past several decades has been quite marked. Previously, science was seen as an attempt to specify and explain situations that gave rise to the empirical phenomena at hand. The current requirement of science, particularly engineering, is that it should tell us what actions should be taken in response to the empirical evidence. To do this our models have to handle what are referred to as 'counterfactuals'. A counterfactual is a counter-to-fact condition. A counterfactual conditional is an assertion that if a certain event had not taken place (or had taken place) then a certain other event would have followed. Thus, the assertion that the use of 'burned-in' components would have made a system more reliable is a counterfactual, as we did not in fact use 'burned-in' components. Our prediction of better reliability cannot then be based on any factual evidence of how the system in question behaved.

A logical or factual inference takes the form

If:

(antecedent circumstances) (x)

Then:

(consequent circumstances) (y)

but the counterfactual inference takes the form

If:

(antecendent circumstances) had been (x)

Then:

(consequent circumstances) would have been (y)

Counterfactuals are handled by the theory of logical and causal modality.

As nomological models handle modalities and have the property of consistency and deductive or statistical closure, they support counterfactual inference. However, the abductive enthymeme, in not having these properties, cannot readily support counterfactual inferences. This can be demonstrated by reference to two well known paradoxes of statistical reasoning, Simpson's paradox and the grue paradox.

To illustrate Simpson's paradox (Simpson 1961), we can reference the example made famous in Cohen & Nagel (1934). Table 14.1 shows the data for the number of people who died from tuberculosis in New York and Richmond in the year 1910. From the data we can make three inferences:

1 If *white* then live in *Richmond* since the death rate is lower, 162 as against 179 for New York.

2 If *coloured* then live in *Richmond* since the death rate is lower, 332 as against 560 for New York.

3 If *white* or *coloured* live in *New York* since the death rate is lower, 187 as against 226 for Richmond.

Table 14.1. Deaths from tuberculosis in New York and Richmond in 1910.

	Population		Deaths		Death rate per 100 000	
	New York	Richmond	New York	Richmond	New York	Richmond
White	4 675 174	80 895	8365	131	179	162
Coloured	91 709	46 733	513	155	560	332
Total	4 766 883	127 628	8878	286	187	226

Thus the inference in **1** contradicts the inferences in **2** and **3**. In recent years it has become recognized that all statistical inferences based on categorizing data suffer in this respect. It is now known that one can always reverse a correlation simply by finding a third category which is correlated to the previous two categories. Knowing this, one can hardly claim that statistical models of this kind are consistent.

The second paradox is the grue paradox as formulated by Professor Nelson Goodman in developing his 'theory of projection' (predictions from sample data) which he published in *Fact, Fiction and Forecast* (Goodman 1983). The central tenet of this work is to demonstrate that there are certain properties that one can project from sample data, and that there are certain properties that are more or less resistant to projection. It is for this reason that I advocate that Goodman's book should be regarded as compulsory reading for all those who believe that prediction is merely a matter of technique or the use of a model.

The simplistic interpretation of confirmation is that a predictive procedure is validated by its past success, but as Goodman shows with his celebrated 'grue' problem, this is not necessarily so. We need to have prior reason to believe that what we are predicting is in fact predictable. Further, we can inspect the formulation of our prediction formulae to ensure, using Goodman's term, that they are law-like, and we must inspect our predictions for their logical implications. Goodman's ingenious 'grue' problem brings all of these issues together. For those who are unfamiliar with the grue problem it goes thus:

> An object X is grue at time T if X is green and T is earlier than $T(0)$ (say, midnight 31 December 1999 AD), or X is blue and T is later than $T(0)$. It follows that an object that exists in both the twentieth and twenty-first centuries can be and remain grue only if it is green before the end of the twentieth century and blue thereafter. Goodman then points out that whatever inductive

> evidence we have for the generalization 'All emeralds are green', seems likewise to be inductive evidence for the statement 'All emeralds are grue'. If there are any emeralds after the end of the century, at least one of these generalizations must be false.

The relationship between the 'grue' problem and reliability may not be immediately apparent. Nevertheless, it is a simple matter to show that it has direct implications as to how we analyse reliability. In the 'grue' problem, we are confronted by two alternative hypotheses as to the nature of an emerald:

1 all emeralds are green;
2 all emeralds are grue.

Ultimately, these hypothesis are contradictory in that in the year 2000 AD they cannot both be true. However, there exists no singular or collective empirical evidence by which one can judge which of these contradictory hypothesis is likely to be true, since the force of all empirical evidence to confirm or disconfirm hypothesis **1**, has equal force in confirming or disconfirming hypothesis **2**. In reliability analysis it so happens that we are faced with precisely the same kind of problems. One can demonstrate this by considering software reliability growth models.

Many software reliability models are based upon the understanding that reliability grows as faults are removed and that we can use the knowledge of the times it takes to discover successive faults to infer what the reliability is, or what the future reliability will be. In this, the sole data of interest are then the inter-arrival times of fault discovery.

Now, if we give the data to a competent statistician and ask him to infer what the current reliability is, he will tell us that there is no way he can estimate this without introducing auxiliary premises (assumptions). The one of greatest importance is that of what the testing efficacy has been over the fault removal time. In deriving an inference of reliability, testing efficacy has to be represented by a deterministic function (currently all reliability models presume this to be a constant).

Alternatively, using the same data, we can ask our statistician to give us a measure of current testing efficacy. Again there is nothing he can do without introducing some auxiliary assumptions. This time though, he will have to introduce some deterministic formula that characterizes reliability over the full fault removal time.

From this we can see that to say anything precise about reliability, we have to have a full knowledge of testing efficacy, and to say anything precise about testing efficacy we have to have a full knowledge of reliability. Thus our two hypotheses take the form:

Given that testing efficacy is $T(t)$, reliability is $R(t)$

or

Given that reliability is $R(t)$, testing efficacy is $T(t)$

No amount of data of the kind normally used in this type of model is capable of distinguishing which, if either, is correct. The reason for this is that reliability growth models do not have the property of deductive or statistical closure.

One can also point out that absolutely no one with any software experience believes that testing efficacy is anything like constant over time. It is surprising that any modeller would attempt to introduce such an implausible assumption, particularly when he knows that any results will be more sensitive to this assumption than any other.

14.8 CONCLUSIONS

In conclusion we can state that practical reasoning based on models requires models to be of a nomological form. By use of this form we introduce the property of completeness and deductive or statistical closure. It is only by introducing these two concepts that a model can be considered to handle counterfactuals, and it is the handling of counterfactuals within engineering that makes engineering practical and not theoretical.

References

Achinstein P. (1968) *Concepts of Science: a Philosophical Analysis*. John Hopkins Press.

Bartlett M.S. (1980) *Probability, Statistics, and Time*. Chapman Hall.

Carnap R. (1950) *Logical Foundations of Probability*. University of Chicago Press.

Cohen M.R. & Nagel E. (1934) *An Introduction to Logic and Scientific Method*. Routledge & Kegan Paul.

Glymour C. (1980) *Theory and Evidence*. Princeton University Press.

Good I.J. (1983) *Good Thinking: the Foundations of Probability and its Applications*. University of Minnesota Press.

Goodman N. (1983) *Fact, Fiction and Forecast*, (4th ed.) Harvard University Press.

Hanson N.R. (1958) Theories. *In Patterns of Discovery: An Inquiry into the Conceptual Foundations of Science*. Cambridge University Press.

Hempel C.G. (1962) Deductive nomological versus statistical explanation. In Feigl H. & Maxwell G. (eds.) *Scientific Explanation, Space and Time*. Studies in the Philosophy of Science 3, University of Minnesota Press.

Hempel C.G. (1970) *Aspects of Scientific Explanation*. Free Press.

Klemke E.D. (1980) Explanation and law: introduction. Pt. 2. In Klemke E.D., Hollinger R. & Kline A.D. (eds.) *Introductory Readings in the Philosophy of Science*, pp. 81–86. Prometheus Books.

Kyburg H.E. (1974) *The Logical Foundations of Statistical Inference*. Synthese Library **65**, p. 209. Reidel.

Reichenbach H. (1956) *The Direction of Time*, pp. 167–178. University of California Press.

Simpson E.H. (1951) The interpretation of interaction of contingency tables. *Journal of the Royal Statistical Society Series B* **13** (2), pp. 238–241.

Chapter 15

Safety Systems for Railways

G. Hagelin
L.M. Ericcson Signalling Systems Dept, S-12625 Stockholm, Sweden

Traditionally, equipment used by railways has been grouped into vital and non-vital equipment. Vital equipment must work in a *fail-safe* way, meaning that *all* single failures should be detected and made non-dangerous. Interlockings and level crossing units are examples of vital equipment, while a train dispatching panel is an example of non-vital equipment. This fail-safe requirement has forced railway equipment designers to use special techniques and components. Standard (telephone) relays cannot, for example, be used in vital circuits because of the risk that two contacts can weld together in a way that cannot be detected. Therefore special safety relays have been developed. Many railway administrations do not trust metal contacts in the relays, so use carbon contacts instead. Special components, however, are more expensive than standard components, and today relays are more expensive than electronic components. Therefore there is a demand to put electronics and computers into vital equipment. But how does one handle the fail-safe requirement in computer hardware *and* software?

As we know, it is quite impossible to totally avoid faults in complex software systems, especially in real-time systems. And even if the software is fault-free, how can we prove it? An acceptance of the fact that faults may always remain in software systems seems inevitable. In vital systems, the results of these faults must be detected and made non-dangerous.

Designers of electronic vital systems are today working with different types of redundancy which have majority voting. Within ERICSSON we are designing electronic vital systems for railways using diversity techniques. This means that we design two different software packages, which are both executed online and the results compared; these must be equal to permit vital operations. The two packages are designed by separate teams and data is, by definition, different in the two systems; the Hamming distance between data is four. Different data, and some rules about calculation order, force the two software teams to design different programs.

Using diversity, we also need comparisons. All output data must be compared and the results of the two systems must agree. If they do not, signals, etc. are turned to 'stop'. Comparisons must be done at every calculation cycle.

However, even if the design is based on two teams, there must be a common specification. Therefore special measures must be taken against specification faults. The most important of these is a validation

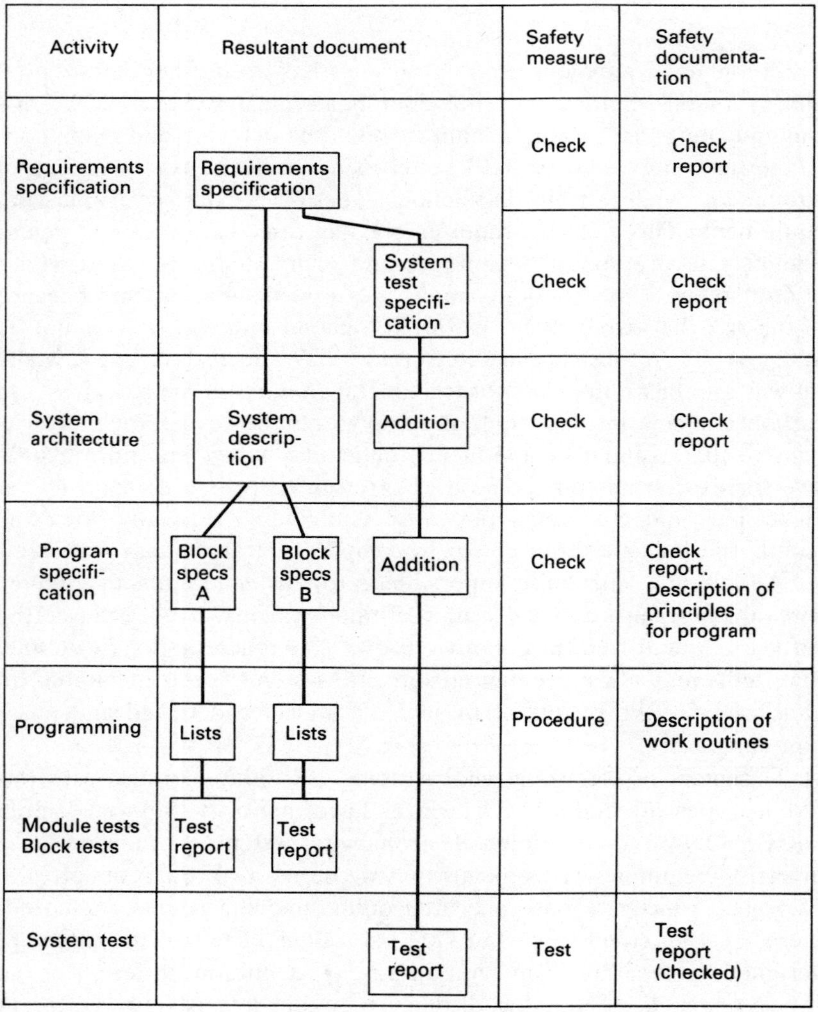

Fig. 15.1

check, which is done by a special checking group. This group later works as a check group for all design phases (Fig. 15.1).

Diversity is now used in computerized interlockings and automatic train control systems (ATC) in operational work in several countries. The first installation was put into work in 1978. Short descriptions of the systems are given below.

ATC is a system which supervises the engine and the driver. At signals (and some other places), data are transmitted to the engine.

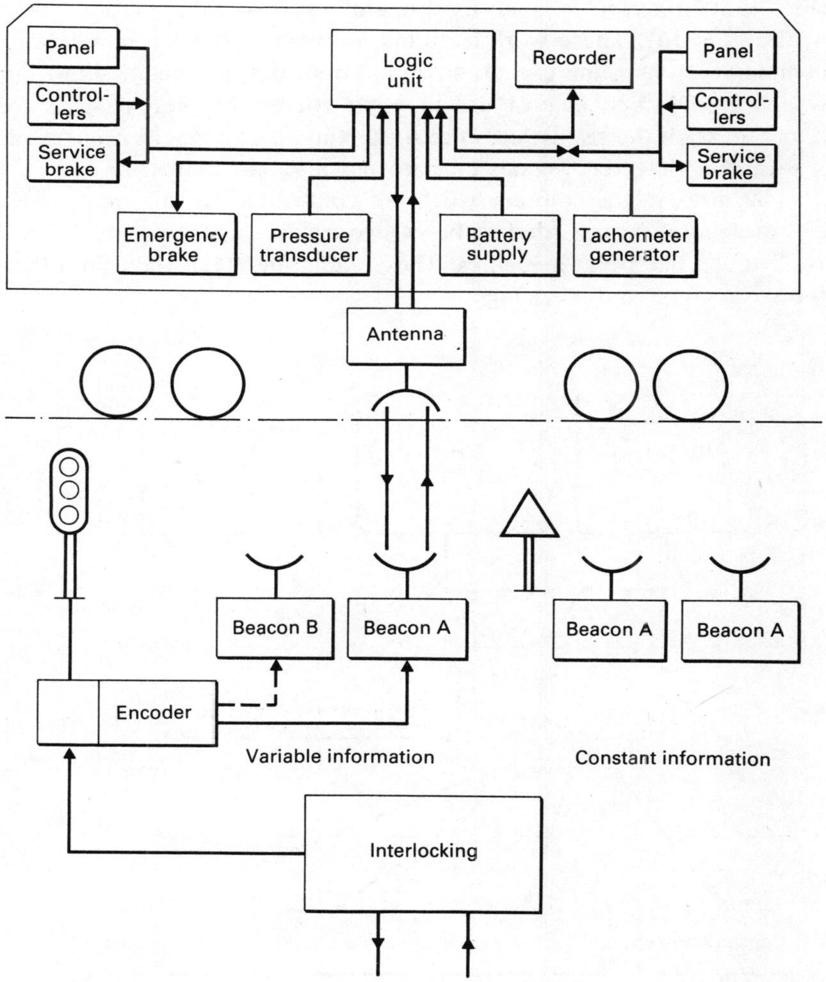

Fig. 15.2

The data basically have information about:

- permitted speed;
- distance to next signal;
- gradient to next signal;
- required speed at next signal.

The data is displayed to the driver and is used for supervision of the driving, train braking capacity, train weight and train length are also taken into account. If the driver is not performing correctly, ATC will brake the train and in the worst case, apply the emergency brake (Fig. 15.2). *Interlockings* are used in stations (normally one interlocking per station). These work as filters, preventing dangerous operator commands from being executed. In addition, devices included in train routes are blocked against use in other routes, blocked devices are released when the train clears the route and all equipment is checked. If a fault is detected, signals etc. are put into safe status.

The units in the stations which are controlled, signals, points etc. can in general be regarded to be of two types:

- Bistable, like point machines. They remain in left or right until they receive a command to change.

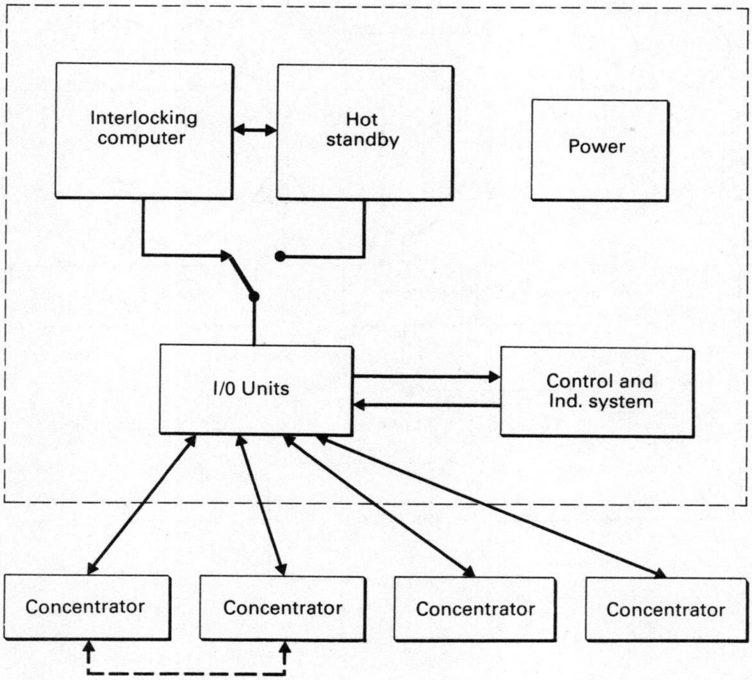

Fig. 15.3

• Monostable, like signals. They have one stable position, showing a stop aspect.

From the control point of view, the monostable units are most dangerous. What will happen if the signal is put to a clear aspect and then the cable is cut off, the computers switched off or anything else that will prevent a stop command is sent to the signal?

To prevent such a situation, the system must repeatedly feed information to the signal as long as it is in a clear aspect. The signal itself, or a controller close to the signal, is therefore designed to revert to the safe (stable) position as soon as this repeated sending has, for any reason, ceased.

Figures 15.3 and 15.4 show the general design of the computerized

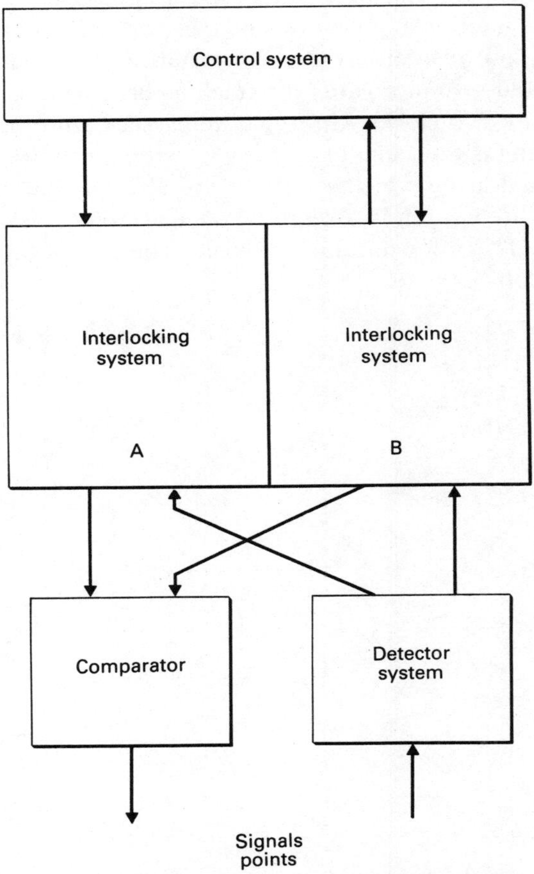

Fig. 15.4. Computer based interlocking system JZS 750 and JZS 850.

system. The two interlocking systems are run in the same computer. The only reason for having two computers is reliability.

The comparison and detecting functions are designed into common units called object controllers. There is one object controller for each signal, point machine, etc. These object controllers are located in concentrator cabinets in the station area, close to the signals, points, etc., and between the central equipment and the concentrators a serial transmission system (19200 Bauds) is used.

When building vital systems it is also important to guarantee that:

- calculations, at all points, are based on current information;
- the data flow forms closed chains, where all breaks must be detected and cause safe action;
- time measurement is correct.

To guarantee current information and also to check the data flow, all data in the interlocking have a time tag. Data which are too old are replaced by more restrictive data. For instance, if the data for a track are too old, the system regards the track as occupied. Time measures are checked by two clocks with separate crystals, and the software in the interlocking is the same in all stations within a railway administration. Individual layouts of the stations are also handled with data.

Programs are written in assembler language and STERNOL, which is a language design for interlocking logic. The size of the programs is about 200 kilobytes.

Chapter 16

Reliable Funds Transfer

J. DAVIES

Systems Designers plc, 105 Fleet Road, Fleet, Hampshire GU13 8NZ

16.1 INTRODUCTION

This paper reviews the requirements for electronic funds transfer with reference to two major national circuits. System availability and security are vital requirements in electronic funds transfer and normally account for a major part of the system cost. As funds transfer circuits become larger and more complex, more sophisticated software engineering techniques will be required in order to assure that integrity is achieved at an affordable cost.

16.2 PAYMENT SYSTEMS

Payment systems have existed ever since man began to trade, and are now an essential part of our daily life. A wide variety of payment systems are used in order to support both our domestic and our commercial trade. Domestic payment systems include:

- cash;
- retail banking services, including cheques, standing orders, credit cards, etc;
- home banking services, which allow customers to access retail banking services via public videotex services;
- point of sales services (EFT POS) which will allow fully electronic retail trading.

Commerical payments systems used by business and financial organizations include:

- automated bulk clearing services for high volume funds transfers (for example, payment of salaries, direct debit collections);
- fast payment services, for guaranteed payment and settlement of high value payments;
- international payment services.

The current trend in banking is to provide these services through computerized electronic funds transfer services. Once a payment instruction has been initially generated and authorized, the entire payment process is automated. The banking industry, and the financial and commercial industries it supports, are today wholly dependent upon automated funds transfer systems. Failure of these systems may have serious consequences.

16.3 SERVICE REQUIREMENTS FOR AUTOMATED FUNDS TRANSFER SYSTEMS

All automated electronic funds transfer systems must meet a number of service requirements in order to provide a reliable service. The key requirements are described in this section of the paper.

1 *Security*. Electronic funds transfer (EFT) circuits must be protected against deliberate and accidental fraud. Funds transfer circuits transfer large aggregate values in a potentially insecure environment, which may include external computers and communications systems. These systems must be protected by adequate security measures.

The main security mechanism used is message authentication, based on cryptographic techniques. The authentication systems used should protect the payment during the entire funds transfer process, preventing the insertion, duplication, deletion or alteration of payment messages. Several communication links or processing functions may need to be secured in order to achieve *complete* protection.

2 *Privacy*. Electronic funds transfer circuits must protect the payment instructions being transmitted against unauthorized access or disclosure, in order to assure users' confidentiality. Privacy is normally assured by the enforcement of strict access controls on operational EFT systems, and by the encryption of data on communication links, or at other points where privacy threats may be encountered.

3 *Availability*. Electronic funds transfer circuits must be available for use throughout the normal operational day. In the case of 'fast response' circuits, for example point of sales circuits, ATM networks, or fast payments circuits, any loss of service may cause serious inconvenience or disruption to system users. EFT circuits are normally specified to meet high availability criteria, and are implemented on continuous processing systems.

4 *Integrity*. Integrity is a combination of all the service requirements discussed in the previous paragraphs. In order to achieve the required integrity of service, an electronic funds transfer system must assure that the funds transfer is authorized, and must securely transfer the correct value between the corresponding payer and payee accounts on the specified value date.

16.4 CHAPS PAYMENT CIRCUIT

The CHAPS (Clearing Houses Automated Payments System) provides an automated fast payment service to the London clearing banks. This circuit transfers high value payments, providing *immediate* advice that a payment has been received, and guaranteeing same day settlement.

16.4.1 Service requirements

CHAPS is an inter-bank payment circuit which *guarantees* same day settlement of all values transferred between the clearing banks. Hence payments made using the CHAPS circuit may be booked by the payee bank immediately advice of payment is received, allowing the beneficiary immediate access to the funds transferred. CHAPS payments represent good money.

Once a CHAPS payment is accepted by the payer CHAPS gateway it becomes a guaranteed payment. The CHAPS circuit must assure that all payments accepted are advised and settled during the current banking day. CHAPS payments cannot be refused or cancelled once they have been accepted by the circuit. In order to provide this level of service the CHAPS system has to meet stringent availability and integrity requirements.

16.4.2 CHAPS system architecture

The system architecture adopted for the CHAPS circuit is shown in Fig. 16.1. CHAPS is a distributed circuit whereby each clearing bank has its own CHAPS facility designed and developed to meet its own specific requirements. These facilities are linked by means of a common CHAPS gateway system.

The main components of a CHAPS circuit node are described below:

1 *CHAPS gateway*. The CHAPS gateway provides the inter-bank communications, etc., required to provide the fast payment service. It accepts and validates payments submitted by the payer bank, and then performs two major functions:

(a) It delivers a payment advice to the payee bank which may be used to book the payment. The payment message is transmitted between

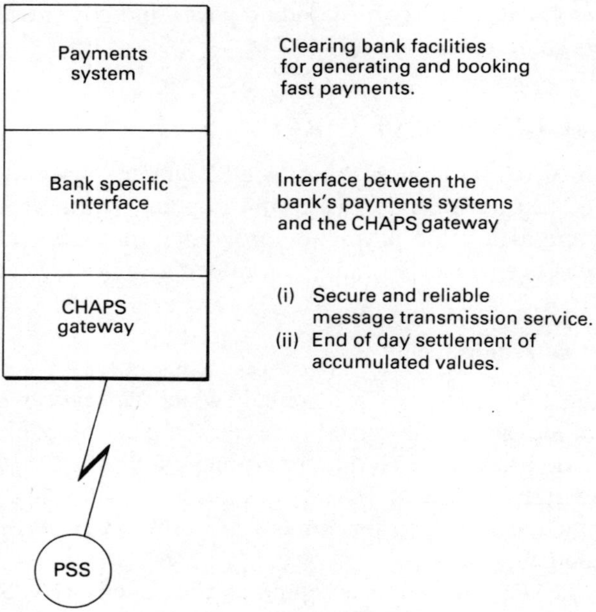

Fig. 16.1. CHAPS circuit system architecture.

the corresponding gateways by a secure and reliable message transmission service.

(b) The values transferred between clearing banks are accumulated, and are settled by the Bank of England at the close of the CHAPS business day.

The CHAPS circuit currently has 13 primary and fallback gateways, some of which are shared by several clearing banks. The gateway was developed by a central CHAPS project team under the auspices of the CLCB (Committee of London Clearing Banks).

2 *Bank specific interface*. The bank specific interface provides an interface between the CHAPS gateway and the bank's payment system. The development of these interfaces was the responsibility of the individual banks.

3 *Payment system*. The payment system is responsible for the generation and receipt of CHAPS payments. It comprises all banking functions necessary in order to accept and authorize clients' payment instructions, notify clients of payments received, and to perform the necessary booking functions. The payment systems are the responsibility of the individual clearing banks, and system designs vary widely. Some banks have integrated the CHAPS circuit into existing payment systems capable of supporting a number of payment methods, whereas other banks have developed systems specifically for CHAPS.

16.4.3 Availability

The CHAPS rules which regulate the operation of the CHAPS circuits state that each clearing bank must be open for business and able to receive payments throughout the CHAPS operational day. In the event of any system failure, the system must be able to recover and re-establish the payment service in less than 30 minutes. This rule applies to any credible failure, including complete failure or destruction of a CHAPS gateway system. In order to meet these requirements the CHAPS circuit has a number of high availability features:

1 *Non-stop systems*. The CHAPS gateway and bank specific interfaces are implemented on Tandem non-stop computer systems. These systems are resilient to any single hardware failure and should continue functioning without interruption to the payment service.

2 *Fallback gateways*. Each clearing bank has both a primary and a fallback CHAPS gateway. These gateways are independent and are located on separate physical sites. In the event of a complete failure of the primary gateway, the clearing bank must be able to re-establish its service and be capable of at least receiving payments at its fallback gateway.

3 *Communications routing*. Each gateway has two separate links to the BT public data network. Each link is routed to separate PSS exchanges via different physical routes.

4 *Contingency communications*. Contingency communications using magnetic tape are provided in the event of total failure of the public data network, or of an individual bank's communication links.

5 *Recovery*. The gateway system is able to recover rapidly from gateway failures involving loss of payment information. It is able to recover from simultaneous failure of two or more gateways.

16.4.4 Integrity

The CHAPS central project was responsible for assuring that the CHAPS circuit was capable of delivering payment instructions correctly, securely and promptly. This responsibility covered four major areas:

1 *The gateway interface*. The CHAPS gateway interface represents the most significant interface in the CHAPS circuit. Once a payment instruction is accepted by the gateway it becomes good money, and

cannot be subsequently rejected or amended. Hence this interface is subject to defensive checks and session controls:

(a) The defensive checks can only assure that the payment instruction is deliverable by the gateway and cannot assure that the payment is authentic (see **4** below). The checks validate the message and field formats rather than the message content.

(b) The session controls assure that sessions can only be opened between authentic gateways and bank specific interfaces. Session controls also assure that messages are not duplicated or omitted, and provide restart facilities. Controls are applied to message serial numbers, and the cumulative values sent.

Note: Equivalent session controls are applied across the internal gateway interfaces.

2 *The gateway system*. The CHAPS gateway is not functionally complicated, acting mainly as a simple message transmission system. The integrity of the gateway system was adequately assured by the use of normal good system development and quality assurance practices, and comprehensive system testing.

3 *Bank specific interface*. The development of bank specific interface software and payment systems was the responsibility of the individual clearing banks. The central project only assured that the bank specific systems were capable of interworking with the gateway, and of fulfilling the banks' obligations under CHAPS rules. This assurance function had three elements:

(a) simple verification of bank specific interface system designs,

(b) certification of bank specific interfaces in order to demonstrate compliance with gateway interface standards and CHAPS rules,

(c) extensive system validation through bilateral and multilateral system testing.

4 *Security*. CHAPS payments are protected by end-to-end message authentication between banks' payments systems. The CHAPS functional architecture prevents authentication failures being rejected by the payee payment system. Such payments have to be accepted, and either validated or returned by subsequent manual actions.

16.4.5 Conclusions

The CHAPS payment circuit is not a functionally complex circuit, and it is possible to achieve the levels of availability and security required by conventional development methodologies — at least with regard to the central gateway facilities. In the period since CHAPS has been operational, there have been several failures which have required use of fallback or contingency facilities, but no loss of the payment service. The CHAPS approach to integrity has been justified in practice.

16.5 THE DUTCH NATIONAL PAYMENT CIRCUIT

The Dutch national payment circuit (NBC) will provide funds transfer services to the entire Dutch banking community. This circuit is currently at the functional specification stage, with a phased implementation which commenced early in 1986.

The NBC is intended to be a truly 'National' circuit, providing a comprehensive set of payment services, and capable of future expansion to incorporate new services which may be required. Currently the following types of payment traffic are envisaged:

- guaranteed fast payments;
- bulk traffic, including both payments (credit transfers), and incassos (debit transfers);
- point of sales traffic.

Immediate on-line settlement of funds transferred will be provided by means of an 'electronic purse' system.

16.5.1 Integrity problem areas

The NBC circuit is technically much more complex than the CHAPS circuit owing to the nature and variety of payments services to be supported, and the amount of data processing performed within the scope of the NBC circuit. The NBC performs some functions which would normally be assigned to the host payment processes in order to simplify transition to the new circuit. The main technical areas where integrity problems may be anticipated are summarized below:

1 *Batch payment processing*. Batch payments have to be processed by the NBC circuit in order to ensure that the individual payment instructions are routed to the correct destination banks. These processing functions must be authenticated to assure that fraudulent or erroneous processing actions cannot be performed.

2 *Authentication*. Simple end-to-end authentication of payment instructions is not possible within the NBC circuit owing to the addressing and payments processing functions which are performed. Each of the data processing functions and data communctions links must be separately authenticated.

The authentication functions performed at the various stages must be chained such that the generation of a message authenticator for each stage is dependent on the successful verification of the preceding stage. Any unauthenticated process may allow fraud to be perpetrated.

3 *The 'electronic purse'*. Settlement is performed using an 'electronic purse' system which contains real value in an electronic form. In settlement, value tokens are transferred between the corresponding banks, allowing the values in their purses to be adjusted accordingly. The electronic purses must be subject to stringent security and audit controls to assure that value is not created or destroyed, either accidentally or fraudulently.

4 *Transaction processing requirements*. The NBC represents a distributed transaction processing system. Each payment action constitutes a separate transaction which is either completed in its entirety or is aborted. This allows the NBC to handle unclean payments which may not be accepted by the payee, and to handle various authentication and processing failures.

It should be noted that the various processing locations in the NBC circuit may use different hardware with different native TP monitors. These hardware and software environments must be able to interoperate in order to realize a single integrated TP system.

5 *Communication requirements*. Substantial data communications are required in order to link the various processing modules, electronic purses, etc., which constitute the NBC. The NBC communications infrastructure is based upon the emerging OSI standards, in order to provide a common standard for the various components, and in order to support future growth and development of the circuit.

16.5.2 The NBC project

The development of the NBC circuit will be a complex undertaking involving approximately 60 banks and financial institutions. It requires the development of a significant number of different systems, all of which must interoperate in order to provide an integrated NBC circuit. These systems comprise various types of data processing module, in addition to external devices such as electronic purses and authentication and encryption devices.

The integrity of the NBC circuit is a major system requirement. The central project assurance functions must ensure that the various system components which are procured will integrate successfully and will interoperate, and ensure that future development potential is not impaired. It must also ensure that the required levels of security, availability and performance are being achieved.

The complexity of the NBC development activity is such that normal 'good development practices' are likely to be inadequate. More sophisticated project assurance techniques might be appropriate; in particular the use of an independent verification and validation authority.

16.6 SOFTWARE INTEGRITY IN FINANCIAL SYSTEMS

Financial systems do not present the 'absolute' risks which may arise in, for example, the nuclear and aerospace industries. In such industries a failure of system integrity may have catastrophic results with major social and political consequences. An equivalent failure of a financial system would hardly be noticed outside the immediate financial and commercial business community. In any financial system, integrity must be justified in financial terms, including:

- actual monetary losses resulting from deliberate fraud, or from system errors or failures;
- consequential losses resulting from any loss of service, or from failure to correctly perform clients' instructions;
- adverse publicity or 'loss of face'.

A risk analysis performed on a financial system must identify all situations or occurrences which may directly or indirectly result in financial loss. These represent the 'assets' to be protected. Threats to these assets, and appropriate counter measures, may then be investigated. The cost of counter measures may be compared — at least at broad qualitative terms — with any potential reduction in financial loss. Cost-effective counter measures should then be implemented and monitored throughout the system lifetime.

The software engineering techniques adopted must ensure that the required levels of integrity are achieved in practice. Any software engineering techniques which would allow systems to be designed and developed to meet specifiable integrity standards would be welcome. Such techniques would assist in the development of more secure and reliable financial systems.

Index